SIXTIES FASHION QUEEN
& ALL THAT JAZZ

By Sue Locke

Other Books by Sue Locke

100 Coffee Recipes
with Heather Lambert
Octopus Books 1983

100 Vegetable Recipes
Octopus Books 1985

Vegetarian Microwave Recipes
W Foulsham & Co 1986

Landscapes on the Edge -
Poems of the Wye Valley and Welsh Borders
ed. with Margot Miller Fineleaf Editions 2010

SIXTIES FASHION QUEEN
& ALL THAT JAZZ

First published 2011
Copyright   © Sue Locke 2011
ISBN   978-0-9541161-7-0
Design   Loulita Gill
Print   SS Media
Published by   Ogma Publications
                    Herefordshire HR1 4PN
                    margotmiller@ live.co.uk

British Library Cataloguing in Publication Data.
A catalogue record for this book is available from the British Library.

Except as otherwise permitted under the Copyright, Designs and Patents Act 1988, this book may only be reproduced, stored or transmitted in any form or by any means, with the prior permission of the author and publisher in accordance with the terms of a licence issued by the Copyright Licensing Agency.

SIXTIES FASHION QUEEN
& ALL THAT JAZZ

By Sue Locke

*For my beloved parents and family
and in memory of Gale and Greville, Sam, and Deidre*

Mark and Sue in Chelsea

Acknowledgements

Great thanks to Margot Miller for her hard work in preparing this book for publication. Also thanks for photographs by Paul Orssich and Luke Kelly; and to Oliver Sharp who put up with many hours being devoted to creating this book.

References Chapter Titles

6. *Come live with me, and be my love* - Christopher Marlowe
7. *How do I love thee, let me count the ways* - Elizabeth Barrett Browning
10. *Parting is such sweet sorrow* - 'Romeo & Juliet' Shakespeare
20. *For age is an opportunity no less
Than youth itself though in another dress* - H W Longfellow

CONTENTS

1. Young days in Petersham...9
   Down by the riverside

2. Chelsea Art School..21
   You're driving me crazy

3. Family reflections - and Shaun.......................................29
   A foggy day in London town

4. Student days..37
   Dream, dream, dream

5. Cocktail hour in Malta..45
   When I take my Sugar to tea

6. The Italian affair...55
   Come live with me, and be my love

7. Kings Road boutique - and Nicky..................................67
   How do I love thee, let me count the ways

8. The wholesale project - and Jeremy..............................77
   All you need is love

9. Separation, divorce & 'Chelsea Nights'.........................89
   Johnny be good

10. Final Chelsea days..101
    Parting is such sweet sorrow

11 New life in Montego Bay 107
Woman - don't cry

12 Seventies - return to London 131
The way we were

13 Life in Dayton Ohio with Kjack 141
Hotel California

14 Starting over again in London 175
Suzanne

15 'Coffee & Spice' delicatessen 201
Lady in Red

16 Tobias School of Art 221
Speed bonnie boat like a bird on the wing

17 Placements - Ford Prison & Blackthorn Trust 251
Layla

18 Moving west 269
May your little light shine

19 Sue Sharp and 'Shieldbrook' 287
You're getting to be a habit with me

20 Sculpture exhibitions - new awakenings 297
For age is an opportunity no less
Than youth itself, though in another dress

CHAPTER ONE
YOUNG DAYS IN PETERSHAM
Down by the riverside

I came into the world rather dramatically in Barnes, London on July 5th 1939. In those days, many babies were born at home. I was born at home in my parents' flat at Seaforth Lodge. There was a midwife in attendance and my Gran; apart from that Mummy was on her own for what was to be a difficult breech birth. I later discovered that it had nearly killed us both. The drama of it consequently made us close. My father had already gone to work in the City at the family electrical business.

He was summoned back pronto to a blood-spattered bedroom to find me gurgling away in my cot and my poor mother exhausted. Gran was in complete control of the situation though and generally saved the day as she usually did. The ordeal of childbirth did not put my mother off the idea because, to my amazement, she went on to have three more children, not to mention a miscarriage. It is apparently true that you forget the agony of childbirth once you hold the baby. The shock of it caused me to be born with my eyes open. I also had a lot of curly dark hair which Mummy said she could tie a ribbon round and I weighed a healthy 7lbs.

I had a happy time in Seaforth Lodge: it was quite social. I was wheeled by my mother around Barnes Pond, meeting other babies in prams. One mother and baby that we always stopped to talk to was Pat Bond with her son Jack. Not that I remember this but I heard about it years later when Jack became my first serious boyfriend. Apparently, we would gurgle to each other and bat our arms about in our prams: amazingly a spark of recognition had occurred. It is extraordinary to me that my destiny even at that early stage was beginning to make its mark. Strangely enough, both sets of parents and babies were born within a square mile of each other: we thought later it made a special bond between us which is maintained today.

Soon after I was born war was declared against Germany on September 3rd 1939. Therefore I was a war baby and grew up with everything this entails, such as sirens going off at all times of the day and night, air raids, and the dreaded rush to air-raid shelters with that horrible damp smell. I have a strange reaction even now, to the sound of sirens. There was rationing but in those early days I was not aware of this. Increasingly I did become aware that I felt a constant ache brought on by the absence of my father.

At that time all able young men were expected to join the Forces. My father joined the RNVR which was the Volunteer Reserve for the Royal Navy. He had an electrical training and experience, having worked for his father's company Locke and Soares in Cavendish Street. The company had been the electrical contractors to Buckingham Palace and for St Mary Abbots Hospital amongst other prestigious addresses. So with this expertise as background he went on to complete torpedo training, joining the Navy as an expert in this area. My mother was pregnant again and about to produce my sister Trisha. The family moved to Helensburgh in Scotland where my father was due to join his ship. He had also been given some time off for the birth of my sister, Patricia Anne. Gran was there as usual offering her loving support and I was excited about a new baby.

My earliest memory is from this time, when my father carried me in the crook of his arm up a steep hill and showed me the devastation of the bombing which had taken place on the Firth of

Clyde the night before. The ships were still smoking from the raid. He stood there transfixed and then carried me down, all the time talking softly about how he was going away to the war, that he may not come back, and how much he loved me. Also how I must look after Mummy and my baby sister. I felt this overwhelming love between us; we had really bonded. I was eighteen months old. In a strange way, all my life I have been searching for this feeling from him again.

After my sister was born we returned to London and stayed with Gran in her East Sheen flat. Mummy had the task of finding somewhere for us to live and eventually we moved into 19 Lauderdale Drive, Petersham. It was a lovely house but I remember it being cold: there was no central heating. We would get dressed in front of an electric fire in the winter. We had a coal fire but that seemed to be lit only in the evenings. There was a great garden with fruit trees and in the fullness of time, we became experts at growing vegetables. My favourite tree was the cherry in front of the house with amazing pink blossom each spring.

During the war we saw little of our father but he would come home on leave occasionally. When he came back, nine months later another baby arrived. So now there were three children: my brother Simon came first and some time later my younger brother John was born. The house was perfect for a family, rather messy, without much discipline when my father was away, but when he was home it was another thing altogether. His family background was rather Victorian, formal, strict and straight-laced. His mother wore dresses to the ground!

We had a normal happy childhood, climbing trees, having crazes for skipping, bikes and horses. Mummy was always there for us to take care of our needs. In the early days there was no TV but we had an enormous radiogram with plenty of good records: my interest in jazz started early because of their great collection of music - musicians such as Hoagy Carmichael, Bix Beiderbecke and Glen Miller to name but a few. It was great to go through piles of old 78's and play what we wanted, always being careful not to break anything. We lived in this house for most of our childhood and there were many happy moments and, of course, the occasional drama, the worst was when John was rushed to hospital with a great gash to his left cheek. He had fallen through the french window when we were playing football with a balloon. He was scarred for life - it was dreadful.

The radio was on most of the time and we would have passions for various programmes, such as 'Listen with Mother' for the boys, 'Womens Hour' for Mummy and my favourite 'Dick Barton Special Agent'. This programme would finish with a little trailer for the next with sayings like 'What will Snowy do now?' This programme was on every evening, so we would be sure to be there to hear the next adventure. Later on we would listen to Radio Luxembourg for all the latest sounds, and 'Take It from Here' and 'Hancock's Half Hour' to keep us all laughing.

My first school was Mrs Taylor's Nursery a five-minute walk from where we lived. The war by now had ended and we, like most people, were struggling to get our lives together. The sad thing was that our father was still not home with us. He did not return immediately because he had decided to remain in the Navy. Although Mummy was on her own much of the time, she had great support from all her family so we were always well cared for and entertained by close relatives.

There was an event which happened at my first school which became a lasting memory. It happened whilst out on a Nature Walk. On these walks we were encouraged to pick up interesting things as we went along such as cones, leaves and feathers. The idea was to bring them back to be displayed on the Nature Table and then have a discussion about the various items. On one of these walks

I took a liking to some lupins growing in somebody's garden. I picked them and triumphantly carried them back, laying them out on the table - only to find to my horror I should not have taken the flowers. Consequently, I was severely reprimanded, which made me cry. A few weeks after this scenario, rushing out of the house to help Fred the milkman on his rounds, I fell down the stairs and broke both my arms. For a while I could not do anything and had to stay in bed. My teacher came to visit me and brought a beautiful bunch of lupins and since then they have been a favourite flower. It also taught me to respect flowers especially if they belonged to someone else. I will never forget planting my first lupin seeds and watching their very distinct leaves develop and then eventually the flower came.

We learned to read early. Books were a central part of my parents' life. There was an eclectic selection available in the house, not to mention in the children's library. My father was a member of a club called 'World Books' and a new title would arrive every month. Later on there was one which particularly fascinated me: *The Life and Works of Leonardo da Vinci*. I would spend hours pouring over it. Leonardo's love of nature, humanity, machines and horses made a deep impression. That publication, I am sure, influenced me greatly and soon I was determined to learn to draw well and become an artist myself. As a youngster I wanted to go in this direction and soon everything I did was geared towards it.

My sister and I joined the Girl Guides as our mother before us. It was a wonderful organisation, teaching us some of the fundamental things about life caring for other people, looking after children and the elderly; and it developed in me a lifelong love and respect for animals and plants. During my time in the Guides I worked for a number of badges which once achieved were stitched on to the sleeve of your uniform. In the end I became a patrol leader and a Queen's Guide. One of the enjoyable things every week was at the end of the session, we sat on the floor in a circle and sang songs as if around a campfire. In the summer we went camping and really did sing around a campfire. The motto for the Girl Guides is 'Be Prepared' which has always served me well.

We were also regular churchgoers. For many years we children walked to St Peter's church in Petersham with a penny in our pocket for the collection. The vicar there was a good old man who obviously loved leading the Sunday School Service. We learned the church calendar there with different colours for every festival Each time we attended, we got a stamp to put into our book. It was always a privilege to be asked to read the lesson and the Reverend Mills carefully selected the children so that nobody was left out. In the Fifties, he prepared me for confirmation and I was confirmed in Richmond by the Bishop of Kingston-on-Thames.

The next school I went to was the Old Vicarage School, which I had to go to on the bus at first by myself, as it was in Richmond. Later, my sister Trisha came with me on the No.65 bus. At this school, I tended my first garden: we planted seeds and bulbs and watched them grow and eventually flower. I remember having to sit on the naughty bench for giving a teacher Mrs. Collins the nickname Collywobbles. She and other teachers, used to write in my school report 'Could do better!' There were one or two dramas here as in any childhood, like the time on sports day in Richmond Park when I was knocked out by a rounder's ball.

I enjoyed my early education apart from when I was sent away to boarding school. Trisha and I were close as children and she has told me that seeing me off to boarding school at Waterloo Station was a terrible memory. I was sent to the Royal Naval School in Surrey, which I absolutely hated. My father had thought it a brilliant idea to send me there. At this point he had been stationed in Haslemere, and had seen the girls walking down Farnham Lane to church in their neat uniforms. They looked rather well-behaved and devout and he thought it would be good for me to have a little discipline in my life. But it was not for me. I ended up organising the Runaway Club from a mouldy old coach dumped in the grounds. We had some successful escapes but I personally never got further than the station. We saved our tuck and pocket money so that we always had cash and supplies for escapees. There was great celebration in the dormitory when somebody got away. Eventually, we were found out and they removed the coach and banned our club. Thankfully, my time there was cut short as my father was posted to Malta. But my stay at boarding school left its mark as any unpleasant experience does. I am sure I became claustrophobic as a result of being held on detention and made to stay in a small room writing out lines. I still cannot go into a lift without feeling sick. So it was a great relief to the whole family, as well as to me, when we went out to join Daddy in Malta.

During the times they were together, my parents were a wonderful, loving couple and certainly had their hands full with us four. My father had been absent for most of our childhood but now we were thrilled to be all together again. In the early Fifties, we sailed to Malta on an ocean liner the Empire Halliday to Valletta, the bustling capital. It was the family's first time abroad and all of our senses were awakened by what hit us as we disembarked. All around the ship were dghajsas, local fishing boats filled with people trying to sell us things. What caught my eye were the horse-drawn kavvozin, which many people used as a taxi all over the island. Our father was delighted to see us at the port and filled the car with all our cases. He drove us to our splendid new home in Rabat. We were amazed at this huge house he had managed to find. It had the most magnificent view, looking out towards Valletta and Sliema in the distance below. We had rented the building from Mrs de Trafford who apparently had met Daddy at a cocktail party. He had mentioned he was looking for a house suitable for four boisterous children. Later she told us she had only let it to us because of the children. She had brought up her own four there.

The house and surrounding area was a youngster's paradise. It had a grand staircase leading up to the entrance. There were pillars supporting a huge veranda outside my parents' bedroom - perfect for nude sunbathing. There were wonderful tiled floors, especially good for sliding on and generally rushing around. For the first time we each had our own bedroom and a maid for the cleaning. There were large reception rooms and sofas for lounging about in, but the hub of the house was the kitchen which had a big table and a magnificent Aga. You could make toast at any time of the day as it was always on, supplying the hot water for the whole house even in summer.

We went to the Naval School in a place called Tal Handaq, going by bus from the main square in Rabat; the school bus collected children from all corners of the island. The school was for the forces' families on the island and in those days - we are talking about the Fifties - there were a great many troops stationed in Malta. There was a primary school, a grammar-school stream and a secondary modern stream all in different buildings on the same campus. One day there was a terrible accident on the journey home; the bus had stopped to let a young boy off. He jumped down and ran across the road and was hit by a car. We saw it happen but the bus did not stop. He was the brother of a friend of mine and it was a dreadful experience for us all - never to be forgotten. His funeral was one of the first I remember going to.

I had my first riding lessons at the Marsa Club. My father was quite a horseman himself and would drive me to the club, and have a ride himself whilst I had my lesson. For a treat we would go and have a drink in the clubhouse afterwards. We spent quite a lot of time at the Marsa as it was a centre of activity for the officers' families. My parents played tennis there, we would go to watch them play, or we could observe other events such as polo and cricket. If it was a family outing, we always took one of our famous picnics to avoid having to eat in the expensive clubhouse. My parents did the usual round of cocktail parties and when they were away, we got up to all kinds of adventures. There was a network of caves in the cliffs just below the house and we constructed a den there where we would go and make supper on a camp fire.

We were always eager to hear what had happened on their nights out at these parties which were special as they did not exactly happen when we were in the UK. I remember one story which we all laughed at after one of these occasions. Mummy, on hearing a joke, was laughing so much on board a ship that her hat blew off into the water below. She could not possibly lose her precious headgear, so after a real hullabaloo - a boat was launched to retrieve it, much to Daddy's embarrassment.

I seemed to have a difficult but loving relationship with him which I think goes back to my sister's birth in Scotland. Then I was the only child, eighteen months old and I imagine, rather spoiled and much loved. My father was in Helensburgh waiting for his appointment to a ship during the war. Luckily, due to the imminent birth of my sister, he missed being sent to HMS Hood, thank God. Later the Hood was sunk in the Atlantic with almost all hands lost, so it was a great blessing for us that my father did not make that posting. As I have mentioned, I had really bonded with him then but it was never really the same again as I hoped it would be.

When he was at home, my father was always the disciplinarian and liked to run the household rather like a ship. This remained so in Malta although there was more of a holiday feeling about our life when we lived there. We had many marvellous trips to the beach in the family car, and we all became efficient swimmers. Another favourite for us were the boat trips which were organized by the various naval ships docked in Sliema or Valletta. There were constant cocktail parties and other celebrations to which we were occasionally invited. Malta therefore was a favourite place for all my family. We were to live there twice, the first when I was twelve and the second when I was nineteen.

After the usual three-year stint, we returned to our home in Petersham which had been let to another family while we had been in Malta. New schools had to be found for Trisha and I, and we opted to go to Notting Hill and Ealing High School. A number of girls in our street had gone here and, although it was a long way for us to travel each day, it was worthwhile as the school had a good reputation. It was also safe for Trisha and I to go on our own as it was door to door on the same 65 bus. This was our routine for the next five years or so.

I worked hard for my 'O' levels and ended up getting eight, though they were in rather strange subjects such as cookery, needlework and above all, art. I had spent most of my last year in the art studio working with a teacher who had become a good friend. She had suggested I take up art and really encouraged me to go in that direction. The idea of further art education was put to my father in 1956 and we had several meetings to discuss it. My teacher, Mrs Lazenby, had approached Corsham Court on my behalf and I was thrilled by her recommendation. For the first time I was planning to do something I really wanted for myself. I did everything I could to persuade him to allow me to go. Sadly, he decided against it as, truthfully, he could not afford to send me to Corsham Court residential art school because he had to bear the considerable expense of both my brothers' public school fees. I was devastated. It was my first major disappointment. Later I found out that my headmistress had offered to pay for the art school costs herself but my father politely declined the offer - too proud to accept a handout. It did not stop me in my tracks for long; in fact, it delayed me for only a year, as I was absolutely determined to go to art school. So, being rather pig headed, I set about making my own plans. I had heard about Chelsea Art School in London, and made inquiries there but was too late for the current year. They suggested I apply again in the spring of the following year. I went for an interview then and, thankfully, I was accepted and proudly paid for everything myself.

In the meantime I had a gap year, as they are now called, to fill. Mrs Lazenby suggested I become a student art teacher and that is what I did. As luck would have it, she knew of a school which needed somebody. It was Dulwich College for boy's public school near Sydenham Hill station relatively easy for me to get to and from Richmond. I happily worked at the college for a year, assisting the art teacher, Peter Sumsion. It was a good experience and taught me how to cope with rather lively boys who did not always want to paint. It was also useful for me later in my life when I would find myself teaching art again in rather different circumstances. It was while I was working here that I arranged my interview at Chelsea Art School.

Collecting my drawings and paintings together mainly from my art classes at school for my interview with the headmaster Mr Williamson, was the most serious thing I had ever done. I especially bought a portfolio to carry my work in because I had quite a distance to travel and I certainly did not want work falling out and getting damaged. I was professional in how I arranged everything, and it surprised me how I applied myself when I really wanted something. The day I set off for my interview was one of my proudest moments and in all seriousness, it was also the first day of the rest of my life.

I mounted the steps to Chelsea Art School and entered the Victorian building, which was comfortable and welcoming, and I had that feeling of having finally arrived somewhere I wanted to be. That day is ingrained in my memory. I climbed the stairs with my heavy portfolio, the Art School being on the upper floor of what was the Chelsea College of Technology. I waited at the top, breathing deeply to give myself courage. There was a smell which I immediately recognised - oil paint - and I loved it.

I waited a moment while I gathered myself before announcing my arrival. This was such an important moment in my life and I truly wanted to get it right. I was shown into the headmaster's office. The interview began. He was charming and asked many questions such as 'Why do you wish to study art?' I said I had always wanted to be an artist and it was the subject I was most talented in; I wanted to paint with all my heart. Surrounded by my work, I said it was my passion. The interview did not last long but he welcomed me into the school and hoped I would enjoy my time there. It felt so marvellous leaving the building knowing I had been accepted to study for the Foundation Course.

CHAPTER TWO
CHELSEA ART SCHOOL
You're driving me crazy

I started the following September. Actually spending the whole day painting or drawing with other colleagues was bliss. We were all hopeful artists, giving the best feeling of belonging. There were moments on the way when I had seriously doubted if it would really happen. The collapse of my first effort with Mrs Lazenby had been a major blow. That original school had been especially good for training art teachers. Interestingly, I would become a teacher of art later in my life and my experience at Dulwich College had been important in that respect.

For my first term at Chelsea I commuted from our Petersham home. It would mean rising early, taking a bus to Richmond and catching the District Line to Sloane Square, then another bus to Manresa Road. It was tiring but I was determined to do it. It became an exciting ritual. I was an art student now and dressed accordingly in rather strange and colourful outfits. I enjoyed and definitely looked the part in a duffle coat with a basket containing my sketch book and painting materials. I wore combinations of exciting colours and textures. By necessity I was making my own clothes so there were some interesting numbers!

I was still involved with my first boyfriend, Jack Bond. He had been the centre of my life for the last two years. We had met at 'L'Auberge', a coffee bar in Richmond. Early in our relationship we were invited to a special birthday party which significantly was a jazz night on Eel Pie Island in the middle of the Thames. Jazz nights were often held there on the island and they became a regular feature in our lives. It was a venue of great importance to us and for many of our generation. Although it was still the late fifties, for me this was where the sixties music revolution began. Bands like the Rolling Stones played there later. It was a must for Jack and I and we went there every Saturday night to jive the night away without a break. We became famous for our dancing, especially our slow jive. All the girls wore full skirts, some with matching knickers. I made many extraordinary outfits especially for jiving; this was the start of my designing and making clothes - the more outrageous and colourful the better. It was not unusual for me to knock up an outfit for a Saturday night session out of some material that I had found either at home or bought in a shop.

There had been a few boyfriends before Jack but nothing serious. He was my first boyfriend and we loved each other with a breathless passion. He taught me how to kiss and was the first person to teach me about the birds and the bees. We seemed to do everything but the real thing. I was very naive and inexperienced about sex, terrified of getting pregnant. He on the other hand was experienced. Later on I never understood how he coped with not going all the way with me. We both had close, good relationships with our mothers but a difficult one with our fathers. We felt we had something in common here. Our fathers had been away for a lot of our childhood during and after the war. They were both disciplinarians and expected us to do their bidding. We were both quite strong individuals who knew what we wanted to do with our lives and I suppose like most teenagers, resented being treated like children. We were pretty naive - just beginning to find our feet in our relationship and in our lives. I don't think either of us felt we wanted to spend the rest of our lives together then.

Jack had a huge motorbike and, later, an old Hillman car. He used to come and collect me from school on the bike and I will never forget pointing him out to my friends as he waited for me by the bus stop, combing his hair just like James Dean in the movies. I felt so proud of him in a schoolgirl way, as I climbed elegantly on to the back of his bike. We would zoom off with a roar all the way back to Richmond for a coffee at our special place, 'L'Auberge'. My father, needless to say, did not approve: ' a most unsuitable boy', he would say. One evening he even called the police because we were late home. We were actually sitting in the bus shelter having a snog. I was furious with Daddy, and we didn't speak for days. It was so humiliating having a police car stop and ask what we were doing.

Jack and I spent a lot of time at the pictures, and went regularly to one of the three cinemas in Richmond. I was enthralled by the clothes, while Jack was passionate about the process of film-making. We discussed each movie endlessly, dissecting every aspect. He went on to be an excellent film director, making many films - such as 'Dali in New York', as well as programmes for the 'South Bank Show'. His love of film started in those early days going to the pictures in Richmond - it was a passion for both of us.

We were often accompanied by Trisha and her boyfriend at the time, Dave Partridge. She too would work in the film business for most of her life and became a famous set decorator, ending up with the greatest accolade - awarded an Oscar for her work on 'Finding Neverland'. It is interesting how early passions make such a deep impression; we all ended up doing something connected to the film business - mine was fashion. My first inspiration had come from watching so many movies.

Jack always encouraged me with my art and often sat for me as I practised my drawing. He was, though, quite fearful of my going to art school and thought it would take me away from him. I told him not to worry as we thought we were a long-term item. I felt I would never meet anybody who could kiss the way he did or dance the way we did together, and I never did meet anybody to match him on both those counts. Like all the young men at that time, he was called up to do his national service. On the terrible day his mother and I went to see him off at Waterloo Station, we both had a very sad feeling that our youth had ended. Jack was absolutely right though - things were never the same after that. My Chelsea art school environment was so different and inspiring in comparison. I was now meeting an extraordinary cross section of people and making new friends. Nothing serious at first, but I felt free from the usual parental pressure of having to be back home at a certain time. Jack was away doing his national service and although we were still in touch, I felt he was very distant. My father was already in Malta, the rest of the family would join him in a few weeks, and then - for the first time ever - I would be truly on my own.

With my new bohemian friends I could go to pubs and nightclubs on a regular basis. 'The Kings Head and Eight Bells' in the Kings Road was a favourite with the added bonus of the jazz club upstairs. Artists like Augustus John would be there holding forth and he especially enjoyed talking to us art students. He had been a student at Chelsea years before, and was a regular much appreciated visitor to the school. He cut a dashing figure in the Kings Road in a flowing black cape with his usual matching fedora. He was well respected amongst us; we used to hang on his every word and loved the privilege of a conversation with him. It surprised me how much he enjoyed speaking with us. I think we were a breath of fresh air in his complicated life.

I was commuting to college but when the family left for Malta to join my father, I had to find somewhere else to live. The house we shared for most of our childhood had to be cleared and the furniture stored for our return. Now my task was to find a flat and I decided to share with my friend Virginia who was also a student at Chelsea, a year ahead of me. Without much effort we found accommodation in Carlyle Square - a large ground-floor room in the front of the house with two single beds, with a shared kitchen and bathroom. It was an eclectic household with an amazing mix of people coming and going, which soon became the centre of my life.

The first year at Chelsea was the foundation course which everybody had to do to find their special talents. By now, my heart was set on sculpture and I spent as much time as possible in the Sculpture Department. We had some wonderful teachers, such as Elizabeth Frink, Bernard Meadows and Willi Soukop. Liz was a great help to me, very enthusiastic and always encouraging, and became a good friend. She advised me that it was almost impossible for a female sculptor to make a living, and that I would probably end up teaching. At this time she was still struggling herself, long before she became an eminent artist. I would not have minded teaching in an art school as things were beginning to happen for women in the sculpture world.

She became my mentor and lived opposite our house in Carlyle Square. She cut a colourful figure, in tight jeans, floppy sweaters and masses of blonde hair flying out behind her. She was a true bohemian: it was certainly the look of the moment which I tried to emulate when I was at Chelsea and later on, with black stockings, colourful skirts and big sweaters, not to mention loads of eye makeup.

Life at college was hard work with, most importantly, regular life drawing, but I enjoyed every minute of it. These days they do not do much life drawing at art school, but I believe it gives students a strong grounding for your future work whatever you might end up doing. For me it would be sculpture. Each Monday we would spend the day at the V&A Museum drawing whatever took our fancy and I became familiar with everything in the museum. Today it is still a firm favourite and I try to go to their new exhibitions which are always beautifully presented.

I got involved with the Students Union and helped with various events. Every Tuesday lunchtime they would have jazz in the Great

Hall and my friends and I would go for a jive. We met the president of the Students Union, who made the profound statement that for sure we would lose our virginity and take up drinking and smoking before the year was out. We were surprised to discover that he was quite right. He became a good friend during my time at Chelsea; sadly for me, he had a girlfriend but he was a wonderful jiving partner on Tuesdays.

The following year at his suggestion, I became social secretary of the Students Union, organising regular events such as jazz nights with bands like Wally Fawkes and The Temperance Seven; some of our students played in the band with them so they were happy to do a college gig. They had a weird and wonderful sound, with numbers such as 'You're Driving Me Crazy'. Their music was fun to jive to and it was great to hang out with them. Later they became a big success and went on to make records and be one of the more unusual groups of the early Sixties. I developed my organisational skills setting up these events, booking bands, arranging advertising and doing the food and drink.

In my first year I had been involved in an annual college event. The students put on 'The Stunt' which was the last college show that Trisha and Mummy came to see me in before they went to Malta. I was in the chorus and in the opening routine I came in a bar too early, to my horror! I was mortified and it would be my last effort as a chorus girl for a very long time. This was a farewell celebration for the headmaster Mr Williamson. Many years later I would be singing and dancing again, this time for a Gilbert and Sullivan operetta group in Hereford.

Our landlady in Carlyle Square was quite an eccentric individual called Meriel Mowbray. She was from the famous building family Mowbray Ltd and by our standards was incredibly rich, but also very generous. She held extravagant parties which we were always invited to and at one of these I met her friend, Shaun Noble. He was a real charmer and seemed to make a beeline for me. He was an actor who had recently split up from his wife and was bemoaning the fact that he did not see enough of his children. His wife owned 'The Boutique' in Walton Street, and the first thing he did was take me there and buy me an outfit: a winner in the impression stakes for an impoverished student and I had my first taste of designer clothes.

'The Boutique' was beautiful and definitely made its mark on me. I took it all in because, unbeknown to me then, just a few years later I would open my own boutique in the Kings Road. For the moment, I had this wonderful new outfit which I wore later that night when Shaun took me out to dinner at the Rascasse Club in Chelsea. He introduced me to his many friends. It was the kind of place I had never experienced before - all rather sophisticated and theatrical, with lots of 'Hallo, darling'. We started to see each other regularly as he was fun to be with and different from anyone else I had ever known. I began to think perhaps this was the man who would finally take my virginity. I thought it was about time I did the deed as so many of my friends had already lost theirs. I would not be surprised if it had crossed his mind as well; it seemed to be a subject that we returned to in conversation on a regular basis. But it was difficult if you shared a flat with somebody!

Virginia and I enjoyed living together; the room was light and spacious but it was difficult to have any kind of privacy. We had single beds and occasionally there would be four of us. It could be a bit crowded with much huffing and puffing. It was here that I finally lost my virginity to Shaun, a man ten years older than me. My great fear was always that I would get 'in the family way' as they said in those days. I felt he knew what he was doing and would be careful, and I am happy to say he did not make me pregnant. On the great occasion, we were on our own in the flat. I had waited a long time for this moment and was disappointed it was not more spectacular. There were no bells ringing and it was all over very quickly with me wondering - was that it? But I did feel different the next day, more grown-up but still not exactly relaxed about the whole thing.

CHAPTER THREE
FAMILY REFLECTIONS - AND SHAUN

A foggy day in London town

Whilst I found my way in the exciting student environment of Chelsea, the family had moved to Malta and for the first time in my life I was truly on my own. We were emotionally close so I was homesick and missed them all dreadfully. I was the eldest of four, my sister Trisha being the closest to me, then came my younger brothers Simon and John. Simon was away at school at Sherborne and joined the family for the holidays. Both Trisha and John were already in Malta with my parents. I planned to be with them all for the whole summer at the end of my second year at Chelsea.

Although I loved the flat, I was feeling a bit sorry for myself. I had the usual cold and flu of that time of year and was miserable. It gave me time and space to think about my family and how lucky I was to have their loving support. It felt strange to be separated from them but at the same time in my stubborn way, I was trying as hard as I could to distance myself. It is often said that girls are attracted to men that are like their fathers, but I think I was aiming for somebody who did not resemble my father in any way. As a child it was difficult to get his attention in the same way I had when I was very young. I started to become naughty and attention-seeking to make my mark, but instead of drawing us closer, the bond we had made in Scotland seemed to vanish. The great love he had expressed to me on that fateful day, never materialised in the way I had always longed for - perhaps I was foolish to have expected it.

Most importantly I knew he loved me: he was a good father to us all and always gave sound advice. Interestingly, I tried to achieve everything in my life for him and for my mother but she was much more appreciative and easier to please. He was the hard taskmaster. Few men were ever good enough for my sister or me, and it was always a relief when he approved of the man in your life. Luckily, he did approve of the man I eventually married and they got on rather well. It might have had something to do with the fact that his family lived on a huge estate called Avington Park in Hampshire.

My mother was a quite different story - she was warm and gentle, loving each of her children equally. She was always there for us as she did not go back to work after she married, having been a successful hair stylist and beautician. She was artistic and had a great colour sense. Her genes have made a huge contribution to my sister's and my artistic achievements. I feel I owe everything I have achieved in my life to my parents' support and enthusiasm. My mother really did sacrifice her own career, whatever that might have been, for her children which was normal in those days. My parents had a good, strong relationship; there was the odd tantrum but nothing serious. My father was the boss and we did everything we could to keep the peace. I was the only one really who was at all difficult.

My relationship with my mother was always special. She loved the fact that somehow I had got to art school and that I was doing what I really wanted. She could be quite critical of the men in my life, but her judgement was always sound and she could often see what I saw in somebody - even though they might not be the kind of man she hoped I would marry. I listened to her advice and there was a moment when I felt, perhaps, I was living the kind of young life that she would have liked to have had, but was unable to accomplish.

Everything was so different for her and her sisters when they were growing up. This gave her a cautious attitude to sexual relations, giving my sister and me the impression that you almost only had to kiss a man to get pregnant. It was her way of telling us to be careful. It certainly had the desired effect; it took me ages to relax and enjoy sex, until eventually, as we have discovered, I lost my virginity. In the fifties, sex education was still limited to biology lessons, and like most teenagers of the time, one learned from one's friends who were already sexually active. I was really surprised when one friend said to me that making love was the best thing in the world; it took me a long time to feel the same.

It was during this time I decided to get a dog. From the past I knew that having a pet gave you responsibility and something special to love. I went to Battersea Dog's Home - a short walk from where I was living - and had a look at all the dogs wanting homes. There were so many to choose from. In those days the staff were not too fussy about the home a dog might go to, as I only had a small flat. Thank goodness Virginia did not seem to mind the dog being there as well.

It was during my childhood that I developed my love of animals. The first dog I remember was a little terrier called Penny. I had found her wandering in the nearby fields without a collar and managed to persuade Mummy to let us keep her. We put a notice up to say we had found her but nobody claimed her. I was not quite so successful with cats: again, I found a kitten and brought her home and hid her in the airing cupboard, where she was discovered immediately. Mummy was not very fond of cats so I had to take it back to where I had found it. Hopefully it found a home, but I worried about the poor little thing for a long time.

After the terrier, we had Labradors. My godfather, Uncle Geoff and his wife Bundy bred a litter of puppies from their bitch. My aunt and uncle were favourite relations and I would often go and stay with them on my own. So when the puppies arrived, it was fabulous to choose one for ourselves. We called her Honey and she was my pride and joy. She would come with us on family walks when we went to Richmond Park or along the Teddington Lock towpath. Eventually she had puppies and I remember being really upset when we were not allowed to keep Jinx, my favourite. I had always enjoyed keeping animals including loads of rabbits and mice. At one time I had thoughts of becoming a vet, but soon realised I was not brainy enough to achieve the qualifications required. Then I learned the training took about seven years, so I quickly gave up on the idea when I knew just how long it would take to qualify.

There was never a great deal of money around when we were growing up. A naval officer's salary was rather limited then but there was enough to clothe and feed us, with few luxuries. The day we got our first car and first television were great events in our lives and of course made a huge difference. Part of the problem was that my parents were, quite rightly, keen to educate us properly, sending us all to private schools. Many of their generation had missed out on further education due to the two wars. Eventually, we all appreciated our education but it was hard on the family financially - as many sacrifices had to be made.

As children what we enjoyed most and yet took for granted, was the fact that we were surrounded by countryside and played in such a beautiful landscape. Living near Richmond Park and the River Thames was a real bonus and we walked there regularly. A picnic in the park was another favourite. I watched people riding their horses and imagined that one day I would do the same. Later I exercised polo ponies at Ham Polo Club, and it became an ambition of mine at an early age to play polo. Years afterwards in Jamaica - I did exactly that.

Finding myself alone made me reflect and appreciate how lucky I was to have grown up in a safe, loving family. It is true that you do not appreciate what you have until it is not there any more, although in reality it was always there for the asking. I was desperately trying to prove that I could manage well on my own, even if I was living off tomato soup and baked beans on toast. To this day, if I am not feeling great - I feel the need for Heinz tomato soup and baked beans on toast to sustain me. Sad but true.

Mixing with students from all over the world made you aware of your fellow students' extraordinary lives. One friend had just escaped from the Hungarian revolution traumatised by the events there. He was a prince and had left his country with nothing except his life and what he could carry. He was extremely talented and went on to do great things as an artist. The college was a wonderful eclectic mix of students from diverse backgrounds - that was what I enjoyed and appreciated most about it. The friends I made at art school set a pattern for the rest of my life: I was always attracted to the unusual or tricky character - the more complex and needy the better. My mother would say that all the men in my life needed looking after. Why not go for somebody to look after me?

She was right of course, and here I was once again setting out on such a relationship. Although Shaun was older than me, there was so much about him that I needed to take care of. He had left the safety of his wife and family and was now dependent on his friends more than ever before and that included Meriel, who had introduced me to him, and myself. He certainly was not able to cook for himself, and I think I can safely say I never saw him prepare a hot meal. My cooking then was limited. I was hardly able to produce delicious meals; they were very simple dishes and we went out to eat sometimes.

At this stage, I was not fully aware that because Shaun was 'resting' as most actors tend to do between roles, it meant that if he went for an audition for a new part - he spent the remainder of the day in the pub. I was at college all day and often came back to find him the worse for the drink. It took me a long time to realise that this was becoming a problem for him. The freedom of living in my own flat was rather daunting but at the same time special; I felt more grown-up and found I was able to make my own decisions - even if some may have been wrong.

It was special too - having a new man in my life while at the same time being at college; I also had to work so that I could pay my own way. I soon found that Shaun was not entirely responsible for himself let alone for me, but I was determined to stay with it. All day I was modelling in the sculpture department while Shaun would either be acting in a film or going to auditions. If there was no acting work, he went to the pub.

During this time I had various jobs working as a waitress. One was in the early morning in a breakfast restaurant called 'Small Fry' where I learned to make the best scrambled eggs - the secret being that the heat should not be too high. One should melt the butter and gently stir in the beaten eggs, then keep stirring constantly until the eggs are ready, and season with salt and pepper. The cafe 'Small Fry' was just around the corner from where I lived, on the Butler and Wilson site in the Fulham Road. When I had finished cooking endless breakfasts, I was ready to start my day at college by ten, usually smelling of eggs and bacon but having eaten a really good breakfast which would last me the whole day.

The second was an evening job at a drinking club called the 'Apron Strings', also in the Fulham Road. Invariably Shaun dropped in for a pint before taking me home. The 'Apron Strings' was an unusual place with all kinds of Chelsea characters coming in for a tipple. It had a distinctive boozy smell in which I felt comfortable. If we had the energy, we would end up at the Chelsea Arts Club for a nightcap and dance. In theory I was not allowed to drink on the job at the 'Apron Strings' so I usually stayed sober. I had not yet developed a taste for alcohol and would just sip a glass of red wine.

Shaun introduced me to his sophisticated way of life. Neither of us had much money, but he took great pleasure in showing me off to his friends in the pubs and clubs. We ate in various Chelsea restaurants such as the 'Picasso' and 'Choys', the local Chinese. Occasionally we would go to West End clubs such as Ronnie Scott's Jazz Club and the 'Blue Angel'. Our life, though, centred around the Kings Road and the Fulham Road where there was always plenty of activity. Our favourite pubs were 'Finchs', 'The Cross Keys', and the 'Queens Elm' not to mention the Chelsea Arts Club.

With Shaun - I felt very much part of the Chelsea Set which was different from just being an art student. Chelsea people were diverse and exotic - mainly writers, actors and artists. They could be rather elitist as well and often a student like myself was frowned on. I did not mind a bit - for me it was amazing to be part of this life, and to enjoy the wonderful conversations going on all around you. In the end, I realised that Shaun's life was drink orientated and that this was not what I really wanted in a relationship or in my life. Shaun remained a good friend but I drifted away from him to form other friendships with people more my own age.

CHAPTER FOUR
STUDENT DAYS
Dream, dream, dream

One person whom I befriended at this time was an extraordinary chap named Douglas Gray. We met in Hyde Park walking our dogs. I had called my greyhound Brubeck after the famous Dave Brubeck Quartet. Brubeck was black with the saddest eyes, and in need of tender loving care after his ordeal on the racecourse and at Battersea Dogs' Home. Similarly, Douglas's dog was also a rescued greyhound called Ginger - so we immediately had something in common. The dogs were the first to meet on that spring day, and Douglas and I inevitably got chatting.

He was a larger-than-life flamboyant character with a bushy red beard and cheekily asked me to come for a drink in a nearby pub. It turned out, not surprisingly, that he was a musician and with his brother was part of a cabaret show called 'The Alberts'. They were in demand in the nightclubs and used to perform all over the West End. Their show involved playing many weird and wonderful instruments including a penny-farthing bicycle. They sang songs to go with it, many of which they had written themselves.

Later that week he invited me along to one of his gigs to experience for myself what their shows were like. It was amazing. I had never seen anything quite like it before. The act was pure music hall, very funny with some good songs. In the next few months I would often go with them in a long black dress, to the gig and pass them the instruments as they were required. They sometimes had a clarinettist with them called Tony. He was a magical character and a great musician and played beautifully. He was the first person I knew to live in a van and used to park it near the Iranian Embassy. Sadly, he died a rather mysterious death, which we all thought was from hypothermia.

To have a steady income both the Gray brothers, Douglas and Tony, used to do the early collection of newspapers from Fleet Street and deliver them all over London and the suburbs. When Douglas had the morning shift, he would leave a pile on our doorstep with a red rose and a love letter, usually inviting me to a show or to walk our dogs. We were a strange-looking couple: he wore exotic clothes - long flowing coats, boots and a hat. I was a typical art student and wore black stockings with colourful skirts or jeans. I remember a pair of tight lilac trousers which were a firm favourite which I wore with a baggy top. I was making my own clothes as it was so much cheaper to buy a few yards of cloth and put them together. I was very experimental in those early days and would often cobble together something amazing on my sewing machine, a prize possession.

Making clothes for friends was another way I could earn a few pounds and it turned out to be a nice little earner. Often people would ask me to make outfits for them from their own material, or sometimes I would find the material, selecting the cloth and making a pattern as I had done for myself in the past: it was exciting work and I enjoyed in enormously. They were always unusual and rather colourful; it all seemed a natural progression and so easy for me to make something truly original.

At the same time I was also printing some of my own fabric designs on the huge printing tables we had at Chelsea. I had decided to do a couple of terms of textile design with Stephen Sykes, one of my favourite teachers at the college. It was great to design a fabric, print it, and then make it up into a skirt or a pair of trousers. As you could print off quite a few yards at a time, there was always some spare to make up for others. It was yet another way of earning a few pounds to spend on other more necessary things.

On one occasion I made a wedding dress for a girlfriend in my year. It gave me a wonderful feeling of satisfaction to go to the celebrations having designed and made the dress. Later on this would happen quite often when I had my own boutique. But by then it was much more professional as I had pattern and sample makers and I just did the drawings and fittings. Making a little money by designing and producing clothes for friends made me realise how satisfying it would be to make a living this way, but I never imagined that I would end up being a sixties' fashion designer and become part of the 'Swinging London' phenomenon.

As social secretary of the students' union I regularly put on events at the college on a Saturday night. It usually involved booking a band such as Wally Faulks, advertising the event and generally getting everybody to come. How I wish I had kept all the posters for those events because they were done by fellow students such as Patrick Caulfield and Natalie Gibson, both of whom developed into well-known artists in their own special way. Those Saturday nights became quite famous in Chelsea: they were the place to be at the time. I also organised food and drink for the occasion but that was always secondary to the music and dancing.

As well as the social events at the college I got involved with the political events of the moment. The most important of these were the anti-nuclear protests. There were marches in the capital but there was also a huge march from London to Aldermaston. We were against nuclear weapons and for me it was the first of the important marches that students organised. Although Chelsea College of Technology did not organise it, all colleges and many students participated. Somehow it had to be co-ordinated. It was well attended and I think ingrained on our consciousness - a devotion to anti-nuclear demonstrations and frankly anti-warfare of any kind.

For the moment I was leading the life of a student and living on very little. I had my various jobs and managed to pay the rent and make ends meet. My parents did not give me an allowance but I knew that if I needed it, they would come to my rescue. Pride, however, prevented me from asking for help. I got an enormous pleasure making my money stretch, whilst at the same time taking good care of myself, and enjoyed making simple meals out of healthy ingredients. Often we would go to other students' flats to sample what delights they might rustle up. I remember one day going to a friend's flat at World's End in Chelsea, which was exactly where my boutique would be.

My diet was limited to standard student fare such as spaghetti bolognese, lasagne, bacon and eggs, baked beans on toast or even a baked potato. An evening out was always a treat, either at a local Chinese or Indian restaurant, but an evening in listening to records - such as Dave Brubeck or Thelonious Monk - with 'spag bol' and a glass of red wine was most acceptable. I still have my jazz record collection from those days, and these records remain my choice to dance to. We would go to jive the night away at 100 Oxford Street, Ronnie Scott's and Cy Laurie's jazz clubs. The dancing was always more important than the drinking; anyway we could not afford to drink much.

Our Carlyle Square house seemed to be a Mecca for parties, not necessarily put on by myself and Virginia. Meriel, our landlady, was a generous and gregarious woman and had many friends. Through us she met Chris, a fellow student and a fine artist. They celebrated their relationship with soirees in the L-shaped studio above our room. It was impossible to sleep if this was going on so we would invariably join the group, often ending up in our flat downstairs for coffee. These parties would happen most week-ends and it was here that I saw people smoking marijuana for the first time.

Shaun was still around but our relationship was not as intense as it used to be. He had got a job working on a film in Ireland so he was out of circulation for a while. As soon as he was back in the UK he was a regular visitor again, often coming to one of the parties and hoping that things would take off again as before. We remained friends but I did not want to have a serious relationship with him because of the drink problem.

One evening somebody suggested we play the Ouija board. I had never heard of this and looked on rather tentatively but at one stage was drawn into it and sat down with the group. There was an upturned glass in the centre of the table, and around the edge were randomly placed letters of the alphabet. About six or seven people sat together with their fingers gently resting on the glass. The medium would call to the spirits to direct it. As if by magic it would move across the table to various letters, spelling out peoples names and often leaving a message. All rather disconcerting. It predicted a car crash which actually happened, but luckily nobody was killed.

I was burning the candle at both ends so at a certain point I become ill again, and ended up in bed, unable to go to college. I must have called Uncle Geoff, my guardian. The next thing I knew he arrived to take me to his home in Dorney near Windsor. He whisked me off to the country, not exactly against my will as I was feeling dreadful. I had a temperature and a terrible cough. The flat was a typical student's pad, rather chaotic including an empty milk bottle on the mantelpiece and clothes scattered everywhere. He reported back to my parents, who realised things were not as they should be. I am sure they were not surprised but needless to say - they now became worried about my London lifestyle.

I soon recovered during the Easter break and returned for the summer term at Chelsea, realising it was time to settle down to some rather serious work. I decided to try for the Christopher Head Scholarship which would enable me to do another year at Chelsea and specialise in Sculpture. To apply I had to produce and select a number of drawings from my portfolio in any medium, which I then displayed on four imperial-sized pieces of paper in the corridor at the art school. My presentation consisted of various pieces I had done during my time there and some which I had done especially for the Scholarship, such as a pen-and-ink sketch of the Albert Bridge and the Embankment. Also various life drawings, and portraits of friends and animals.

We were then asked to make a presentation of our work and talk a little about our hopes and aspirations for the future. I told them my desire was to go to the Royal College of Art and study in the sculpture department. At Chelsea we had the best sculpture teachers a student could wish for, thus enabling many of us to go on to get our NDD at the Royal College which was what I wanted to do. So I emphasised that with my present teacher's help, I thought they could get me accepted by the College. It was all very nerve wracking, talking about life-changing dreams which felt almost unobtainable.

To my surprise, I won the Christopher Head Scholarship and was thrilled to pieces. I was determined to complete a third year at Chelsea and then apply to the Royal College of Art to finish my studies. My last few weeks were busy; and we always had an end-of-term party. I was largely responsible for getting this event together as I was the social secretary. It was fancy dress and we dreamed up some outlandish costumes and generally behaved outrageously. I certainly had my fair share to drink - a good few glasses of wine. But it was always the dancing and not the drink that interested me - madly swirling through the night, knowing I was about to set off to a completely different lifestyle, leaving behind my bohemian student life. I was looking forward to seeing the family again, spending the summer in Malta with them, swimming in the sea, playing tennis and generally relaxing.

I left college at the end of term with the full intention of coming back to Chelsea in September for another year as an art student; with that intention I flew to Malta for the holiday. Brubeck my faithful greyhound stayed with friends for the summer.

CHAPTER FIVE
COCKTAIL HOUR IN MALTA
When I take my Sugar to tea

They were at the airport to meet me, even my father who should have been working as the Electrical Commander on HMS Forth. It was good to see everybody and be back in Malta. The family had spent time there before in the early fifties when we were young and we had gone to a school for the services called Tal Handaq. As mentioned, we lived in Rabat then and used to go there in the school bus which would pick us up in the square. I remember one morning a policeman coming up to me to stop me doing somersaults over an iron safety bar. I was showing my knickers in a most unladylike way and he fairly ticked me off. The Maltese are very religious and I was unaware that I was being most offensive.

Back to the airport: the smells, the sounds and the dry-stone walls all seemed familiar. Great excitement: greeting the family and telling them a little about what I had been up to in London. Simon, my elder brother, who had been at Sherborne School had arrived earlier in the month. So finally we were together again and there was much to catch up on. My younger brother John and Trisha had been there with my parents and had already made some new friends. We were close as a family and valued each other's individuality. It would be a special time as it would not be long before we would all go our separate ways.

We loaded everything into the car and drove to Balzan in the centre of the island, eventually arriving at our rented home, Villa Violette.

They showed me my room and I unpacked my few precious belongings. I had not brought a great deal: a few sketch books, my records and in particular my clothes, which were all rather bohemian, more suited to the Kings Road. I would have to get busy with my needle and knock up a few summer outfits to wear in the heat of Malta.

The sun and the sea were fantastic and the first thing we did was to go on one of our legendary family picnics prepared by Mummy. We piled into the car and drove to a special beach called Ghajn Tuffieha, which is beautiful but dangerous. I heard the story in detail about how my father came to rescue John, my young brother, who had got into difficulties in the strong current a few weeks earlier. Trisha and Daddy had been playing and surfing in the waves together. Unbeknown to them, John had been struggling to put his flippers on in rough water. He felt more confident wearing them but on this occasion was swept out of his depth without them. He was frantically calling to them on the beach and they were looking everywhere for him.

Finally, my father spotted a little head bobbing in the distance. He was in the water in a flash and swam to rescue him. They were both swept further on to the rocks, but with great difficulty he managed to bring him back safely to the beach. At that time, John was only twelve, so it was a dreadful moment when everybody realised how close we had come to losing our darling brother. My father's relief was palpable as he retold the story. Apparently on that day, it was one of the few occasions when he openly cried with the emotion of nearly losing his youngest son.

The first few days were probably a bit too much for me because I became ill again with a similar bug to the one I had a few months before in London. It was a truly dreadful cough which would not go away, along with a temperature and night sweats. During my recovery it became clear that my parents did not want me to return to complete my studies in September. They were sweet about it but firm, and as I was not feeling my usual strong self I agreed to stay in Malta. They said my sister and I would have the time of our lives there. We did of course have a great time; the place was buzzing with eligible young men but they were not particularly artistic, in my opinion. Most importantly would I ever fulfil my dream of going to The Royal College of Art to study sculpture? Probably not.

Trisha by now had a boyfriend called George de Trafford who had invited a group of his friends to his family home on Gozo, a small island north of Malta. And I was invited to join them. It was my first taste of life in the sun and it felt as far removed from my London existence as you could imagine. We were staying in this rambling farmhouse and I shared an attic room with Trisha. It was in the village of Xlendi, a picturesque fishing village with a wonderful beach nearby. It was during this weekend that I met Richard Nevil who was also one of the guests at the house party and who happened to be in the Royal Fusiliers. My first thought was 'Oh my God, he is in the army and Daddy definitely would not approve!' He had dreams of Trisha and me getting married to naval officers! But Richard would soon become a good reason for me to stay in Malta.

It was a beautiful relaxed time - when we walked around the village in the sharp, bright sunlight, shopping for food became quite an adventure. We took it in turns to prepare meals - spending our days cooking, drinking, reading, talking and getting to know each other. I met people that weekend who have remained good friends ever since. On the Sunday we hired a fishing boat and took it round the island to a nearby cove to picnic and swim in the amazing turquoise water. Although Richard was supposedly with somebody else at the time, I felt his penetrating blue eyes watching me as I attempted to place myself in this group, trying not to let it be too obvious that I was attracted to him.

I had noticed him immediately, but our first moment was when our gaze had met as he helped me on to the boat. The sea was rough and it was quite difficult to get on board. He had held out his hand and our eyes met for longer than was really necessary. We savoured the moment of that feeling of something extraordinary happening and would always remember that second as the instant when a special spark ignited between us. It is strange to declare love at first sight - but it was like that for me and Richard. At the time I thought it was monumental; this auspicious meeting was obviously the reason why I decided to stay.

I did not know what might happen because he was with somebody else but, as she was a guest on the island, I knew she would be leaving soon - so I was not too worried. As far as I was concerned something extraordinary had happened between us and it would continue throughout the weekend. I had to bide my time and see what would transpire. Having had doubts about wanting to stay in Malta, I now had a very good reason to stay. I had met somebody exciting who was different from the kind of people I had known in London. A straightforward army officer - not the kind of man I usually went for - yet attractive and fun.

As usual I needed to get a job, because I had to have my own money. I had heard over the weekend in Gozo that George's brother Gerald ran a pottery in the garden of the family home, Villa Bologna, in Attard near where we lived in Balzan. I telephoned Gerald and arranged to meet him for an interview at the pottery. It was just a ten-minute walk from our house, through the gardens of the Governor's Palace. He showed me over the premises and brought me to the upstairs studio where he pointed out a table where I would be working decorating plates and tiles. He wanted me to start almost the next day and my pay would be piecemeal. So each week, Gerald gave me a buff envelope with my pay and a list of all the work I had completed. Soon after I started there, Richard came to visit me and we chatted and made plans to meet.

He would collect me in his car, a nippy little red MG, and we would rattle off around the island to have something to eat. We were both still rather innocent, holding hands and sharing a few passionate kisses. I was still too nervous about getting pregnant to go any further. Once we arrived home late and my father was up waiting for us. He was furious and had a real go at Richard for keeping me out so long. I was in tears and I think Richard was embarrassed and cooled off a bit because of my father's outburst.

Life continued with boat picnics and cocktail parties, some organised by the Royal Navy and others by the Royal Fusiliers or the Royal Marines. My sister Trisha and I had the most amazing time, often going out in groups but sometimes individually. Trisha had met Henry Beverley, a young officer in the Royal Marines. Our favourite haunt was 'The Griffin' which happened to be in the grounds of our previous house in Rabat. We often went out with a group of a dozen people or more celebrating somebody's birthday. My speciality food at this restaurant was chicken maryland: grilled chicken served with a banana. There was a dance band that played mainly swing with some jazz. Old favourites included Ella Fitzgerald hits and some big band numbers which we danced to; my favourite was 'I would be a king among kings if I had you'.

Although on these occasions we danced with everybody, it was about this time I noticed Richard holding Caroline, the Governor's daughter, just a little too close for my liking. It was not long before I realised that I was losing my great love - he was falling for somebody else. Within a few months of our meeting, Richard came to our house and announced he was engaged to Caroline: he had just left the Palace where he had asked the Governor's permission to marry Caroline. I was devastated and howled my eyes out. Deep down I was certain he still loved me. In reality he did not think I would make an army wife and, of course, he was right. Mummy said, 'Well if he prefers the Governor's daughter - that is his problem'.

For the next few months I was heartbroken, but life continued at a pace, and I often saw Richard at parties. He always asked me to dance and managed a squeeze, but it was not the same. I met other people and tried to put the hurt behind me. I was introduced to Tony Smith - a good man who, like me, loved jazz and played a mean saxophone. He was in the Marines and we had some good times together. Sadly for him, I was on the rebound and not very responsive to his ardent attention. He was fascinated by my life in the Kings Road and wanted to know all about my past adventures as an art student. Which I have to admit, Richard was not in the slightest bit interested.

Something happened to me over my heartbreak with Richard: it brought a bit of a devil-may-care attitude to my relationships. So the next exciting person I met in Malta was an Italian - and he was to be my next big love. He was a naval officer who was in the area performing exercises with the British navy in his ship Frigate Castore. He was Captain Gianandrea Fazio, a man of the world, sophisticated and charming who spoke excellent English. He was ten years older than me. I had been invited with my sister to a cocktail party on board his ship. A special relationship soon developed between us, much to my father's horror, as I seemed to have acquired a taste for older men. He was good-looking with a typical Italian Marcello Mastroianni look about him.

Soon after we met on board his ship, he was off again on various exercises at sea. We started to write to each other on a regular basis. This continued throughout the last few months of my stay in Malta. I became interested in all things Italian and attempted to learn the language. He returned to Malta a couple of times and we were thrilled to be together again, and although the relationship was emotionally charged, we had not gone to bed together yet. It was difficult to make love on board a ship especially as he was the captain. I still had this fear of getting pregnant and did not believe it was possible to make love carefully as he tried so hard to explain he would. Months later I met him in Italy and we would have my first real affair.

Meanwhile, for the moment I remained with the family; it was a wonderful sun-splashed life. I continued enjoying my work at the pottery, decorating plates and tiles. Towards the end of my stay I did a number of large wall murals. One of which, a few years later, I would discover in the reception of a hotel on Comino when I went on honeymoon with my first husband, Nicolas Head. Comino is a romantic island situated between Malta and Gozo: the ideal place for a honeymoon couple and for boat picnics, especially at the idyllic bay - The Blue Lagoon.

Mummy had finally passed her driving test while in Malta and so we travelled around together, visiting some of the sights and spending days on the beach. There was an awful moment though when she gave the car a knock going through a narrow arch and we had to face the wrath of my father who was not at all pleased. My granny came out to visit us and we enjoyed showing her the island. She had always been special for me and we had many good conversations over the years so I was able to share my heartbreak regarding Richard and my fear of what might happen with Andrea. I told her he was a Catholic and we discussed how that might affect my future.

On July 5th 1961 we celebrated my twenty-first birthday and the family had planned a fantastic party for the occasion . My parents were good at giving parties and both my sister and I had taken after them. There was always marvellous food and masses to drink. The music was of the moment and consequently amazing to dance to. Friends always looked forward to these occasions and this one was no exception. A formal invitation had gone out and to my surprise, I found I still have the replies from everybody who was invited. It had a tropical theme with palms and greenery adorning the balcony, fairy lights were everywhere and real banana trees growing in the garden. All the family helped decorate the house and the food looked splendid laid out on a long table. My father made a lethal punch with a sugar cube soaked in brandy in each glass. We were all ready for a splendid evening and it was a beautiful starlit night: as expected the weather was superb.

My present from my parents was a set of beige leather luggage which was appropriate with my current love being in Italy. He unfortunately could not attend as he was away at sea on naval exercises. Trisha and I were dressed to kill, both looking healthy and really brown. Soon our guests started arriving. I was tense waiting for Richard and Caroline: they were late and had just returned from a visit to Ireland where his family had property. They would eventually live there when they got married.

Unforgettably, they gave me some Schiaparelli perfume called 'Shocking' and I assumed that Caroline had bought it. It made me smile, knowing that she knew something about our relationship. I wore it with pleasure even if it was not quite me.

I did not allow all this to affect my evening. I was determined to have the best time of my life and I did. The food was excellent. There was non-stop booze and everybody looked amazing and enjoyed themselves. Terry Moles and Mark Tucker did the music. It was mainly jazz with some swing, with everybody jiving. We danced until we dropped: it was a fantastic night. For me the music was the most memorable and flamboyant of any party I had ever been to in Malta. The older couples, friends of my parents, were on the terrace away from the loud sound system, having a comfortable drink and a chat. They too had an enjoyable time and some ended up on the dance floor.

Terry Moles was another great friend at the time but rather too keen for my liking. Like me, he loved jazz and jiving. During the build-up to the party we had made a list of the music and tried out a running order. It was all the greats such as Oscar Peterson, Erroll

Garner, Gerry Mulligan, Dave Brubeck, George Shearing, Barney Kessel, Chris Barber and Acker Bilk, to name just a few. All came from our joint collection of records. He was a fantastic mover and I had some great dances with him that night. Trisha was with Henry Beverley; he and his sister Rosemary both had a terrific time.

The summer of 1961 was to be our last in Malta. Daddy's time on board HMS Forth was drawing to an end and the family would be returning to the UK. The final event implanted in my memory was the Governor's Summer Ball at Verdala Palace, his summer residence. Always a special occasion and for my sister and me it was a final chance to dress up and dance the night away. My partner for that evening was Mark Tucker who was a lovely man but not exactly my type, and Trisha was with her great love Henry. The young men were in dress uniform and we were dolled up in our party regalia, all looking rather fine. We certainly did not realise we would seldom do this again as times they were a-changing.

It was a grand occasion, dinner first and then the dancing. The men looked wonderful in full evening dress, and the girls in their magnificent colourful evening gowns cut a delightful sight. We could wander in the spectacular gardens of Verdala Palace and be amazed by the history of the place. In the dance floor, for example, there was a carved-out chess board which had been used during the siege of Malta by the prisoners to pass the time. It was a chance to say goodbye to our friends because soon we would be leaving on a jet plane. We had come to the end of our Maltese fantasy; there would not be many more nights like this for me. As it turned out there would be big changes all round as within the next five years the services virtually departed from the island along with almost everything connected to them.

Malta would never be the same again and many people would miss the presence of the services and all they had meant to so many families, over the years. Malta was fought over during the war with the Maltese behaving heroically and winning the George Cross. There had almost been another siege situation during that time with food and medical supplies being in short supply. Many were intimately involved and had been connected to the services for years and would miss everything life had offered them in what had been an excellent working relationship. The Maltese still hold special memories of the British as I have heard many times from various taxi drivers on my later visits.

We said our fond farewells to our many friends that night and realised what a marvellous time we had had and that probably we were the last generation to experience it quite in this way. Malta would soon change, a new government was sworn into power with Prime Minister Mintoff at the helm. He had ambitions for tourism and wanted total separation from the British, starting off with the dockyard. We thought we were leaving at just the right time. We spent the last few weeks packing up the villa and our possessions ready to fly back to London and an exciting life ahead.

We would not be going home to the house where we had all grown up. It had been decided to let it go as it was only rented. In those days most people seemed to rent but now it was becoming fashionable to buy so that was the big plan for the future. Where it would be, would depend very much on where our father would work because he was coming out of the navy. Most of the furniture was in store though relatively easy to access. For the immediate future - we would rent something in London.

CHAPTER SIX
THE ITALIAN AFFAIR

Come live me and be my love
- Christopher Marlowe

We arrived back in London in time for Christmas. As a family, we found the festive season special so we had to get moved in, unpacked and ready for a suitable celebration in record time. Mummy had found a new flat to rent in Latimer Court on the Hammersmith Road. I remember it being long and thin and uninspiring. My sister and I thought we would not be there for long and we would soon be looking for our own place. But not before I had sorted out things with my Italian naval officer. In the meantime I got a job at the Briglin Pottery just off Baker Street, working with the potter, preparing the clay and decorating some of the pieces.

It was while working there that I had one of my past-life flashbacks which have often happened throughout my life. My job was to knead the clay and then fashion balls for the potter to make mugs from: they had to be one pound balls. It felt so familiar that it came to me that I had done a similar process before when I was a baker centuries ago. I used to knead the bread and make one pound balls of dough for loaves. When I have this kind of memory, it is different from recalling day-to-day events. It comes in a flash of recognition and is usually accompanied by a shiver and a cold feeling. Consequently, I could knead clay very quickly.

The letters and cards continued to arrive from Andrea and I was still trying to learn Italian. Also I thought it important to look more deeply into his faith so I ordered a series of booklets about how to convert to Catholicism. We had always been a religious family and had attended church regularly. I had gone off it a bit when I became a student but I did study the booklets. When I read these, there did not seem much difference between the Anglican and the Catholic faith, but there were, however, major divergences. The Pope was the head of the Catholic Church and the Queen of our Anglican Church. They were stricter on matters such as birth control and abortion, confession and mortal sin.

In the summer of 1962, Andrea and I eventually agreed to meet. It became possible because my sister and I had arranged a holiday in Italy approved by my parents. We were to stay with Henry's sister Rosemary Beverley in St Margarita. We spent a week with her then Andrea arrived and carried me off to Spain. Trisha stayed on a few more days before returning to London. My parents knew I was going to Spain on holiday with Andrea, but not that I would not come home for a few months. The truth is that I did not know for sure that I would stay myself; it could have been a disaster.

We had a beautiful drive along the coast of northern Italy through southern France, and down to the Costa del Sol, ending up at a fishing village called Peniscola. I felt very grown-up as it was the first time I'd gone on holiday with a man. I realised he was surprised that I was able to leave my family and come away with him. He assumed, wrongly, that this was something I had done before and quite early on there was some tension about what I might have been up to in my past. Which frankly was not very much. I managed to convince him that I loved him and that he was the one.

The holiday in Spain was extended. I could not bear to leave him. He invited me to come to Taranto to accompany him on his next posting. We stopped in La Spezia for a few days, staying with a friend of his while he spent time making arrangements to rent a house for us. Eventually, we drove to Taranto where his ship was based. He had found a villa in the bay near the beach and we drove straight there. By this time I had let my parents know that I planned to stay. They were not pleased but felt that I was now old enough to know what I wanted to do. I was completely smitten by my beautiful Italian and, for the first time, was enjoying a full sex life.

He was the most tender and amazing lover, considerate and accomplished. He took his time in everything he did, so that when he entered me I was totally submissive and ready. He muttered sweet nothings to me in Italian, which was fantastic and made me feel beautiful. He did not want to make me pregnant so was very careful not to come inside me. There were a few occasions when he thought he had, and there was a little performance of douching with lemon juice. It was a time of discovery for me: my whole body seemed to change as I relaxed and enjoyed blissful lovemaking. It was interesting to me that I had to go to Italy to lose my inhibitions and enjoy sex. Later, I realised I was lucky to discover all the wonderful things that two people can do to each other within a truly caring love. He prepared me for what was ahead in terms of understanding the desires of the men in my life. He also gave me an insight into the very different attitude that men had towards sex and relationships.

Andrea was the first man in my life who could actually cook and he taught me some wonderful Italian recipes; together we made amazing meals. We made a big pot of minestrone soup which would last for days. Once a week he would take me shopping to the market in Taranto and help me buy vegetables, fruit, meat or fish - whatever we needed. It was a good place to practise my Italian. Years later somebody asked me why I spoke Italian with a southern accent and I realised it was from doing the shopping in that market. Life was blissful for a while but I knew it would eventually come to an end. Daddy wrote saying the family expected me back by December 25th and that most Italian naval officers had a woman in every port, which, not surprisingly, I found out to be true.

Andrea drove me to Milan station, via Florence and Bologna. On the way he showed me the sites and was the first person to take me to the Uffizi Gallery, which became one of my favourite places in the world. I really enjoyed being in public with him; he was so tactile. He put me on the train and we made our fond farewells. Stupidly, I cried all the way to London. The other women in the train thought I was mad. They had brought masses of food with them for the journey which they offered to me, but I could eat nothing. I was so devastated at having to say goodbye to Andrea.

I returned to the bosom of the family and we had our usual special Christmas with everyone present - the wanderer was back. It was a strange feeling, having had all those life-changing experiences including the thought that I might be pregnant or perhaps I would marry him one day. We continued to write and I did go out to see him in Italy in the Spring, but it was never the same again. The relationship had run its course and my father had woken me up to the fact Andrea would probably be an unfaithful man.

When I came back Trisha and I talked of sharing a flat. She was working at the General Trading Company, a fabulous shop in Mayfair. After a few months there, she had fallen madly in love and was having an affair with the owner, David Part. As you can imagine this did not go down well with Daddy either. David was a married man though not exactly happily. There was a moment when we all thought they would end up together. First, he sent her on an extended holiday to Malta whilst he arranged his divorce. He did leave his wife but in the end he married someone else and broke my sister's heart. We all thought he was an absolute rotter for hurting Trisha and causing terrible disruptions at home. He did the same again to the next wife.

This seemed a good opportunity for us to branch out and start sharing a flat together. Our first place was in Fernshaw Road,

Chelsea. There was nothing special about it: just a kitchen, bathroom and a large studio. By now Trisha had decided to leave the GTC as it had become rather painful and a huge drama. She found a job at Jaeger. I left the Briglin Pottery where I had been employed since I got back from Malta, and I started to work at J. Walter Thompson in the Art Department - a large, successful advertising agency and just the place to be at that time. Soon we were both earning reasonably good money so we decided to look for another flat where we could each have our own bedroom and ended up at 103 Flood Street. We had an amazing social life with so much happening in London. The Beatles were just starting their extraordinary rise to fame and the Rolling Stones were playing in places such as Eel Pie Island. It was exciting to buy their first records and see their early appearances on television. We seemed to be at the centre of the activity, just off the Kings Road, Chelsea, and very much the centre of the London 'Swinging Sixties' revolution.

The next important thing to happen was meeting Nicolas Head. I was invited by a friend to a New Year's Eve party at the White House Mansions on the Euston Road. We arrived and went up to his flat. The friend's name was Tony Warren and he had been part of our group in Chelsea but I was not actually with him. We were early and Nicky was having a shower. He came out of the bathroom, brown, dripping wet, and looking as if he had come off a beach. He was the best-looking man I had ever seen: tall, blond, and charming. He attempted to get dressed, only to discover that he had left the trousers he wanted to wear at a girl's flat so he rushed off to get them. I thought this strange but he returned quickly and soon we were in the bar having a drink.

We were a group of about ten, all of whom seemed to know Nicky. I knew nobody except Tony. It was a party with dinner first and then dancing we were just one of the noisy tables. I was observing everything and felt a bit on the outside. I noticed all the girls were chatting Nicky up and that occasionally he would glance in my direction. To my surprise I found myself dancing with Nicky and as the New Year came in - we had a passionate kiss which took my breath away. At this point, I had no idea if any other girls had a claim on him: it seemed not, as from that moment on - we were together. Finally, in the early hours of the morning, a few of us went up to his room while he sang and played the guitar. I discovered his passion was songwriting and that he also did some acting with the Pat Larthe Agency. It was unlike me to sleep with a man I had just met, but that night my usual inhibitions were lost and we had a beautiful first night together. He must have played me every song he had ever written and a lot more besides - before we eventually got some sleep. Our meeting was a night to remember for both of us. After a slap-up breakfast together, he took me home to Flood Street. I shall always remember the smell of him - it was of sun, sea and Ambre Solaire as if he had just been on holiday. It was this in particular that captivated me from the first moment.

His acting and modelling took him abroad and for those initial few weeks he was away often. There were plenty of phone calls and postcards and we met a few times. After one call in March of '63, he arrived on the doorstep at Flood Street with his suitcase. He had returned from Paris without a place to call his own, his lease having run out at the White House. I was thrilled to see him, brown as a berry and wearing a pink shirt. Without more ado he moved in there and then. Things were changing anyway at Flood Street. Trisha wanted to have her own place and had found somewhere in nearby Redburn Street and I had decided to move into the basement - so our first home was down there together. It was a momentous decision for me to make, it all happened so effortlessly and seemed absolutely right at the time.

I was still in advertising but by now I had moved to Garland Compton art department. For some reason, I can remember the conversation there always being about hot-air balloons, basically it was quite a lot of hot air. I helped design some packaging for

Rowntree's Fruit Gums and I enjoyed doing the fruit for the new pack. Nicky was successful acting and modelling, and encouraged me to have some photographs taken and to have a go myself. It was in the days when it was very professional and the models on the whole were well looked after by their agents and not as thin as sticks.

Following his advice, I left Garland Compton, got some shots taken and joined the Pat Larthe Agency. Then I started the hard slog of taking my portfolio around the photographers. I did not enjoy dressing up and found it soul-destroying. I went for masses of auditions with lots of glamorous girls usually much thinner than I was and invariably did not get the job. Eventually, I did start to get offers and best of all I occasionally worked with Nicky. He was great to work with - always encouraging me to relax and be myself. The best fun I had modelling was appearing with him.

Although Nicky did some photographic work, Pat Larthe was better known for successful films and commercials. I decided I wanted to do more photography and cat-walk modelling so I did not stay with Pat Larthe long. I left them and joined an agency called 'New Faces'. I wanted to try my luck on my own and knew I would still be cast with Nicky which was always great. We did some memorable trips together, one being to Morocco for some Thomas Cook travel brochures. Eventually I found more work doing catwalk modelling.

Life together in our basement flat was the best fun: we were madly in love, both working hard with Nicky especially doing incredibly well. He would sometimes come back from a job with a great wad of notes and we would fly off to Paris for the weekend or go out for a delicious meal. He still continued with his songwriting, and he also wrote several successful jingles for commercials. But his writing began to take second place as he became more and more renowned as an actor and model.

In those days money went a long way. One day he arrived outside the flat and hooted the horn and there he was in this gorgeous white Jaguar XK150. He immediately took me off for a spin around Richmond Park. He was full of wonderful surprises like taking me shopping and buying me exciting new clothes from Mary Quant's shop called 'Bazaar'. Trisha by this time was working there along with Mary Bee, who would become my first manageress when I opened my boutique. My housekeeping budget in those days was £10 per week, which bought an enormous amount of food and flowers. Life in the fast lane with Nicky was very exciting and tremendous fun. My father had been a rally driver so I enjoyed going for long trips. All the men in my life were excellent drivers, fast but always safe. I was never afraid to go on a car adventure and we went on many - such as a trip across Europe. The only thing we ever booked beforehand was the ferry.

We decided to aim for Split on the Dalmatian coast in the former Yugoslavia. Although it was communist, we had no difficulty getting across the border at Trieste. We had a beautiful drive along the coast until there was a horrible crunching sound as we went over one of the many potholes and we came to a grinding halt. The suspension had gone and if I remember rightly, it was a public holiday. Two soldiers with rifles came up to us wanting to know what we were up to. We tried to explain that we had broken down and that we needed to find a garage. One pointed to what looked like a shack, saying his brother was the mechanic there. They fixed it between them but the car now was absolutely solid with no suspension whatsoever. We hoped and prayed it would get us back to the UK. Somehow, doing anything with Nicky was great fun but at the same time nerve-wracking. We set off slowly and soon realized the car had lost all acceleration. We limped home, doing 40mph on the German autobahn and just making our ferry booking in time. Finally, as we turned into Flood Street, the car gave up the ghost and just stopped. Between us we pushed it in to park just outside our house. What a relief, we had made it! Brown and exhausted, we fell into bed wondering what kind of money it would cost to get the Jaguar back on the road.

I soon began to realise that I was not the only kid on the block who fancied Nicky: Women loved him and would flock around him. It was almost unsafe to go to a party with him as by now he was becoming rather well known. Slowly, it dawned on me that I could not trust him out of my sight. Every job he went on, I was convinced he would be off with whichever beautiful bird he was working with. The car was a great bird-catcher too. So we began to have rows and eventually I said I was going to move out and find a flat on my own. I found an unfurnished one in Rectory Chambers in Old Church Street. Conveniently, it was near my favourite cinema, the 'Essoldo'. So if I was miserable without him, I just went to the movies.

I shared the flat with Sandy Moss, another model, and started to make new friends. We gave dinner parties and enjoyed going out to clubs. At the time she was seeing Chester Jones and I had met Jon Bradshaw, a young writer from New York. I was modelling and making clothes for friends. At this time I had a big order from the Chanel Gift Shop in Knightsbridge. Some of the items I was creating were called Gonks and I had managed to get a big order through Yvonne, a new girlfriend of Nicky's, who worked there.

Whilst still living in Flood Street, Nicky and I had bought a Dalmatian puppy. We called him Mark because of an extra big spot on his face. He was a character and obviously needed serious walking which we enjoyed doing. He came with me to Old Church Street because Nicky was often away. Mark got up to all kinds of mischief but the worst thing he did was attack my completed Chanel order. I arrived home from a celebration lunch, and the entire flat was covered in kapok. I had to work all night with my friend Katie to repair and remake half the order for delivery in time the next day.

Trisha was also doing exciting things with her life. She moved from Jaeger to 'Bazaar' and then she was invited through a friend to help promote a band. They were an up-and-coming group called The Who with Kit Lambert as their manager. She well and truly helped put them on the map. Attending their concerts was always an event because they would end up frenziedly destroying their guitars, costing them a small fortune in new equipment. The next thing she would do was start up a new model agency called 'English Boy', with Mark Palmer. This would be a great success and many of the dashing English Boys such as Mark were on their books creating an up-to-date look for that special phenomena of the Sixties.

London was a wonderful place to be living during that decade. It was full of young people bursting with good ideas. The Liverpool sound was making its mark and many musicians were forming bands and recording their own music. For the first time I was enjoying popular records: the only genre I really had liked before was jazz but now rhythm and blues was flooding London and the sounds were just jumping. Against this background, and after a long rather boozy lunch at the 'Casserole Restaurant', Nicky, John Bell and I, decided it was a good moment to open a boutique in the Kings Road. It would be up to me to find a suitable shop. Nicky agreed to design and do it up in preparation for opening. I would be responsible for the clothes and John Bell would keep an eye on the finances.

The two designers I liked most were Mary Quant and Coco Chanel. As far as I was concerned these two women had changed the face of fashion. Coco was first, starting off with her quirky hats for the races she used to attend; followed eventually with her Chanel suit and the little black dress. In those days they were a must for any follower of fashion. Now Mary was bringing new exciting ideas with her short skirts and bold colours. I had lusted over her designs when I was a student; now I would try to compete with her as best I could. I started designing my first collection of clothes with great excitement but with some trepidation. Could I survive in this very competitive market and did I really have the know-how and courage?

Our team did not have much money so it was my job to get a bank loan. I decided on the Midland in Sloane Square as my father had banked with them for many years but I did not expect him to guarantee any business of mine. In those days it was relatively easy to chat up a bank manager and I persuaded Mr Hewitt, to support the business with a loan of £10,000. He agreed, provided I would match it with the same amount from the other directors, which we managed to do.

We realised we needed more support for our venture so we invited Paul Orssich, a photographer, and Geoffrey Mattingly, a car dealer to get involved too and they became directors. We therefore were able to match the money and now the search was seriously on for the right property. It had to be in the King's Road because that was where everything was happening. A friend had quoted to me 'location, location, location' so I knew how important it was. It simply could not be in the Fulham Road then; though later that would become fashionable. But the best available premises I could find were really at the wrong end of the road.

Property to rent in Chelsea was already at a premium and the only place I thought we could afford was this old empty gas showroom on the bend, opposite the 'Water Rat' pub. Frankly, it was just a little bit too far round the bend, but the rent was at least possible for our budget. Our landlords came by the rather wonderful name of 'The Loyal Order of Ancient Shepherds' and were based in Cheshire. The rent was £1000 a year and stayed at that for most of our tenancy. In those days properties certainly did not come done up, so there was a great deal of refurbishment work to do on the building. It was absolutely filthy and needed to be scrubbed from head to toe - not to mention all the old gas appliances in the backyard.

CHAPTER SEVEN
KINGS ROAD BOUTIQUE - AND NICKY

How do I love thee, let me count the ways
- Elizabeth Barrett Browning

Nicky did the most amazing design job; it was thrilling to watch him making the shop presentable, helped by many friends too. The whole place had to be gutted and completely replastered. The only thing we saved was the loo, because it was absolutely necessary to have one. Finally, with much hard work all round, we were ready to meet the public.

The 'Susan Locke Boutique' launched with a flourish on a brilliant summer's day in July 1964. The opening party was full of the faces of Swinging London, with press and friends in abundance. It was a great occasion, and such a relief to be happening after the performance of finding the shop, the clothes and getting the money together. Jon Bradshaw wrote the press release and between us we had invited everybody we thought should be there. He was an American freelance writer, working for Queen and Vogue magazines. He had just written an article for Queen about what was 'U or Non-U' in British society and was the flavour of the month. Much to Nicky's annoyance, I went off with Bradshaw to 'Nick's Diner' to celebrate afterwards. Although he had done the shop, we were not together any more - just good friends.

Nicky had done a marvellous job in converting the filthy, boring gas showroom into a colourful boutique. He was very talented at creating the right atmosphere, and the boutique had a rather

Spanish feel. There were six dressing rooms at the back, along with the loo, which were approached through an arch made in wood. The colour scheme was shocking pink, orange, and white. In the main part of the shop was a huge, elaborate mirror with a patchwork chaise longue in front of it. I'd had it reupholstered and we would sit and have our coffee there. The rest of the shop was fitted with rails for the clothes. Some were my own design, others I bought in from other designers, such as Gerard McCann, Roger Nelson and Martha Hill. The first window was done by Yvonne, who happened to do the windows for Chanel: it was amazing and very eye-catching with fairground carousel horses charging through the window.

When we opened, the lovely Mary Bee was our first manageress. She had been working at Bazaar along with my sister and had decided she needed a change. Working with her was Gale, who had married a great friend of ours from Malta days. He was a very entertaining chap called Jonathan Benson and they lived nearby. We had gone to their wedding and in the early days in Malta, we had had a lot of fun and much banter over curry lunches. Later Gale, sadly, left Jonathan and got involved with Hakim Jamal and that is a very sad tale - more about this later.

The well-equipped workroom was on the first floor with an enormous cutting table along one wall for the pattern cutter, Nina Jordon. Then there was a sewing machine and over-locker for the sample maker, Margaret. They had both come to me from Mary Quant, along with our driver, Jack, who collected the clothes from our seamstresses and outworkers. The other wall housed the cloth rack piled with material. Then my desk with pencils and pads to design the clothes on. We made a good team and would go on to produce three collections a year with alacrity and style. I wanted desperately to be part of the London Fashion scene and it slowly happened.

I gradually began to believe in myself, that it was my clothes which people wanted, so this was where I decided to concentrate my time and effort. We were getting good write-ups in the paper one of the first being by Barbara Griggs in the Evening Standard. I decided my great push would be for well-cut trouser suits which I personally liked to wear along with many of my friends. All my garments had names, such as Sinbad and Edwardian. The trouser suit Sinbad was the first item I sold in the shop; it was well-tailored, fully lined and sold for only 18 guineas. The trouser suits and trousers were my best sellers because they were very reasonably priced, well-made and the trousers were longer than usual. As well as making good-value-for-money garments, I wanted to produce unusual outfits for tall, larger girls. In those days it was so difficult to buy anything interesting if you were not a size 8, 10 or 12. For years I had to make my own if I wanted anything different. Finally, with bigger ladies in mind we made up to size 16. So with the help of an efficient cutter who could grade a pattern well and my ever loyal sample maker, I began designing my range of trouser suits, miniskirts and party clothes for each season's collection. Right from the start I set out to produce a Spring/Summer and a Autumn/Winter collection: ambitious, but that was what all the other design houses were doing and the way it had always been done in the past.

As mentioned, I delighted in calling my clothes names such as Zhivago, Burlington, Hardy, and Refifi. I usually had a theme which might be based on a film or a writer. For me, choosing the name was an important part of the creative process; by combining the special name and by using beautiful materials, I gradually built up the range and my reputation as a fashion designer. It was also an important part of my promotion strategy to get friends - who were also models - to wear my clothes and be photographed in these new designs at the various nightclubs of the moment. I made sure that my clothes were of good quality and well made; my outworkers were excellent and many of them made up clothes for Mary Quant. Mary's driver Jack also worked for me and often suggested the right outworker for particular garments I had just designed; for example, mentioning someone who was skilled at working with materials or designs that needed special care - such as lace.

Gradually, I brought in less of other designers' work, and concentrated entirely on my own designs. In the end, the only things I bought in were shoes from Terry de Havilland and some accessories. In due course, I felt I had achieved a certain style suitable to present the clothes in a fashion show. I decided to set up my first show at a London nightclub - the latest hot discotheque called Sybilla's in Swallow Street, which happened to be owned by friends. The fashion shows would become an important part of my work in the future and would often be held in other discotheques. This was quite a new way to display clothes especially as the models danced their way through the show.

I usually had special accessories made for the occasion - such as hats and shoes; the most important being Terry's shoes, which he made to complement the clothes. I had sold his creations in my shop from the start. We had started our fashion careers together. A few years later he too opened his own shop in the Kings Road. His father had had a factory in the East End and had been making shoes there since World War II. We used some of his old lasts for his famous wedge heels - which are collectors' items now!

The shows were marvellous affairs with beautiful models dancing to the latest sounds as they paraded in my designer clothes. Previously, fashion shows had been staid affairs with the models walking in a stiff formal way. For our new style of show - the sounds were important and loud, introduced by the club DJ according to my specifications. The music was of the moment: the Beatles, Rolling Stones, Chuck Berry, Bill Haley and his Comets. I still loved jazz - so Dave Brubeck and Thelonious Monk also featured. The wine flowed with everybody - including the models - ending up on the dance floor afterwards. It was a gathering of friends, press, customers, and also buyers from the larger stores. The magazine fashion editors were invited and many came.

These fashion shows were exciting happenings of those times. In their way they really were pioneering events; nobody had ever seen anything quite like it before. It was part of the excitement for the team in the workroom to get the outfits ready, and the outworkers who made up the clothes for the shop would back up everything in the show - timing had to be perfect to tie in with the shop and the specific season. It was great fun to be part of the fashion explosion which was happening in Swinging London.

People were coming from all over the world to see what this phenomenon was: it was a passionate and productive period, though at the time you did not realise what an impact we were making on fashion.

Journalists and photographers would fly in from every continent to do a piece. There were many articles and endless words written about what was happening. It was strange to be at the centre of something the world had never experienced before. The miniskirt, trouser suits, all kinds of boots and shoes for the ladies and great men's clothes from shops such as 'Granny Takes a Trip', 'Hung On You', 'John Stephen', and 'Mr Fish'. These retail outlets along with mine were changing the face of fashion once and for all. Even today the Kings Road is a mecca for the avant-garde.

Young creative people for the first time had their say; they were feeling their power and challenged the stuffy image of London. Three groups strove for recognition, or so it seemed to the press. Those who worked hard keeping body and soul together in the City, boutiques, advertising agencies and restaurants. Then there were the artists, groups, musicians and all the marketing and promotion involved with records and concerts. Finally, there were those who decided to drop out. Cannabis was readily available if you knew where to get it, as was cocaine, heroin and LSD. I think that old quote from Paul Kanther of Jefferson Airplane 'If you can remember the Sixties, you were not really there' does not exactly apply.

When I opened the shop I lived in the flat above and was going out with Jon Bradshaw. He was an American writer, freelancing in London mainly for magazines. He lived in Tregunter Road and was great friends with Nigel Dempster and Gerard McCarten. Dempster worked for the Daily Express and introduced us to a young Anna Wintour at this time and I like to think that my shop, which she was well aware of, had something to do with her career choice. She went on to have a relationship with Bradshaw herself and famously became the editor of American Vogue. Later the film 'The Devil Wears Prada' was supposedly based on her character and career.

The early sixties were great; just relishing being part of it and the new freethinking of the time was exhilarating. We went to all the shows, the movies, and the pubs together. We would regularly eat out at places such as '235', 'The Casserole', or 'Nick's Diner' in Ifield Road. The conversation was always stimulating, be it discussing Vietnam or the latest play or book being reviewed. The whisky and wine flowed. I often laughed until I cried with some of their stories: probably from Dempster, spouting off about somebody he was writing about such as Princess Margaret.

Nicky had not vanished and was still part of my life but now he was getting serious; he seemed not to like the idea of my going out with anybody else. To my amazement, he proposed. He had always been hesitant to make a commitment. I was so surprised I agreed. I wanted to focus on my work and career; the inevitable dramas with relationships were getting me down. It was a great relief to have that part of my life sorted. I knew Nicky was not likely to be a faithful man: were we both ready for the commitment of marriage?

I made my decision knowing I would have to put up with his infidelity. I was now twenty-seven; it felt the right time for me to marry: I loved him and we had had many good times together over the years, even if there had been several dramatic blips. We knew each other well, and there was a part of me that thought, naively, that when we were married things would be different. I knew he loved me; perhaps he would be faithful to me... So after much discussion, we started to plan the great day.

The wedding took place on July 9th 1966 at St Simon Zelotes Church, just off Cadagon Square in Chelsea. The reception was in the roof garden of the Carlton Towers Hotel. Our wedding breakfast with both families was in one of our favourite places - The Rib Room at the Carlton Towers. The party was held the night before and was a truly magnificent occasion. Some of the family stayed in the hotel, others were dotted around the capital. My sister Trisha and Nicky's three sisters Georgie, Sarah and Catherine were my bridesmaids. It was exciting for them to be measured up for their dresses which would be made in our work- room. John Bell, Nicky's great friend, was his best man. My father certainly did us proud that day and paid for everything, including the Rolls Royce cars.

I designed my wedding dress, made from pure Swiss capure lace: it is still hanging up in my wardrobe. I also designed my going away outfit, a white satin trouser suit and the bridesmaid's pale yellow dresses. My dear friends, Nina and Margaret, had made everything up lovingly in the workroom. Nicky and all the other men were in grey morning dress. The lilies and pale-yellow roses in the church were beautifully arranged with delicate arches of them across the aisle. It was breathtaking, looking and smelling magnificent as I proudly walked down on the arm of my father towards Nicky. My heart was pounding so loudly I felt everybody could hear it.

The sad thing for me was that none of my grandparents attended the wedding. They had all passed away by then, but I am sure they were watching from above. In particular, I missed my precious Gran who had been an important part of my childhood, not to mention my birth. She did at least meet Nicky before she died.

I remember the vicar who married us wore odd socks. We both noticed it at once as we waited for him to proceed and we burst out laughing. Later, we were told Nicky had a hole in his left shoe: not a good omen, I thought.

After the wedding, we jetted off to our honeymoon in Malta. We both had good memories of it, and I still knew people there - such as Geoffrey Aquilina Ross, a boyfriend of my sister, and the de Traffords for whom I had worked. We stayed at the Blue Lagoon Hotel on the tiny island of Comino, where there was privacy and plenty of sun, sea and surf. The first thing I noticed in the hotel reception, was a large tiled mural of a fishing scene which I had made when I was working at the Malta potteries in 1960. It even had my name on it. The hotel had been built in the intervening years and what a surprise it was to see it there. It was a special welcome!

It was a happy and exhilarating time with the odd dramatic incident which frightened me. When Nicky was around, something unexpected always happened, but that was what made life with him exciting. On this occasion a group of us had gone out scuba diving in a dhjaisas fishing boat with an instructor. At the time I had not done my British Subaqua Training so I did not dive. The others and Nicky were trained and experienced enough to do so, though they did not go in pairs or as 'buddies' which is the safest way. The water was beautifully clear, so we could see them. They each had about twenty minutes of air in their tanks. I sat happily sunbathing, reading a book, waiting for them to return.

They all came back safely except Nicky. He seemed to be away for ages, way beyond the twenty minutes. He was nowhere to be seen and we were getting anxious. Eventually, he turned up, really green around the gills, coughing and spluttering, having followed a sting ray and run out of air. The instructor and I were not pleased; he fairly ticked him off, much to Nicky's embarrassment. Everybody was very quiet in the boat going back to the hotel and I was thinking 'What if I had lost him and had to return to London a widow?' We had all been quite traumatised.

We also had another quite different dramatic event. It happened one evening, while we were out in a boat on a trip along the coast with some friends. We glanced up and were convinced we could see two UFO's doing a dance in the sky. When we got back to the hotel we discovered that two spaceships, one from America and one from Russia, had docked for the first time ever. It certainly felt as if something extraordinary was going on. It was the beginning of better relations between these two superpowers. This was a great relief after the drama of The Bay of Pigs in Cuba a few years earlier when John Kennedy was US president.

On our return to the flat above the shop, we found loads of mail and everything fairly chaotic. There always was a disaster or two to sort out if I went away. I was responsible for so much of the daily running of the shop, the ordering, deliveries and payments and, of course, organising the workroom. It was a difficult balancing act keeping a good supply of clothes to keep business going well in the shop, and also making sure the outworkers are paid and have enough work to keep them busy. It was a fine line financially too. Mary Bee was still the manageress and she ran the shop in my absence. Her great friend was Pattie Boyd, George Harrison's girlfriend and later his wife. Occasionally the Beatles would come into the shop to our great delight.

Consequently, we always had the latest Beatles records, often before they were released. This somehow became known and so the shop was really buzzing on Saturday mornings - 'The Susan Locke Boutique' in the Kings Road was the place to be if you wanted to hear the newest Beatles records. This period was the most successful time for the shop; we were well and truly on the map of Swinging London. Newspapers and journalists published articles about us, and magazines such as Vogue were using our clothes in their fashion pages.

Soon after we got back from our honeymoon in Malta, we moved into our new home in Shawfield Street. Nicky had worked hard to get it ready in time and decorated the house with his usual style. It had a basement flat which we let to John Bell, his best man at our wedding. We were all good friends by now with a bit of a 'Jules et Jim' feel about us. We did everything together; dined out together and went to movies sometimes with his girlfriend, Liz Brewer. John worked in advertising as an accounts executive at the advertising agency Bensons.

Everything was going well and we were getting requests to supply other shops and large companies. So we started talking about expanding into wholesale business as well as continuing with the retail side, It made sense, as we were being approached by large companies to supply them. There simply was not enough finance to make up any further orders. It got out that we were looking to expand the business and we were approached by Panton and Leila Corbett with this in mind. It was all agreed so we began to make plans to set up 'Susan Locke Designs Ltd': this became the wholesale side of the enterprise. From now on it would have a more professional feel about it.

CHAPTER EIGHT
THE WHOLESALE PROJECT - AND JEREMY

All you need is love

A number of serious meetings took place in the flat above the shop, which now had become my office and design studio. It was apparent that there needed to be two separate companies: one for the retail side and one for the wholesale business. We made plans for the wholesale market, with the Corbetts and myself being directors of the new company 'Susan Locke Designs Ltd.' Although the business was financially sound, the retail side was always a tricky balancing act. An accountant did the annual audit but the day-to-day feasibility plan depended on me and I was never great with figures.

We had already started in a small way to supply wholesale goods to other shops, an early client being 'The Hollies' Boutique' in Liverpool. It was great fun when they came into the shop and selected straight from the rails. Sometimes we made up designs especially for them. But gradually bigger fish, such as 'Peter Robinson' and 'Miss Selfridge', approached us to create collections for their stores. The biggest store was 'Lord and Taylor' in New York, who had found out about us from various write-ups in the fashion press. For me, 'Lord and Taylor' was the most important client we could ever hope to have.

We were also approached by 'Wigfalls' mail-order company in Sheffield who wanted a boutique collection for their catalogue. We did this for a couple of seasons but it was rather soul-destroying. They always took off the special things, like the pockets or buttons, to reduce the cost. The wholesale market was new and exciting; a great challenge for me because I did not like losing my special features. For the first time I was designing for a much larger clientele, quite different from my rather wacky Kings Road clients. I did, however, always try to keep a touch of the exotic about my designs. The cloth was the most important feature of my garments. Apart from the designing and making, selecting and ordering the cloth was time-consuming. Suppliers would come from all over London and even from Scotland, to show me their fabrics. I loved this process of selecting and ordering. For years I kept a huge collection of sample lengths.

The photography and marketing aspects of the wholesale trade fascinated me. The clothes from the latest collections had to be photographed, ready to send out in time for publication: the magazines being always months ahead. This would usually be done by Paul Orssich, one of our original directors. He was the shop's photographer, having photographed the clothes from the start. Some times the magazines chose to use their own models, but we also used models such as - Patricia Hodge, Marilyn Rickard and Judy Oswald.

On joining 'Susan Locke Designs', Leila Corbett became our house model. We would shoot the entire wholesale collection on her over a couple of days. Thankfully, this time Paul was paid properly. He worked at Michael Dunn's studio, which had wonderful facilities. I still have the entire set of photographs he made for our 'Lord & Taylor' trip to America. Preparations for the US visit were exhausting - everything had to be right, the samples had to be beautifully made, and slightly longer than for the UK because the mini-skirt had not yet arrived in the States.

On October 8th 1967 I flew to America for my first visit to the States. The Corbetts met me at JFK airport in New York. I brought with me the portfolio with the photographs and designs, which we presented at a meeting with 'Lord & Taylor' in our Waldorf Astoria suite. I wore a green mini-culottes outfit with long, over-the-knee, green leather boots made by Terry de Havilland. London fashions had not really arrived in New York by that autumn. That day I got a few strange looks and was relieved to arrive safely at the hotel.

Luckily, the clothes I had designed for 'Lord & Taylor' were very English and a little more traditional than my usual outfits. They were mainly made up in some lovely lightweight Scottish tweed. Leila modelled the designs and we both presented the sales pitch. 'Lord & Taylor' gave us a good order for most of the collection, but all the clothes had to be made even longer, which I thought spoiled the balance of the dresses. Instead of being short, fun creations, the designs became somewhat frumpy. Despite this, we were thrilled with the order and were soon celebrating with a bottle of champagne and canapés ordered on roomservice. I remember we threw ourselves down on the beds in absolute exhaustion.

While I was in the city I went to as many museums as I could and did the usual sightseeing. It was fabulous to be there after everything I'd read and heard from friends. By a stroke of luck, my old Italian boyfriend Andrea was in USA at the same time. He was stationed in Washington DC doing a naval gunnery course and flew to New York especially to meet me and we had a grand reunion, and we shared some memorable dinners, especially one at 'La Lettuce' restaurant. I was newly married and he had a serious lady in his life, whom he went on to wed. Nothing happened in the bed department; we parted the best of friends but I would never see him again after that.

'Susan Locke Boutique' continued to be part of the grand tapestry which was the Kings Road. When I opened in 1964 there were only six boutiques in the road. Almost every month another one opened, mainly selling jeans and cowboy boots which everyone was wearing - men and women. In order to compete, I started selling jeans and boots too, but I continued to design a new collection of clothes three times a year while doing some special promotions. But it was now much more competitive.

Sadly, things were not going well with my marriage. We were both working hard; I was involved with the boutique and wholesale fashion business; Nicky was acting and modelling, mainly in Germany. We seemed to spend little quality time together. As so often happens, neither of us noticed that things were falling apart. We were both too busy and engrossed in our own separate lives. I had a business to run and he was up to his old tricks of having affairs with work colleagues and with close acquaintances. I was aware of a number of my friends having a taste of the cherry and there were others in Germany too. You cannot dwell on it when you are busy; life had to go on, and I regret to say that I did not work hard to save my marriage.

In the spring of 1968 I met Anne Lambton, who was working freelance in public relations and marketing. After long discussions, she became part of the team and started taking care of our publicity and generally promoting the 'Susan Locke' label. One day over lunch at the 'Casserole', we planned our first promotion - for a new collapsible Raleigh Bike. I designed a cycling outfit for the model to wear riding the bike and we did a photography shoot to promote it. The bicycle took off and luckily for us had nationwide publicity. This was the first of several exciting promotions we did together.

The most important and wide ranging of these were for the Hilton Hotel Group in collaboration with Middle Eastern Airways, which to my great joy - was a series of fashion shows. Over lunches at the 'Casserole', we planned and discussed in detail an event we called 'A Chelsea Night'. These plans and arrangements had a significant effect on both our lives for the next few years, and Annie ended up living in Tangier.

For the moment, the idea was to travel all over the Middle East to promote British fashion with a Swinging London theme. The designers selected for these events were Mary Quant, Susan Locke, Tony Armstrong, and Michael Fish for the men's clothes. Michael had a reputation for well-cut suits and especially flamboyant shirts and ties, using striking colours and unusual prints. He was a good friend and was enthusiastic about being part of the show, and designed some great outfits for the Chelsea Nights. The format of the fashion show was four female and two male models - dancing to a band rather than a recorded music. Annie introduced the show and I was one of the models. The first band we hired was Gary Glitter's - but at that time he performed under the name of Paul Raven. He produced a good sound but he was arrogant, and convinced he was going to make it big. Imagine our surprise when he did. He was older than most of us and always performed wearing a toupee. One day, we threw the wig into the swimming pool. Paul was not amused by our antics; we treated him very unkindly with our teasing him about it.

We had several dramatic moments on these trips. One happened on a visit to the Lebanon. Michael Fish sent the two male models Rudi Patterson and a German called Walter. Both of these delightful chaps were his boy friends - one past, the other present. They were sharing a room together and had fallen madly for each other. The plan was to rehearse the show with Michael joining us later. He arrived, to discover what had been going on. The next thing we knew Michael had collapsed with an overdose of his prescribed medication. Thank God - he was rescued, and we were able to go ahead with the show.

On the same visit, the timing of one of our performances at Hotel Al Bustan had been changed. Instead of performing after dinner, the management decided to have the show early, 7.30 pm instead of 10 pm. We needed time to prepare, makeup, hair, and so on, but Paul needed to take speed to get himself psyched up. He took too much too quickly and was incoherent when we went on. I was at the end of the catwalk with him singing 'Johnny B. Goode'. On my return run, I saw him keeling over backwards and then he fell flat. But, ever the professional, he flipped up and continued the number.

Over the years we visited many places in the Middle East - Lebanon, Cyprus, Malta, Turkey and Iran, always staying in the Hilton hotel in various capitals. My relationship with Nicky was to deteriorate even further during this time, as increasingly we led more and more separate lives and each had our own agenda. It became apparent to me that this was not the kind of marriage I wanted. I needed more support and somebody I could rely on even if we were both involved in different careers. I realised I was the one who would have to do something about it, and in due course I started divorce proceedings. But before that a dreadful event happened which was to shatter our carefree lives.

My dear friend Gale Benson, who had worked for me in the shop in the early days had been murdered in Trinidad. She was divorced from Jonathan Benson and gone out to the Caribbean with Hakim Jamal. He was involved with the Black Power movement working with Michael X on a Montessori School project. Gale had found out that there were some less desirable things going on and - being the kind of person she was - she decided to find out more. She was attacked and possibly buried alive, as dirt was found in her lungs. Michael X was convicted of her murder.

You can never come to terms with such dreadful events. It was heartbreaking that someone so beautiful should be taken and cut off in her prime, never able to fulfil her hopes and dreams. Her twin brother Greville tried to find out more about what was behind the killing, and some months after Gale's murder, he also died in mysterious circumstances in Africa. I had lost two wonderful people who I imagined would be my friends for life. For that reason, I have dedicated this book to them to keep their memory alive.

Life had to go on and I soon got back into the day-to-day running of the shop. It was a good place to put my head down, cut myself off from the world and try to decide what to do about my own situation. It all came home to me as I was preparing to celebrate my thirtieth birthday, sitting - weeping - on a bench beside the river. My marriage was not working out and, as usual, Nicky was working abroad and not there to celebrate my birthday with me. I had planned a party and invited a few friends, including Deirdre Hamilton-Hill who was married to Corin Redgrave. She came and she brought the actor Jeremy Brett with her. As soon as we met, we clicked and spent a great deal of time together that night, talking and especially dancing to 'All you Need is Love', which had just been released by the Beatles. Jeremy and I became firm friends and decided to meet up again in the future. He was a shoulder to cry on. He had split up with his boyfriend, Gary Bond, so we could share our sorrow. Interestingly, Trisha met Gary at about this time and started seeing him. On at least one occasion we all went out together for a delicious chatty dinner.

Although Nicky and I had not actually separated yet, Jeremy was rather freaked out that I was still married. He was adamant that he did not want to be named in a divorce case. He was gay so nothing happened in that department but we did love each other truly, madly, deeply. I appreciated that bad publicity might harm his image as an actor, so we were careful not to be seen together in public. He was at a crucial point in his career, and in those days you had to be very discreet.

He was working on the National Theatre's all-male production of As You Like It at The Old Vic Theatre which opened in September 1967. Jeremy played Orlando, a wonderful part for him and it was quite an experience to go to rehearsals and later see the performance. As I watched rehearsals progress, I could see how his portrayal of Orlando's character developed and grew. I must have seen the play two dozen times at least, and every time I would point out something to him which was either brilliant, or did not work so well. I think he valued my contribution, as it was fresh and from a woman's point of view. He introduced me to the other members of the cast when I went backstage, and made me feel part of the company. He stayed with the National Theatre for some time and was in a number of productions, such as *Much Ado About Nothing* with Joan Plowright, directed by Lawrence Olivier. How exhilarating it felt to be involved with these productions even though I was an outsider. The National was still working in the Old Vic building and there was always so much intrigue and gossip going on around the productions and the company. I felt relieved that I had decided not to go into the theatre. My acting efforts had always been a bit of a dead loss. As a friend said after seeing me in a school play: 'You will never be the next Greta Garbo'.

Jeremy was fascinated by the shop and soon wanted to become involved. At the time of our meeting, I was planning to buy a new model for the shop window. I was looking at samples and the ones I liked best were designed by Adel Rootstein. These mannikins resembled real-life celebrities and did not appear to be stiff window dummies. I took Jeremy to have a look and we chose one modelled on Sandy Shaw, the recent European Song Contest winner. They were rather expensive but we managed to do a deal. Jeremy agreed to pose for the sculptor who made the mannikins. In due course, Jeremy's figure appeared in all the West End of London shop windows, and I got 'Sandy Shaw' at a very reasonable price.

Jeremy became a director of the boutique and volunteered to put in some money to get us through another difficult patch. So much of my time had been spent on the wholesale side that the shop had been neglected. By this time, Panton and Leila Corbett had gone off the boil, and I realised there was not an enormous amount of money to be made from the rag trade. So Jeremy and I decided to put new life into the shop by giving it a makeover, starting with the window. He brought in another designer, Nicholas Bullen, to make up 'specials' for customers such as Hot Gossip and Pan's People, two successful dance groups. It was fun making the clothes for television shows because they needed new outfits every week.

Jeremy enjoyed being involved with the boutique, but his acting career always came first, and he became totally immersed in every role that came his way. The next thing he worked on was *The Merry Widow*. I always loved this operetta and it was a great privilege to help Jeremy with rehearsals. In the process I would learn and sing some of the songs with him, and later Jeremy invited me to BBC Broadcasting House for the show's preview. I was very proud to know all the numbers, and understand all the hard work that had gone into the preparation. It was also fun to meet all the members of the cast, especially as I knew the ones who had been difficult. There is always somebody in a production who is a real pain in the neck.

After *The Merry Widow* had been completed, Jeremy, myself and Alan Bates with his agent, Judy Scott-Fox decided to go to recuperate at Grayshott Hall, a health farm in Surrey. We wanted to lose weight and to our delight, we each lost a half a stone. Strangely enough, we all struggled with our size. We swam in the pool, used the gym, played croquet on the expansive lawns and ate healthy delicious food, not to mention the amazing treatments. Jeremy gave me this visit as a present for my help with the show. Judy and I were not exactly happy with the boys sharing a room though. Deep down I had always hoped that Jeremy and I would have an affair, but it was not to be. Some gay men are bi-sexual so I had felt secret longings, but it had been silly to think that I could change Jeremy.

Nicky was away working most of this time in Germany and I wondered what he was up to. Nicky and a pretty girl were never just having a chat. I had consulted a medium, Douglas Johnson, to find out what was happening with my relationship and asked if the time was right to sue Nicky for divorce. The medium advised against it, and told me Nicky had somebody else in Germany and that our separation would take its natural course sooner than I thought. In a way he gave me the green light to have an affair myself. Although Jeremy was a good friend, a director of the shop and we loved each other dearly, he was definitely gay and not the one to come on this particular journey.

Soon after my consultation with the medium, on an evening out at Alvaro's, I met the art critic Robert Hughes. We had a wonderful night with good food and animated discussion.

Robert was writing a book on the life and work of my favourite artist - Leonardo da Vinci, so I had plenty to contribute to the conversation. At the end of the evening Robert invited me to come to Vinci and Florence to help him in his research.

The trip to Italy was in about a month's time so we had an opportunity to get to know each other a little first. We were both married: my husband was in Germany with his mistress, and Robert's wife Danne was in Africa with an actor from the Living Theatre, a travelling company which was currently all the rage. She had fallen madly in love with one of the actors and followed the group, leaving her young son Danton behind with Robert. We spent ages talking about our respective divorces and the meaning of existence. I told him I wanted a man to share my life and aspirations as well as to appreciate, respect and love me. We both seemed to need the same thing from a partner.

Bob travelled ahead of me to Florence to set up various meetings for his research and I went by train to join him. He met me at the station and took me to meet his friend Laura's parents with whom we were staying. They owned the Bonni Cossi Palace and also a special private collection of paintings which was not open to the public. It was wonderful to see these magnificent paintings with an expert. We went to the Uffizi Gallery and the Baptistery together. I was in my element discussing them but at the same time feeling a little out of my depth. He asked me to choose a particular work from everything we had seen and I choose Titian's Flight into Egypt from the Bonni Cossi Collection. Then he wrote a fully-fledged critique about it especially for me. I must admit to being lost half way through; the painting did not seem to be the same one I had admired. It was all too intellectual for my limited appreciation of art.

The summer of 1969 with Bob was pretty spectacular. We went to plays and movies; the film 'Easy Rider' really blew us away. We spent time at his large mansion flat in Regents Park Road with his son Danton. He had a live-in nanny but he did need special time with his daddy and with me. Late that summer Bob was offered a job as the art critic for Time Magazine. He hesitated; it had been quite a summer for Australians as many of his friends had been involved in the OZ trial. Eventually he accepted the role and I talked about selling up and accompanying him. However, the timing was bad for me - I had the shop and a husband to sort out and could not go comfortably.

That autumn the decision was made to get divorced, after a spectacular confrontation with Nicky. He burst into the bedroom expecting to find me in bed with Bob. Luckily he did not. There seemed little point in our remaining married as we both had other relationships. Once a man is unfaithful on a regular basis, there is no marriage left. I found out that he had been living on a houseboat with Gabriele Hobisch while he was working in Germany. When I told Rose, my cleaner, what was happening and that arrangements would be changing, she said 'I've got something for you'. She went home and came back with a pile of letters from Gaby. Rose had been squirrelling the letters away for months to give to me when the time came. They were full of damning evidence, which I later used in the divorce court. But there were a number of other women I could have named as co-respondent, including Nicky's secretary Charlotte.

The legal process was straightforward and uncontested. We both knew the relationship was over and had other people in our lives. It was sad that our marriage had not worked, but somehow I was not hurting any more. All I had to do was appear in court, answer a few questions and agree that the marriage was irretrievably over.

In January 1970, I moved out of Shawfield Street into the flat above the shop. I converted it back into a bright living space and brought as much colour in as possible, re-hanging the wonderful purple curtains I had had at Rectory Chambers. There was not much furniture so it was rather minimalist, but I remember taking all the wedding presents my friends had given us and all the photographs of our time together - including the wedding album.

Mark, the Dalmatian, came with me to help me start over again as a single girl. Nicky travelled so much, it was impractical to leave the dog with him. Throughout my life, I have had dogs to accompany me. They have always been an inspiration and there has never been a time when I did not have a dog companion, not to mention the cats - who are also precious to me. I now believe that my animals have been a compensation for not having children; I have a kind of telepathy with them and never feel alone if there are animals to care for. They need you as much as you need them; there is nothing to compare with the unconditional love you receive. You are never lonely or afraid if you have pets to care for. If you have developed a strong bond, they know exactly how you are feeling and can sense what you are thinking. At the end of a bad day, there is nothing more comforting than a dog's head on your knee. Similarly, there is such pleasure in sharing a dog's delight when he jumps up - ready and eager - to join you on your daily walk.

CHAPTER NINE
SEPARATION, DIVORCE AND 'CHELSEA NIGHTS'
Johnny be good

When you open a shop, every day you have to be there bright and early and ready to go, however you might be feeling. This discipline was good for me and kept me motivated during this difficult period in my life. It was a sad time: I was in the process of a divorce and my great love Robert Hughes had taken up his position at Time Magazine and had gone to the States. We kept in touch but it was never the same again. Later his wife came back to him but eventually they divorced. Robert and I met up again years later, but I thought he had become rather pompous which I suppose happens with great success. Now he is a well respected art critic and has written many wonderful books such as Barcelona.

With all these dramas going on we needed a new manageress. Her name was Annie Cossins. We decided to smarten up the shop and introduce some new lines. She had set up a small business of home workers with knitting machines, producing some amazing knitwear. We thought it a good idea to make these a feature and she arranged a great selection of beautiful hand-made sweaters. They became big sellers, especially one of the first which we called 'Rainbow' composed of bands of spectral colours. 'Mr Freedom' copied Annie's design and made a fortune out of it. By now I had managed to convince myself that if somebody copied an idea, it was best to accept it as a compliment.

That winter my sister Trisha got married to a producer called John Edwards who worked for Benton and Bowles advertising agency. They had met when Trisha was working as a stylist on one of his agency's commercials made by Ridley Scott. Trisha and John fell in love as soon as they met. John pursued her relentlessly, wining and dining her in places like 'Mr Chow'. John was a very funny chap always making people laugh but he could also be serious. It was a most romantic affair; it all happened very quickly, and Trisha soon became pregnant with her first baby. They did everything back-to-front because John did not have a decree absolute from his first wife Anne. The honeymoon came first with a romantic trip to Ireland; they stayed in a log cabin where it is thought their first child was conceived.

Then they had a memorable wedding celebration party held in Nigel Greenwood's gallery in Glebe Place. Nick Bullen had designed and made her dress in a soft appliquéd velvet. John and Trisha both looked beautiful and it was a very happy day. I remember my niece Tonia being attracted to my dog Toggles who had come to the wedding with me and it started her great love for dogs. A week later they got married at Chelsea Registry Office with just family present and we had another celebration meal. It was the first time in a long while that I had been on my own without Nicky and I missed him briefly, as he was always brilliant on such occasions. Again, I felt sad that it had not worked out for us and was not the happiest pea in the pod.

Life continued. Nicky would appear in the shop from time to time. I remember on the day that our decree absolute came through he took me out for lunch at Parsons, a restaurant which had just opened in the Fulham Road. We decided to remain friends though he did not tell me he already had his second wife lined up. We did just that and still talk regularly. He told me he had bought an old naval Fairmile which he was converting into a living space, and planned to travel the seas and hire the boat out for Mediterranean cruises. He had a number of adventures including helping refugees escape from Lebanon. He was the same old Nicky with his usual enthusiasm and, of course, the new lady, Brandy, would be sailing with him. She became his second wife, but not for long.

One day in the spring of that year a young man appeared in the shop with a portfolio of his work to show me. He was Irish and had the bluest eyes I had ever seen. His name was Luke Kelly and he strutted confidently into the shop, asking if he could photograph some of the clothes. As I was always in need of publicity shots, I agreed and he ended up spending the whole day shooting various items from the collection. One thing led to another and as it was late we decided to go out for dinner. He came back to the flat for a drink, and stayed that night and then moved in for a while.

He was a great character, a songwriter as well as a photographer. But more importantly for me, he was a great lover and made me feel like a cherished woman again. He was writing songs for McGuiness Flint's next album. The rehearsals for the recording were great fun - drinking endless cups of tea around Ruth's kitchen table in Blackheath.

The fashion shows with Annie Lambton continued and this time Nick Bullen came with us to model the men's clothes. We performed at the Hilton in Teheran, and then we took the show to Istanbul. When I was in the States with the Corbetts, I had met the Foreign Minister of Iran, Ardeshir Zahedi. I let him know in advance that we were doing a fashion show and he came to watch, accompanied by his flunkies (probably his bodyguards). They wined and dined us royally and made a great fuss of all the girls, showering us with gifts of jewellery and caviar.

This time there was a different band with us - the Masters of Mediocrity, with a lead singer named Jamie Longie. I had met them performing in the 'Teddy Bear's Picnic', a local restaurant and had asked them to play for us. The Masters were a special bunch of boys, great fun to be with and, above all, good musicians. After our first show in Teheran, we were offered some good quality opium. This was one of the hazards of travelling with a band. We made a special arrangement to meet up with Joseph the next day and he introduced us to a man whose father was a registered user, which made it possible to go to his home to try the drug legally. This was in the days when the Shah was still in power and relations with the West were good.

A few of us, mainly the band and models, were driven to the outskirts of the city to a beautiful villa with a walled garden. It was like stepping into another age; we walked into a large, gloriously tiled courtyard surrounded by pillars and statues; then we went through an arch into a lounging area with priceless Persian carpets covered with large colourful cushions. We were invited to take off our shoes, relax on the cushions and sip mint tea. Then the ritual of smoking the opium began: the gardener showed us how to take it in a special antique porcelain pipe, not inhaling in deep breaths but taking quick shallow ones. Soon we were feeling the effects - a gentle kind of floating high but where you were not completely out of it, just very relaxed. It was pale brown opium - the best available in the world.

After the pressure of the show it was wonderful to let go and feel safe in these beautiful surroundings. Soon, the most amazing meal appeared with many different dishes, delicacies made up of everything imaginable. We feasted on these savoury delights, which were followed by a selection of delectable sweets and more mint tea. It was another of my specially memorable meals. This superb, exotic meal was probably made even more delicious because we were stoned.

After a suitable time of relaxation, we were taken to visit the bazaar. We walked around the market which was full to bursting with beautiful objects. I felt like Alice in Wonderland there were so many glittering urns, terracotta pots, glass vases and bottles, shining jewellery and clothes sprawling over the narrow aisles in haphazard displays. So much to take in; a feast for the eyes and difficult to decide what to buy, as you were continually hassled by stall owners. The colours of the garments in silk, linen and cotton were amazing. My eyes were dazzled by kaftans, blouses, skirts, trousers and gorgeous brocade jackets. I bought some scarves and fine lawn kurtas to sell in the shop, long before anyone else had them.

The clothes and the colours were a real inspiration for me as a designer. My collection changed dramatically after this visit. The beautiful silks, linens and brilliant cottons had to be seen to be believed. It truly was an Aladdin's cave, but in reality we were still high from the opium, so we were seeing things through rose-coloured glasses. Many of us bought presents to bring home, then finally, after another mint tea and an extraordinarily memorable day, we were returned, loaded with stuff, by our driver to the hotel.

Soon we were leaving for Istanbul. It was always difficult packing up after a performance - I not only had my own clothes to pack but most of those from the show as well - which ideally had to be kept in some kind of running order for the next show. Still in rather a delicate state, we set off for Tehran airport and prepared to fly on to Turkey. On arrival at the airport we were checking all the bags outside on the tarmac, and I realised one of mine had not come off the plane. I had to go with the baggage handlers to show them which one it was. When it was eventually found I was so relieved; it was only then that I finally came down to earth from the opium.

The Istanbul show was another tremendous success. We were wined and dined at great expense and visited the local sights and night clubs. I was becoming attracted to Jamie, the lead singer of the band, and we started hanging out together. He was American and had grown up in New York. He had been staying with a friend in London so by the time we got back to the UK, I had invited him to come and stay with me. Luke by now had moved on to pastures new. Annie absolutely did not approve and made it obvious that she did not think a relationship with him was a good idea.

Whenever I left to go away for a show or a holiday I would ask a friend to take care of my two dogs. This usually worked well, and I avoided the cost of putting them into kennels. But this time when I was abroad, to my horror, Nicky had come and taken away Mark, my Dalmatian. He had spirited my dog away on his new boat called The Sea Victory, and had sailed off to Minorca with his new girlfriend, Brandy. They were soon to be married, and she was pregnant with Christopher. I was livid, but there was nothing I could do because of the quarantine laws. I eventually visited my dog Mark in Minorca, taking him for our final walk together. But this was the last time I ever saw Mark.

The business was now beginning to falter and it was becoming increasingly difficult to compete with the other Kings Road boutiques. Every other shop seemed to be selling jeans and T-shirts. Perhaps the time had come to think about selling. The final nail in the coffin came when our landlords, 'The Loyal Order of Ancient Shepherds', raised the rent from £1000 per year to £4000 per year. I knew we could not pay that kind of money for long. I began to mention that we would be putting the business on the market, and waited to see what would happen - with some trepidation.

One of my wholesale clients was an old girlfriend of Bradshaw's called Anne, who was living in Jamaica. She was now married to Jeffrey Selznick, son of David. They had a boutique called 'Temptation' in Ocho Rios and used to buy from us whenever she came to London. She was a real character: tall, brown, beautiful and very bright. When she heard I was selling up she said 'Come and work for us, design a range of beach clothes for 'Temptation' and organise the manufacturing with our Jamaican outworkers.'

What a wonderful idea, I thought, and I started to consider moving into their business.

There was one more 'Chelsea Night' before I sold the shop. This time at the Cyprus Hilton, in association with Cyprus Airways. The shows had always been fun to plan and prepare with Annie. She got the go-ahead and then we would meet and choose the designers and models. I designed and made the outfits for the show and also brought along some of our existing stock, because we always sold everything we took.

Our accompanying band was The Masters of Mediocrity, which pleased me as the lead singer Jamie and I were now together. They had developed a good sound which was very individual and sometimes I too sang with them. Jamie bought me an autoharp for my birthday, which I was learning to play so that I could accompany myself as well as sing with the band. I made a recording with Jamie and (to my embarrassment) he took it to Chris Blackwell, a friend who was married to Marilyn, one of our tour models, to see what he thought of it - but he was not impressed.

The fashion show at the Hilton in Nicosia was a big event: the local gentry turned up for a special dinner followed by the 'Chelsea Nights' spectacular, followed by dancing. Everyone wanted to be there because we showed the latest London designs accompanied by amazing music. Annie introduced the show wearing one of my outfits and a marvellous choker necklace which she had designed herself - part of a range of jewellery she sold in the boutique. The audience had never seen anything quite like our show before - it was fast, punchy, right up to the minute, a great example of Swinging London life. At the end those who would like to, were invited to come backstage to see the clothes and could buy them directly off the model's back.

After the show a charming Cypriot, Panos Kyriakidis, came and asked the band to come and play for a week at his Famagusta hotel. They were delighted and I was invited to join them along with some of the other models. Annie was not pleased but somehow we managed to persuade her to change our flights. We then went at Panos's invitation for a week's holiday to Paphos before our Famagusta gig, leaving Panos with a little time to promote our event before we arrived. He arranged for us to stay in a hotel on the Paphos seafront called the 'Pelican'. It was named after a pair of these birds which had a nest there and were obviously cared for by the owners, and you could ask at the bar for fish to feed them.

We swam, sunbathed, went for long walks and generally had a relaxing time, because Paphos was unspoilt in those days.

One member of our group had brought some 'Californian Sunshine' with him and several of us decided to take it for our day out on Aphrodite's beach. 'Sunshine' is acid and we took it with our breakfast coffee, delicious Greek yogurt, and cereal - just half a tab for me as it was the first time I had taken it. Most of the others had some experience of it before and said they would take care of me so I knew I was in safe hands. Two taxis arrived and we piled in and were driven a few miles to the stunning Aphrodite's beach, said to be the goddess' birthplace. It consisted of a huge rock rising ominously out of the sea, where supposedly Aphrodite had emerged from the waves on a scallop shell attracting the birds and the bees as she approached the beach.

The acid slowly began to take effect. The sun was shining brightly, the wind was blowing a gale and the sea was crashing on to the beach. Everything seemed magnified and intensified. I strolled down to the shingle and felt as if I was walking on eggshells though I was on pebbles. I seemed to be in a real wonderland. Everything was shining. I started to pick up shells and accumulated a small collection, some of which I still keep. They were sparkling and beautiful, luminous and bright. I began to play with them and make a design; amongst them, I found a tiny red spider. I watched it closely for what seemed like a long time until it vanished into one of the shells and I lost it. I was devastated by the loss of this little creature and started to cry. Jamie came to my rescue immediately; and stayed with me for the rest of the day.

The next thing I knew he was peeling an orange and we were sharing this deliciously juicy fruit - the best I had ever tasted. Having brought some paninis from the hotel, we gathered round to eat, some of the others had wandered off for a walk. To start with it was a glorious day but later it began to deteriorate; it looked as if we were in for a storm, or was it my imagination?

It all became windswept and the sky darkened. To our relief, and just before the weather broke, the taxis arrived as arranged. We stumbled aboard and they took us back to the hotel. En route it poured and poured with rain. When we got back, Jamie, Ant and I went out on to the headland to watch the lightning. I was wearing a long multi-coloured gingham skirt which was cut on the cross, with a yellow sweater as it had become chilly. We were absolutely soaked and we lay on the rocks looking up at the swirling clouds. What slowly unfolded before us was an amazing electric storm. I have never seen such lightning: it lit up the sky and was breathtakingly beautiful and dangerous, and we thought it was the best spectacle we had ever seen. But we were still spaced out on acid, though it had worn off somewhat by now. When we got back to the hotel again, we found a feast set out for us on long lines of tables. We were leaving the next day to go to Famagusta for our gig, so they had made a farewell party to which the whole village seem to have been invited.

To this day, I am not sure if it was Panos who arranged every- thing but I know he paid for the whole party. The tables were covered in small dishes of fish, meat, aubergine, tomatoes, olives, taramasalata, almonds, sardines, frog's legs, sheeps' eyes, prawns, squid, spinach, lettuce, and beans in olive oil..... all washed down with retsina and plenty of water. There were also great bowls of salad and bread. The meal finished with baklava, a speciality dessert of the area and Turkish coffee. Then the dancing began and went on until late into the night. It started with one of the young men strutting his stuff; they were all wonderful dancers and it was exhausting to watch him whirling around.

At any Greek gathering it is customary to get up and dance or sing to enhance the evening. The men started the proceedings, then the women had a go. We were obviously expected to do our bit and play for them and we did not disappoint. The guys went to get their instruments and played a few numbers. Then I sang my number 'I'm leaving on a jet plane' which I had recently recorded with Jamie. It was a great night, which included another of my memorable meals - something you simply never forget. Their hospitality was incredible, so gracious and kind, always with much laughter and clapping.

The next day, we left sadly and were driven across country to our Famagusta gig. At eight o'clock Panos came to collect us from our flat to take us about one hundred yards along the beach to the hotel. We went in the hotel's back entrance and down to the nightclub to set up. On the way we met a little white dog without a collar, rather scruffy but very sweet. I befriended him and when we had finished the gig, he was still out there waiting for me. A few more pats then he followed us home; we carried him inside and gave him bread and milk: he was starving. We bathed him with my shampoo, getting rid of his ticks and fleas. He was a little beauty, a bundle of fluff. He looked like a poodle but I was later to discover he was probably a pedigree Maltese Terrier. A complete surprise!

We did the gig every night for six nights. I held the beat with a tambourine and sang the odd number with the band. It was fun and fulfilled my ambition and aspirations of wanting to go on the road with a band. The little dog, whom we had named Paphos, waited patiently on the beach for us every night. The moment came when we had to decide what to do with him: apparently strays were rounded up and shot on a regular basis so it seemed we would have to take him home. An important decision had to be made. In those days we were keen on throwing the I Ching. We decided to throw the coins to find out if it was a good idea to take the little stray dog back home with us. The hexagram we threw was the one which represented 'the family.' It talked about travelling over water and remaining together as a family. So we all felt it confirmed that we should take the dog home with us. He would have to be sedated so I decided to give him some of my Mogadon sleeping pills which I knew were not too strong and would not harm him.

I dosed the little dog and put him into my model bag on a towel with the zipper open. I had given him two pills so he dozed while we set off for the airport in a taxi. We arrived and checked our luggage in, each of us taking our own hand baggage. In the meantime - surprise, surprise - the dog woke up. I had to take him into the 'ladies' and give him another sleeping pill. I thought all was going well, then, to my horror, found myself in a queue with our bags being searched before we boarded the aircraft. All seemed to be lost and our little dog would be confiscated. The customs officer looked into the bag and said, 'It's a dog, go ahead.' Without hesitation I did and scampered on to the plane as quickly as possible, taking a window seat trying to hide the dog-bag by my feet. I stayed there until we arrived at Heathrow. Paphos slept throughout the journey, only popping his head out after the plane had landed. I zipped him up before setting off with him to collect our bags. We made a plan for me to go through 'Nothing to Declare.' Although I felt guilty - there was no way I could have left the little dog behind to such a deadly fate.

We took Paphos triumphantly home to the boutique to meet the other animals. I had a bearded collie called Toggles who had belonged to a friend, and Tiger who had been Jamie's cat. We had a bottle of champagne to celebrate our safe arrival whilst they all got to know each other. Because Paphos had grown up on the beach, he was not house-trained. It took a while but he soon learned that we went out for 'walkies' in Battersea Park. As soon as possible I took him to the vet who checked Paphos over and found the dog was fine, and the vet told me she thought he was a Maltese Terrier.

CHAPTER TEN
FINAL CHELSEA DAYS
Parting is such sweet sorrow

We had now reached the last phase of the boutique. It was 1972 and it was obvious the time had come to sell up and move on. Anne's knitted sweaters had become very successful and she left in order to run her own knitting business from home. So when we came back from Cyprus, Rudi Paterson, one of the models from the shows, became the manager. He was our last one and cut a handsome figure as he tried to sell our remaining stock. I had had masses of jeans made up, as that was what everybody was selling. By now it was no longer feasible for me to keep on my pattern cutter Nina, and the sample maker Margaret, though they both continued to work for me on a freelance basis when I needed them for the shows. It was sad knowing that I was on the last leg of the boutique. It had been a wonderful journey, an unforgettable way of life for me since we opened in July 1964 but we were not prospering and I needed to make sensible decisions quickly.

In the autumn of 1972 I had been approached by Patricia Speirs to do a fundraiser for 'Shelter', the charity for the homeless. I was always up for a show as they were exciting and great fun. The show was to be held on HMS Belfast which is moored on the Thames in London. I invited Vivienne Westwood, Malcolm McLaren and Zandra Rhodes to be part of it as well, and all three agreed. Vivienne's shop was called 'Let it Rock' so we decided to call the show 'Let's Rock Shelter'. Felix Topolski designed a wonderful poster and programme using a great drawing he had made of Elvis Presley, which he then offered for auction after the show. Felix was a famous World War 11 artist and father of my great friend, Daniel Topolski.

Vivienne and Malcolm had opened their shop in the Kings Road in the previous autumn. It was only a couple of doors down the road from 'Sue Locke's Boutique'. We were good neighbours; I remember there was a time when they used our loo and we warned each other about shoplifters - the bane of our lives. You could always tell the serious ones as they came in gangs with one chatty leader. Vivienne and Malcolm's shop was full of Fifties gear, featuring teddy-boy clothes which Malcolm used to wear with aplomb. On a Saturday their shop attracted all the mods and rockers of the surrounding counties, dressed up and flaunting their teddy-boy outfits and hairdos as they paraded ostentatiously up and down the Kings Road.

By now our fashion shows were famous and it was extra special to do a fundraiser for 'Shelter', and exciting to have Vivienne Westwood and Zandra Rhodes joining me. It was probably Vivienne's first show with many more great successes to come. The 'Shelter' show was also a great success; Jamie's band 'The Masters of Mediocrity' supplied the music, and a group of my friends modelled for us and we all danced through the show. Working on a ship was extraordinarily difficult, especially when negotiating the anchor chains. The whole show was fun and, best of all, we raised £2,700 for 'Shelter' - a fair amount of money then.

In November I was invited to Jamaica to stay with Jeffrey and Anne Selznick in their beautiful home on Montego Bay. I had been supplying clothes to her shop 'Temptation' for some time, and we had discussed the possibility of my working for them in their boutique. It seemed an amazing idea to me - just too good to be true.

They sent me money for the air fare which was certainly more than I could afford in those difficult times. They met me at the airport and drove me to their house through the most exotic countryside. The vegetation was so green, massive and full of bright flowers. It was the first time I had been in the tropics: everything was enormous and full of superb colours. I knew I would enjoy life here.

The reason for my visit was to check out what it would be like if I decided to come to live on the island, though I certainly would not have such a glamorous lifestyle as the Selznick's. They lived in great luxury with a cook, houseboy and gardener. Their elegant house was built on a hill with a magnificent view across the bay. I was pampered for my two weeks stay with tasty, mildly spiced Caribbean food, extraordinary fruit and vegetables. They took me to see their shop in Ocho Rios and I worked there to get familiar with the clientele, the stock and find out what materials were available for making up.

We spent time looking at the island's startling diversity, swam in a cold river, and they introduced me to their friends and took me to numerous parties. One was a typical Jamaican Sunday Lunch with a barbecue beside the swimming pool. Dessert was treacle tart with ganja sprinkled on the top - delicious and hallucinogenic. I was in this state when I met Kasimir Korybut, an architect who was also a Polish prince. It was all a bit unreal, but we hit it off immediately and laughed together for the rest of the party.

I told him the Selznicks had offered me a job at 'Temptation' and I was looking at the island before coming back in the New Year to take up my position as designer for them. I told him all I had to do was to sell my boutique and tidy up my financial affairs. Later Kasimir invited me for dinner at his house called The Jetty set right on the edge of Montego Bay. He had designed and built the house and pool, and landscaped the large garden. The Jetty was stunning with a veranda running the length of the house facing the sea. Further along the coast, he had also designed and built many properties in the Round Hill development. All of these houses had a sunny, tropical feeling of space about them - ideal for an easy, relaxed lifestyle.

Like the Selznicks, Kasimir lived in absolute luxury with three servants. On the night of my visit, he organised the most impressive meal - all done very romantically. Over coffee and liqueurs on the veranda, we listened blissfully to Tosca. He chatted me up and invited me to stay at The Jetty with him when I came to Jamaica the following year. I said that would be lovely, and agreed, but at the same time I told him I wanted to find my own place and I planned to bring at least one of my dogs. Luckily, he said he did not mind, and by the time I left the island, he had agreed to have both my dogs.

I arrived back in London, having made up my mind what my next move would be: I set about selling the shop as quickly as possible to enable me to move to Jamaica to work at 'Temptation' with the Selznicks. I agreed to stay with Kasimir until I found my own place in Montego Bay. He was a lovely man but not my type exactly; he was a terrible snob and not brilliant in bed, but he was a good friend during my time in Jamaica, which was more important than being a great lover!

A number of people had shown an interest in the shop. The most promising was a friend of Jamie's called Jane, whom he had known in Rome. She wanted to open a florist's there. I pursued this option and eventually everything was agreed. She paid £10,000 for the remaining lease and wanted to move into the place in March. It was sad closing down that part of my life, especially as the Sixties had been so exhilarating. Selling-up left me heavy-hearted, but this feeling did not last long. I have a capacity to gird up my loins and get moving on to my next project.

Most of the money from the sale went on paying-off the bills, not to mention the rent which had mounted up. It had been hard towards the end of my time at the boutique; the competition in the Kings Road had become very intense, and I would be left with little capital when I got to Jamaica. The important thing was to have a big sale and get rid of everything. Cloth, stock, patterns and my precious machines all had to go. Vivienne Westwood took my sewing machine and the over-locker, so these just moved next door. Vivienne was now doing well in the Kings Road, and went on to have enormous success and, some time later, was voted designer of the year.

As I could not take much with me, I left some things with my parents and gave away a great deal. This left me with a good feeling of new beginnings and bright expectations for my life in Jamaica. I liked starting again with a clean slate. I took my precious border collie Toggles with me; he had a rabies injection and I had a travel kennel made. Paphos, my Maltese Terrier from Cyprus went to live with a colleague in the country, and Tiger stayed with Jane.

The time came for me to leave so there were farewell parties with friends and family. After these celebrations, I eventually made it to the airport with Toggles in his expensive 'kennel' which looked rather insubstantial. We boarded the plane at Heathrow, heading for Montego Bay refuelling in Barbados. At Barbados, I got off to check on the dog as I saw they were unloading some bags. Some premonition had made me make sure that Toggles was safe, because, to my horror, I found that he had escaped from his box and had run off across the airfield. To bring him all this way and lose him would have been dreadful. With the help of one of the baggage handlers, I set off to search for the runaway dog on a motorised buggy. I must have looked an idiot sitting on this uncomfortable vehicle, with tears streaming down my face, calling helplessly for a dog which did not seem to hear me. Luckily, we found him, sniffing around the staff canteen; typically, Toggles had gone to find food. I whistled him and he came immediately, jumping up beside me. I was so relieved to find him that I hugged him and burst into tears again.

When we got back to the plane, which had waited for me, the pilot kindly agreed to let Toggles come into the passenger compartment, albeit in the feeble kennel from which the dog had already chewed his way out. We flew like this to Kingston with me sniffling and the dog beside me in the back of the plane. A feeling of great relief flooded over me and made me realize that he would be my protector, that he was absolutely meant to come.

During the next part of the journey, I tried to make the kennel a little more secure without much success: on landing the same thing happened. Once again, a baggage handler rescued him and we were reunited. We waited a long time for the vet to come to check Toggle's paperwork, and consequently missed our connecting flight to Montego Bay where dear Kasimir was going to meet us. The business with the vet was completed at last, and I phoned Kasimir to let him know what had happened and I left a message with Victor, his houseboy.

There was no connecting flight that day so my only option was to take a taxi, as it was impossible to stay in a hotel with a dog. I found a cabbie who agreed to drive me to Montego Bay for 50 dollars, which happened to be all I had. My luggage had gone ahead with the plane, and I was left with only my hand baggage and the dog. We had about a four-hour drive ahead of us and by now it was dark. I admired as much as I could see of the scenery and slept for most of the ride. We finally reached Montego Bay Airport around midnight; amazingly, my bags were just sitting there out in the open waiting for me. We collected them and drove the last few miles to The Jetty where a very relieved Kasimir welcomed me with a stiff drink.

CHAPTER ELEVEN
NEW LIFE IN MONTEGO BAY
Woman - don't cry

When I agreed to take up the position of designer at 'Temptation', I thought I would stay with them for a couple of years and then set up my own business in Jamaica. Right from the start I had my eye open for suitable premises, bearing in mind that trade there was almost totally tourist orientated. I also needed a partner to share the responsibility and costs. I had always had directors in my Chelsea business so I knew the value of having the support of associates. I had a little capital of my own but not a great deal. Kasimir and I had already talked about the possibility of working together and this discussion continued.

As soon as I arrived in Montego Bay, we talked again about what kind of shop to go for. That same weekend Kasimir invited friends to stay at the Jetty, even though I was due to start work at 'Temptation' the following Monday. I soon discovered I was meant to be the hostess with the mostest, planning menus and discussing food with the cook. In the middle of all this, I had a call from Jeffrey Selznick to say that one of his Ocho Rios staff was sick and I was needed to go immediately to take care of the shop. I had no car and it was quite a drive to Ocho Rios and I had Kasimir's guests to deal with too; so without too much thought, I told Jeffrey that I could not come to help out at the shop. He sacked me on the spot - and for a moment - I was devastated.

My initial reaction was one of enormous shock and disbelief. How could they get me all the way from England just to sack me at my first refusal of a request? My second reaction was one of immense relief. Jeffrey had a reputation for treating his staff terribly, and not only that, he had already made a pass at me when I had stayed with them the first time. He had managed to get me in bed with both him and his wife, so maybe it was best not to be employed by such a man. Without too much pain, I managed to have a most enjoyable weekend with Kasimir and his friends, but I was anxious about being in a new country without a job. In other words - I was up the Swannee without a paddle.

All through my life I have been lucky with my friends. Kasimir was wonderful: he assured me I had somewhere to live and that I could stay as long as I liked. Although it had been a while since I had gone out and looked for a job, I have always been confident that I could find something. Obviously, I wanted to work as a designer. Montego Bay was a small place, everybody knew what was going on and word soon spread that I was available. I found out about the other fashion businesses and made some calls and enquiries. The one that appealed to me most was an American company called Ruth Clarage, a husband and wife team running a number of boutiques around the island. They had developed their business over a number of years, and had outlets in Kingston, Montego Bay and Ocho Rios. They printed and made up virtually all their own garments and accessories in a small factory on an industrial estate not far from the Bay. About a month after my drama with the Selznicks, I had an appointment with them about a job as a designer.

From the moment we met, I knew we could work together. They were charming and delighted to have somebody with experience in the trade; after all, I had come straight from Swinging London which was the centre of the fashion world. They showed me over the premises where there were rows of noisy machinists making garments with loads of stock piled up, ready to go. There was also a sample maker in a small studio, who made up the first prototype, with whom I could work closely. They showed me the tables where they printed the cloth - a mixture of cotton and polyester - not my favourite but practical material which washes well.

I was back in my element. In my London business all the making-up had been done by outworkers. I had spent a great deal of time delivering cloth or ready-cut garments to out-workers all over London. Working in this way, there was always problems with what was called cabbage - where the outworkers felt it was their right to make extra garments to sell for their own profit in local markets. It was well known in the trade, had been going on for years, so it was almost impossible to stop. You could control this cabbage, though, if you cut the items yourself. I did this sometimes but doing this was enormously time consuming.

To my delight, I got the job and a company car too. It was very difficult to work in Jamaica without a vehicle. The pay was not great but I did not mind; it would cover my expenses. I told them I was looking for a house, and they knew a family with a plantation where there was a cottage to rent. I went to see it and, although it needed some work doing, I gratefully took it. The Cotch, my wooden house on stilts, was on the outskirts of Montego Bay - a ten-minute drive to the Clarage Factory.

Throughout all these negotiations Kasimir was supportive and helped me a good deal, driving me around to appointments. He introduced me to his friends and we had a pleasant social life together. When he had to go to Miami on business, he would leave me at The Jetty with Victor and the cook to look after me; the cook taught me Jamaican recipes. Kasamir also left me his car - a large white Cadillac. On one occasion I went into Montego Bay to do some shopping with Victor. The streets were narrow and somehow I managed to scrape the paintwork against a wall. Victor was horrified and insisted we took the car to a friend of his to get it fixed. The guy at the local garage did a touch-up-job and you really could not tell that the car had had a little knock. It was great to have Kasimir back in the house especially as he was none the wiser.

At the beginning of May I moved into The Cotch a home of my own at last. I had spent time doing the place up and had given it a lick of paint. It was sparsely furnished but comfortable enough for me and Toggles. I was pleased to have the dog with me as friends were nervous about my being a white lady alone out in the bush, so I decided to get another dog for extra protection. Orlando was a Rhodesian Ridgeback puppy and he went everywhere with me and Toggles. A few months later I was given a pair of kittens so my family was complete. I felt safe there and nobody ever bothered me, unlike other friends who were burgled regularly.

The company car arrived - a new bronze-coloured Ford Escort and from that moment I could drive to work. Although Kasimir had been good to me, it was wonderful to be free and be able to do exactly what I liked. We remained friends and were still considering going into business together. First I would have a look at the market and see where the pitfalls lay. Occasionally, we would bump into the Selznicks at a cocktail party and it gave me real pleasure when I told them about my new job. In many ways it was better than the one they had offered me because my remit was for fabric and dress design.

On my first Monday I went into the office and had a meeting to discuss what was wanted for that week and our future plans. I was asked to produce two fabric designs for their collection. I spent the morning looking at the style of the existing ones, then went home to The Cotch where I had set up my sitting room as a studio. It was a perfect place to work - light coming in from north and the south - exotic Jamaican smells wafting in from the veranda. I had air conditioning, which I put on when it became very hot in the summer - but it made a terrible noise sounding as if it was going to blow up - but it never did!

My first design was based on the sea grape, a native coastal plant, using two greens and black. The second design was in yellow, red and black based on the ackee, a colourful Caribbean fruit from which they make the national dish, saltfish and ackee. My fabric designs were colourful but quite basic. I had great fun drawing them and planning the repeat on graph paper and then testing the designs out on paper. After creating the designs, it is always good to see the next step - when the fabric you have designed is made up into a garment.

One of the most disconcerting things about working in Jamaica was that there was only one season: summer. My first collection was called the Cruise Collection as one of our largest outlets was where the cruise ships came into Montego Bay. It was pleasing to start with but I did miss the winter and autumn fashions which I had been used to designing. The summer season in London had always been the most difficult and least interesting, but in tropical Jamaica clothes could be backless and more frivolous. I created a skimpy sundress which was still being sold when I returned twenty years later!

I soon settled into a working pattern and my old life of cocktail parties was left behind. This was partly because The Season in Jamaica is from November to February. Now I was meeting a different crowd - mainly professional people - teachers, nurses and those working in the hotel business, and I also got to know a group of mainly white Jamaicans. This was far removed from any social circle Kasimir had in mind for me and he did not approve.

Kasimir had taken me to Blue Hole to watch the polo. It had always been a favourite game of mine so when my friend Annette came to stay with me at The Cotch, I drove her there. This was the start of my connection to the polo club, and I remember meeting most of the players that day. We were having a drink in the bar after the game when I noticed Patrick Brownie. He came over with some of the team to speak to us. He was hot and sweaty, having just come off the pitch, and greeted us with a warm smile and a strange soft Jamaican accent. At the end of that afternoon, he asked me for my telephone number. I gave it to him and could not wait to hear from him.

That evening Kasimir was coming for dinner to meet Annette. We told him about our trip to the polo club and I could tell he was annoyed that we had gone without him. He invited us back to the Jetty for a meal later in the week. It was a splendid meal and over dinner he suggested that Annette come and stay with him for a few days. As I was working it seemed a good idea and he had taken a shine to her. She was delighted to accept the invitation as it was luxurious and a bit of a treat. I certainly did not mind and they had a bit of a fling. It left me free to pursue other friendships, which I was looking forward to doing.

Sure enough Patrick called me. We started seeing each other and it soon became quite serious. It all centred around Blue Hole and the polo club. He played most weekends and I helped to care for his polo ponies. Each player had at least three, all of which had to be exercised to have them in tiptop condition for the weekend match. I worked most mornings, often from home, leaving me free to ride after lunch. Sometimes Patrick would visit me during the afternoon. Love in the afternoon somehow always seemed so decadent, finishing with a delicious long glass of something alcoholic. I soon developed the local habit of drinking rum and Coke rather than wine.

All that summer I was involved with Patrick and with polo. I became part of his crowd and knew many of the players, their wives and girlfriends. Amongst them was a young American man called Kjack. He did not live in Jamaica but came regularly to the island on business. He was a numismatist and worked for the Paramount Coin Company. Then he was just part of our group but later he became an important man in my life.

One day, a group of us, including Patrick and me, went for a picnic at Blue Hole. After a magnificent picnic many of us decided to swim in the very cold river. We were fooling around, enjoying ourselves. In the fracas he started dunking me in and out of the water. When I got out of the river I was disorientated, dizzy and immediately had terrible earache. I completely lost my balance, fell over, and had to be put to bed. Patrick was embarrassed and thought I was attention seeking, but Kjack was the only one who kept coming to see if I was alright. I noticed what a caring man he was and was grateful for his understanding. I found out that he was good when I was ill, as I discovered in dramatic circumstances a year later.

The relationship between Patrick and me was never quite the same after that. He really did think I had been playing the hypochondriac, pretending I was worse than I was - something I would never do. I was furious with him and I cooled off pretty quickly. I was well established at the polo club and could go on my own with the dogs, watch a match and exercise other people's horses. One chap who needed help with his ponies was Gilly Byles as he had six to keep fit, so I started to ride for him. He became a good friend and invited me to the opening of his hotel on Negril Beach waterfront. At that time the beautiful, long, empty stretch of beach was being spectacularly developed by him and others. They changed Negril Beach beyond recognition - not necessarily for the better.

My severe earache happened so suddenly because I had just taken up scuba diving, joining the British SubAqua Club at Chalet Caribe. This was something I had wanted to learn to do ever since my honeymoon. I met Dr Es Hamid, the president of the club at a party, and he had invited me to start training, which I had done earlier that summer. What I had forgotten was that just before I came out to Jamaica, I had had an operation on my ears to stop them sticking out. Unbeknown to me this had left quite a lot of dried blood in them. After my little drama at Blue Hole, I made an appointment to have my ears thoroughly syringed. This cleared the dried blood and my ears were better afterwards, but even now I still continue to have a problem with them.

Once I had completed my 'buddy training' with the BSAC, I went diving regularly. Often Es would lead, taking about six of us along the spectacular Chalet Caribe Reef. There were many amazing underwater sights and experiences - such as dozens of parrot fish moving along with you as you swam past colourful sea anemones and sea ferns. The sound of the tanks and the bubbles were exciting; at the same time you were always on edge looking out for shark and barracudas. There was something special about swimming with the fishes - perhaps it was a memory of long, long ago. I loved the parrot fish and was convinced they enjoyed accompanying us humans. They had a habit of nodding their heads at you as if in acknowledgement, but they were probably just trying to get away.

There was one dramatic excursion I went on with Es. I was following him as he led two novice divers. We were plunging in and out of caves and then suddenly they disappeared - I could not see them. I was circling around waiting for them to appear. Later Es said, 'You were brave'. They had been hiding from a barracuda which I had not seen, which then followed us back to the shore. Barracuda are inquisitive fish and are simply attracted to the tanks and the bubbles. As we arrived safely ashore, a French couple we knew were going out. We warned them about the barracuda. They came back almost immediately as the fish was attacking their tanks; barracudas are not only inquisitive but also dangerous creatures when they are angry and not to be messed with.

The next time that Kjack came to the island he contacted me, wanting to know what had happened after my visit to the doctor. Over dinner

I told him what had occurred and that my relationship with Patrick was over. So whenever he came to Montego Bay I would see him, which was good as I got to know him over a longish period of time. He always worried about me as I lived alone. We would go out for dinner, smoke a little dope and have good slow sex. His speciality was 'A Chevy Chase Special' which was oral sex; apparently this was named from the area in Washington DC where he had grown up and a group of his friends had coined the expression as it was their speciality or shall we say 'preferred expertise'. I remember a time at the polo club when, for some unknown reason, we were discussing this expression and one of the older players, Gerald, wanted to know what we were talking about. We explained and he said how utterly disgusting it was. So we said he would never know until he had tried it and suggested he give his wife a treat as most women enjoy it. To our surprise he did and continued to give us the thumbs-up for some time.

Autumn and the rainy season were now in full swing, with wonderful colours everywhere. It really poured and I was regularly soaked through. I often went to Kingston to arrange the windows of the Ruth Clarage shop at the Sheraton Hotel. I would fly in a small air-taxi from Montego Bay, complete the display and come back the same day. The plane would go over the Cockpit Country, collect and deliver mail, then fly on to Kingston. The area we flew over was where much of the ganja was grown and you could see long stretches of it below. Officials turned a blind eye to it.

One day, up a ladder in the Sheraton Shop in Kingston, doing the window dressing, I heard a huge shout go up: 'Grimmey!' I knew the voice immediately. It was my old friend Pinky: besides, nobody else called me by that name. There she was, larger than life, and really pleased to see me. We went for a coffee and discussed the possibility of her coming to stay at The Cotch. She arranged for her friend Richard Melville to fly her to Montego Bay as he was going there on business. They both arrived together, he stayed for supper and she stayed for a week. She was great fun - with endless stories and huge, bursts of laughter.

We had a lot of giggles together and some serious talks in particular about her sleeping with my husband Nicky before, during, and after our marriage. I was miffed because I did not know that Pinky had spent the night before our wedding with Nicky. I had been with my parents, and had not imagined in my wildest dreams that he would have spent his last night with Pinky. But that evening at The Cotch, it did not seem to matter any more. We smoked dope and listened to the Eagles and the Stones. It was hot so we gradually took off all our clothes and ended up dancing around naked. It was isolated, hopefully nobody saw us, although it would have been a sight to behold. Later in the week Richard joined us for dinner and took Pinky back to Kingston and that was the last I saw of her for a few years.

Kjack came back regularly. It was always good to see him - somehow he was a breath of fresh air. This time we went for dinner combined with a film night at the Half Moon Hotel. The evening had been organised by an old girlfriend of his, Jennifer. They introduced me to the German manager, Marc Wagner. The beautiful hotel had a golf course, tennis courts, and wonderful beaches, all of which, as Marc's friends, we were allowed to use. The film club became a regular event, and was a fine opportunity for me to see up-to-date movies; Marc often asked me to join him and in this way I was able to see many amazing pictures which I would otherwise have missed out on completely.

In November my parents came to stay. We shared my bedroom which had just two single beds which we pushed together. We had a good and special time, and it was especially pleasant to introduce them to my friends, Kasimir, the Clarages, and Patrick. They had all been so good to me and had made my time there exciting and very different from my old London life. I showed them as much of the island as I could, especially my favourite places - the polo club and the Half Moon Hotel. At the time the Half Moon was closed because the staff were on strike, Marc allowed us to spend time on the beach with the use of a room with a shower. We passed lazy days on the magical tropical sandy beach sunbathing and picnicking.

On their last evening, I invited a few friends, and prepared a stuffed chicken for a farewell dinner. Daddy had been very curious about this thing called ganja; I told him it was a herb that the locals smoked and also cooked with. I suggested that I stuff the chicken with it so that he could experience it himself. To my surprise he agreed. We all had a little with the meal and slowly it began to take effect. Daddy, of course, said he could not feel anything. After dinner sitting outside drinking coffee, suddenly he exclaimed, 'Look what has just flown on to the veranda.' It was a huge Chinese paper kite in the shape of a dragonfly. I knew that he was feeling a little high on the stuffing, but of course he denied it the following morning.

They thoroughly enjoyed their visit; it was a really memorable holiday for them. It was made even more special by another friend Richard Pavitt, the BA manager in Jamaica. He upgraded their economy tickets to first class for their flight home. We had been invited to a cocktail party at their house and Richard had said then that he would arrange for them to have champagne on their return flight. He was true to his word and did exactly that. It was talked about for many years to come in the family, as none of us had ever travelled first class before.

During the parent's stay, we visited the Green Grotto. It was a series of underground caves with stalagmites which you had to negotiate by boat - a wonderland with marvellous colours and a few surprises added by the owner. We got talking to Audrey Semple who was on the booking desk. She was living on the Runaway Plantation estate with the proprietor helping him with the marketing and running the business which also included a pimento plantation. I gave her my telephone number and somehow I knew she would be in touch. When she called it was coming up to the festive season and as I love a party, I had arranged my first Christmas celebrations. I invited her to join us for the evening, and as she was coming a long way, she stayed the night. By now I had an interesting cross section of friends as I was involved in many different groups and clubs, and there was a wonderful mix of people for that Christmas party. Sadly, the only person who did not come was Kasimir. It was not his cup of tea at all, but I was sorry that he did not even give it a try.

The normal beverage for a Jamaican 'get together' is a strong rum punch containing pieces of tropical fruit. Food was usually a selection of curries, such as chicken, goat, and one for the vegetarians. I managed all these, served with rice and peas with a callaloo dish, which is rather like spicy, spinach with potatoes. I loved Jamaican cuisine and I soon accumulated a number of recipes that I wrote down in a little book - enough recipes for a small cookbook which I published later.

It was a marvellous feast with loads of food and drink and amazing music. Bob Marley and the Wailers, and Jimmy Cliff were popular at the time, and we danced until we dropped. I had brought out with me some of my favourites the Eagles, Rolling Stones and Cat Stephens records so we were really rocking. Audrey had a ball and I seem to remember her falling over and a bookcase collapsing on her. Quite a drama. As she stayed over, we had plenty of time to get to know each other. I found out that she was keen on sailing and had recently been on a Caribbean trip with her good friend, Chris. After that we met up regularly and we are still in contact, though she now lives in France.

My work continued at Ruth Clarage. Now I designed more clothes and was asked to prepare a collection of Cruise Wear for a fashion show to be held at our local Holiday Inn. I could use all my previous experience in arranging the shows so that I was able to create show-stoppers as well as bread-and-butter best sellers. My favourite role was backstage - fitting the models into the clothes, and getting special accessories to go with their outfits to make sure they all looked stunning.

I made up some of the outfits myself for the fashion show, others were made up in the factory studio, and some came straight out of stock. The show was backed by reggae music, and took place in the open around a pool. The whole thing was well received and good for the business; it was quite different from my earlier shows and much more relaxed. In London and the Middle East the shows had been serious affairs, sometimes rather traumatic with the press there - fingers desperately crossed for a satisfactory review. The Caribbean show was very laid back with guests drinking and sunbathing. Despite this, the show successfully promoted and sold the clothes.

Riding had now become an important part of my life. I had been exercising polo ponies and also riding out with Mel, the Kerr-Jarrett manager at The Great House. This family owned my home and the sugar plantation. They had horses which worked in the sugar cane fields and also needed to be exercised at the weekend. Mel arrived with the horse already saddled and ready to go, and we would ride out through the plantation which stretched across the entire Montego Bay area.

These were some of the most beautiful rides of my life, with sugar cane growing way above our heads. On a hot day it was cool galloping along the paths criss-crossing the plantation. As we rode up into the hills, Mel would tell me his life story. One day I remember a worker jumping out of the cane into the path of the horses with a machete. My mare reared up, and I came off, but Mel caught the horse and helped me remount. He told me never to ride on my own, but I am afraid I did later. It could be dangerous, but nothing ever happened to me. I received nothing but kindness from Jamaicans and always felt safe.

One day when we had been out riding, Mel had to pay the plantation workers. It was payday and, as we were late, he asked me to come and help him. There was a long queue of men lined up to collect their buff pay-packets. I was astonished to find that more than half signed with an X. It left me feeling absolutely furious to think that the British had been in Jamaica all those years and no-one had taught the local people how to read and write. It was generally believed the British had a good reputation on education. Now most of the young children very proudly go to school in their uniforms, but to my great surprise, there were still many people who had not had an elementary education.

Later that year, I was offered the opportunity to buy an ex- racehorse. His name was Salzburg, a beautiful bay gelding who could go like the wind. At first I stabled him at the polo club for free if I exercised some of Gilly's horses. I tried to do a bit of stick and balling with Salzburg but he was rather too big for polo. Keeping him at the ground turned out to be really hard work and I became absolutely exhausted. He was my first horse and I was responsible for feeding, grooming and cleaning out the stable. I decided to move him back to Montego Bay where I could pay a groom to do most of the hard work. I stabled my horse at the Delisser's yard which was much nearer, where he would be comfortable and well cared for. All I had to do was exercise him. I used to ride with Nick, the younger son, and we went on wonderful jaunts together. We were both keen on jumping and had been practising to compete in the Kingston Horse Show. All the arrangements were made with the animals going by train with a groom. I drove my car with my saddle and bridle and clothes for the competition. It was a long drive but as I tried to enter the showground the police stopped me. Horror of horrors - my tax disc was out of date. They prevented me from entering and impounded my car on the spot. As much as I pleaded with them, I saw that it gave them great satisfaction doing this to me.

I begged and cried and used all my feminine guile to try to persuade them to let me through but they would not. As I had a competitor's badge, they let me into the ground on foot. I struggled with my saddle, bridle and bag to where the horses were quietly grazing and told my sorry tale. There was nothing I could do: the car would not be released until the tax was paid and neither I nor the Clarages had noticed it. I tried to forget about it and concentrate on competing as best I could. I did not win anything and I remember getting four faults in the jumping. The problem was how to get back. I had animals at home and had to get back to see to them. Nick was staying in Kingston with friends, so I had to find a way somehow and wandered round the show to see what I could come up with.

Jamaica, rather like England, is divided into counties and each had a stall at this annual show, all displaying their local agricultural produce. I went to check our county's stand - the St James's stall. It was beautifully laid out, with oranges, mangos, breadfruit, sugar cane, sweet corn and masses of vegetables. I found the main man in charge and explained my dilemma. I begged for a ride back to Montego Bay; as usual I had little money with me so I could not even offer to pay my way. He agreed to take me in the rear of the lorry - along with the remaining fruit and vegetables. Harry told me to return at 6 o'clock - which I did. I was still in my jodhpurs and arrived with my saddle and bridle over my arm.

The vehicle was a typical battered Jamaican truck with an open back and a plank tied across for any passengers. Three quarters of it was packed with the produce with my saddle on top. The rest was filled with young men, a few of them sitting on the plank. I was lucky enough to be offered a seat here; obviously I was the only white girl on board. So began my adventure home with the smell of oranges and youths in my nostrils. It was quite intoxicating, if a little frightening. I had my jacket on so I hugged myself to keep warm. It was now dark and we seemed to be driving at top speed through the lanes. I was aware that they had made a protective shield around me to keep me warm and safe; we continued like this until our first stop.

What I did not realise was that we would stop in many of the villages along the way for a drink. I did have some money on me so I was able to buy a round. This was a popular move and from that moment on there was much laughter and chatting. They were wonderful to me and could not believe that a white girl would choose to go home this way. For me it seemed practical. I could not have afforded to take a taxi which was the other alternative. After the stop I was invited into the cab of the lorry as friends had been dropped off at that village. It had become cold in the rear so I was pleased to be invited into the warmth with the driver and his mates.

It soon dawned on me that they would be dropping off the various farmers and their produce all the way back to Montego Bay and this was their usual way of celebrating after the annual show. Almost the last stop was in Newcastle. I remember it now as one of the highlights of my entire stay in Jamaica. We piled into the bar where neat rum was served to the men, I had mine with Coke and a slice of lime. Sitting at the end of a large table was a fine Jamaican with a joint of jerked pork in front of him, a huge knife and fork already carving the meat which he began serving to us. It was a delicious spicy marinated roast often made with a secret family recipe. We crowded round him with our drinks and he passed slices of carved pork to us, individually, on the fork. We were ravenous and ate our fill until the whole joint had gone. There was much laughter and endless stories especially of how I happened to be with them. I think somehow they were expecting us but I did not realise it at the time. It just seemed fantastic to arrive at a place and eat and drink without having to pay for it. I later discovered that the owner of the bar was Harry's brother.

By now it was really late and I was a bit worried about my dogs: they had been on their own all day. We were relaxed, happy, and rather the worse for wear. But I had gone beyond worrying about drink-driving and had put my life in God's hands. Eventually, the familiar site of Montego Bay was before us. I directed Harry to my home and asked him to drop me at the top of the drive. It was narrow for the lorry, I could walk to the Cotch. He would not let me, and insisted on coming with me and carried my saddle all the way to the door. I thanked him and gave him a hug. It had been a heart-warming experience, which I never forgot. I did not see him again but think of him as a guardian angel who popped up in my life just when you need them most.

I had a hard time explaining that the car had been impounded in Kingston. They thought I should have realised the tax was out of date and I thought the office should have known. It was eventually sorted out and one of the workers from Kingston brought it back to Montego Bay but I was without transport for a while which was always a blow. They were a little frosty about it and felt I was irresponsible to have allowed it to happen which was true. I worked hard for them in the coming months hoping to make up for it.

It was always exciting when friends from London came to stay with me. The best time was meeting up with Chris Blackwell, who owned Island Records, and his lovely wife Marilyn who had modelled for me in some of my fashion shows. We went to a party at the Pringles home, a stunning estate near Runaway Bay. They would come to Jamaica for the season and always entertained lavishly. While we were there, Chris and Marilyn invited me to spend Christmas with them at their house in Nassau called Sea Pussy. Although it meant I would have to get someone to stay at The Cotch to look after the animals, I accepted gladly.

I flew out to Nassau for Christmas taking a couple of weeks off work. I remember it was difficult to buy presents for them as they were the kind of people who have everything. I gave them a painting which is always a good solution when you are an artist. Chris met me at the airport and drove me the short distance to his home right on the seafront. He had a recording studio there and spent some time on the island recording various artists such as Bob Marley and Jimmy Cliff. He had created Island Records in Jamaica and had success with hits such as 'My Boy Lollipop' with Millie and also many recordings of Bob Marley and The Wailers. Just before I came out to Jamaica I had gone to the premier of 'The Harder They Come' with Chris Blackwell with which he was much involved. It was a great film and gave me a good idea of what to expect in Jamaica.

They were generous hosts. A dozen of us had a marvellous time, though I can never get used to celebrating the festivities in hot climes, going water-skiing on Christmas Day and eating turkey in the sunshine. We played a lot of games almost all of which were for money. We watched racing videos without the soundtrack and bet on the horses. I did not have the resources for these kinds of activities but many made a bit while others lost out. It was enjoyable but I did notice that Chris and Marilyn were not getting on well. His jokes seemed laboured and there was no spontaneity in their relationship any more. I think she had tired of the constant entertaining and travelling. It was not long before they would be divorced. I was devastated for them as it is always so painful. Although I fancied him like mad I was not involved though I would go out with him later on in London.

I returned to Jamaica to get on with my life. For me the New Year is a time to make plans for the future and my thoughts went to the possible commercial scheme I had hoped for in Jamaica. I continued to make enquiries but it became increasingly apparent that running a business there was much more difficult than getting started in the UK. It was almost impossible to borrow money from the bank and there seemed to be corruption almost everywhere you looked - or shall we say there were a lot of backhanders. Kasimir had gone off the boil; he did not like the fact that I had such a wide group of friends so my thoughts of starting a Montego Bay boutique went out the window.

The political situation at this time was also quite volatile. The country was steeped in dishonesty and violence. Michael Manley was in power and he created a kind of prison called 'Gun Court' where people could be arrested for carrying a firearm or even having ammunition. This got many gang members off the streets especially in Kingston, but it also meant many suspects were imprisoned unfairly. Eventually this would have a drastic effect on tourism and generally create an unsettling atmosphere in the country. It was strange to feel these changes and many white people began to feel afraid and were thinking of leaving.

So my Island Paradise slowly became quite a scary place to be living in. You heard of friends of friends being murdered and having their homes ransacked and burgled. I felt safe in The Cotch with my two dogs; apart from anything else I did not have a great deal worth pinching. People advised me not to go on long journeys alone, to be careful after dark and to lock my doors. I did all of that but it did not change my life too much. I still drove to Negril beach usually with a mate or two and we would have wonderful weekends at the Rock House, which was owned by Gilly Byles, as I always got a good deal. It was a series of small chalets built on the rocks at the end of the peninsula. One time Paul McCartney was there with a friend before he married Linda.

Although there were many places of worship in Jamaica, I did not go to church often when I lived there, apart for carols at Christmas. I developed my own kind of spirituality through meditation and my relationship with nature. I still had a strong belief in God and considered myself a Christian but central to my belief was reincarnation, which I slowly realised was not the way most Christians felt. From my own research, I discovered that all reference to this had been edited out of the Bible when it was translated from the Greek and again in the King James Version. I had known about reincarnation from an early age and am one of a number of people who can remember previous lifetimes. The knowledge of reincarnation was important to me and later in my life I found a group of friends who believed the same as I did about what happens after death.

Jamaica was a perfect place to develop spiritually in this way. I could commune with nature, spending a great deal of my time alone. I was working from home mainly and I would ride out regularly with my horse. I took the dogs for long walks daily, usually along the beach which was just a ten minute drive away. The countryside was spectacular in its beauty and diversity. The colours were amazing yet I missed the four changing seasons of the UK. Here it was summer all the time though there was a rainy season where it could be really wet or even blow a hurricane. Every day there would be a little miracle like the wild dog I saw with nine puppies.

Kjack would appear regularly for his work but I began to realise that he had other business as well. With a group of his friends they were doing what was called a 'Ganja Run' or two, where they would arrange for a pick up of this potent drug and fly it to the States. Often the small planes they used would land on roads; as they were building a number of spanking new ones they were ideal landing strips. It was dangerous work but many seemed happy to suffer the consequences. Sadly, his great friend Bo got caught doing exactly this and landed up in a notorious prison in Kingston.

Bo had come to stay with us at The Cotch and I knew something was up as we talked over dinner. He stayed the night, and the next day set off on his consignment. Within a week we found out that he had been arrested and incarcerated in jail. I do not remember there being a trial. It was all devastating and we wondered how Bo would manage in prison. He was a tall, good-looking basketball player from the Midwest and had plans to be a sports commentator. He spent his time in prison teaching other inmates how to play the game as they had a basketball hoop there. The one thing he wanted was soap, he showered three times a day, so I sent him some.

Life continued and riding my beautiful horse became a central part of my existence. Most weekends I would set out to a nearby sawmill to collect wood shavings for his bed, often taking my groom with me and a couple of the children who used to hang out at the stables. On the way home one day, with the car full of shavings and children, I was involved in a terrible crash. They had been building a new road and I came out of the old road straight into a bus. No stop signs had been put in place. I tried to steer out of it's path but we basically had a head-on collision. I felt out for Sam, my groom, and said, 'Are you OK?' there was a grunt in reply. He died on the way to hospital. It was the worst moment of my life when I found this out.

I did not know a great deal about what happened next. Apparently a taxi driver pulled me out through the window and took Sam, myself and the children to Montego Bay hospital. Luckily, it was close and even better a medic I knew was on duty. It was my friend Dr Fraser who told me Sam had died. He arranged to have me admitted to the women's ward. The little girl was fine; but Billy, with a broken leg, went to the childrens' ward. First of all, he had to set my broken ankle, arm and nose. I was in a terrible mess. I soon realised though how fortunate I was to be alive.

It was strange coming round in that hospital as I could see it from my cottage. It was quite newly built just beyond the grounds of my estate. There were some terrible groans and loud noises in the ward and a strong smell of disinfectant. A whirl of fans tried to keep the place cool in the extreme heat. All I could do was lie there and feel terribly responsible for Sam's death. I cried a lot. My first visitors were his family. Most Jamaicans are superstitious, but usually Christian. The first thing they said to me was it was not my fault: the Ouija Man had come for him. They told me how the grooms at the yard had been cursed due to a groom being unfairly sacked. All subsequent Delisser grooms were vulnerable. I did not know what to make of it but they prayed and chanted around my bed for ages. And after they had gone I felt better and was able to gather my composure before friends arrived. There were not many nurses on duty and I remember whenever visitors came they had to help me on to a bedpan and with washing. I was relieved when I eventually learned to walk on crutches which was a long time coming as I had broken the opposite arm and ankle.

It was terrible to be responsible for a person's death and I dwelt uncomfortably on it whilst I was in hospital and long afterwards for that matter. It did make me aware of how it could so easily have been me and I kept asking myself 'Why not me ?' The answer that came back loud and clear was that it was not my time to go. I wondered why it should be Sam's time, especially as he was the eldest son in his family. Each year on October 14th the date, it happened, I think of him and hope he and his next of kin have forgiven me. I thought the stop sign for the new road was not adequately marked and was actually in the wrong position. So, not surprisingly at the time, I did not take full responsibility.

The wonderful Kjack came to my rescue. He had heard about the crash and arranged to work in Jamaica that month so he could get me out of hospital and look after me. He literally carried me most of the way to The Cotch, which, was on the outskirts of the hospital. He was tender and attentive and took great care of me. It is always interesting how men want to make love to you when you are feeling vulnerable and not exactly attractive. So strangely it was rather a sexy time and slowly but surely we fell in love with each other. It was a tender episode in our relationship.

He stayed for a month and helped me get used to a wheelchair and crutches. We also discussed our future together. It was another month until I felt anything like normal. During that time I made a few radical decisions. The car was a complete write-off. Kjack and I had gone to see it. And it was a bit much to expect a replacement from the Clarages. I gave in my notice and worked the final few weeks from my studio. He had invited me to Washington DC, his home town, for Christmas but, interestingly, we did not stay with his parents but with friends of his: Chuck and Sheila Wagner. It was an exciting prospect for me to be going to the States especially as I was beginning to feel I might well end up living there with him.

The idea was to see if our being together worked. If it did I would come and live with him in the States. It was by no means a foregone conclusion; there were a few differences between us. I was an artist after all, and he did have a dreadful temper which I discovered on that first trip. Whatever happened I decided I wanted to see my family first, especially my brother's and sister's children; some had been born in my absence. The whole family obviously had been very worried about me. So I went back to Jamaica and in the next few months sorted out my affairs, got rid of stuff and packed my things. I sold the horse to a friend who wanted to jump him, Kasimir had my dogs, and Felix the girl who took over The Cotch had my cats. Sadly she was burgled the first month she was there. The dogs had been a real safety factor for me.

I thought it would be a fun idea to return to the UK on a banana boat. It would be relatively inexpensive and I could take a huge trunk with me. I booked my place to arrive in April 1975. I bought a large black-and-white box and over the next couple of months started packing it rather well. The first thing to go in was a couple of pounds of beautifully cleaned ganja. I then put it in a tea urn with some tea on top. I then packed everything else around it. You could not go home without a little of this natural weed. The sticks and twigs from it make a stimulating tea to start the day - which is exactly what I did with them!

I had a hilarious leaving party. I prepared a feast of suckling pig and curried goat, the former cooked the true jerked-pork way and served with rice and peas and various salads. It was truly delicious and was accompanied with the usual rum punch or beer. It was a long drawn out affair with people arriving all day to say their good-byes. My time in Jamaica had been amazing and I had made many extraordinary friends, some of whom I would stay in touch with for the rest of my life. For me, it was always very emotional saying goodbye, so I had a heavy heart as I packed my final things.

It had been an especially sad ending with the loss of Sam but it was time to go home. By now I had decided I did not want to start my own business there which had been the original intention. Jamaica had changed as a place even in the short time I had been a resident. It was more corrupt and really quite dangerous, not a suitable place to embark on a commercial venture. I also thought that there just might be some repercussions from my car crash. The police were notoriously slow at following anything up and I had not heard from them. Best to leave before they start any investigation; though, to be honest, I did not really expect one. I felt I had learned a few of life's harsh lessons in my time there. It was another reason to be going home. Also I had been smoking quite a bit of ganja and I did not want that to become habitual. It creeps up on you and suddenly represents a pleasant way to live but it was not for me. I certainly had not been smoking on the day of the crash, I hasten to add. Audrey had come to my farewell party and stayed the night. Early the next day, with some excitement we set off for Port Antonio to catch my banana boat home.

CHAPTER TWELVE
SEVENTIES - RETURN TO LONDON
The way we were

The banana boat was Norwegian registered and did regular trips to and from Jamaica, carrying about a dozen passengers. It was a popular form of transport and you had to book it well in advance. I had a small cabin where I had a suitcase for my immediate needs, the trunk being in the hold. Some of the crew and the rest of us ate together; it was generally a huge spread of many different kinds of pickled herring laid out in true Scandinavian smorgasbord fashion. It was delicious and quite a change from Jamaican food. The only complaint was that it was pretty much the same every day. I soon got to know the captain who told me that on the previous trip somebody had been caught carrying ganja! My heart missed a beat or two, but all I could do was cross my fingers and hope for the best.

It took a good two weeks to get back to England, starting with beautiful weather and clear blue skies. When you live in the sun you do not exactly sunbathe all the time but now was an opportunity to top up my tan and get a good colour. There was a small pool on board so I spent most of my first week there reading, lounging and doing a few aquarobics as it was not really big enough to swim in. On all voyages you meet the most unexpected people and get to know them well as there is plenty of time for conversation. The other passengers were interesting: I was fascinated why they had chosen to return on a banana boat; my reason had been financial as it was the cheapest way to travel.

One of the best things about the trip was meeting a blues singer called George. He was Jamaican and played a very cool guitar every night for us all, unfortunately for me he was married. He kept us entertained with his music and sense of humour for the entire trip. He was travelling to London to do a gig and was coming by this means to get in the mood. As I had discovered it was definitely the most interesting way to return home. It really gave you time to adjust to the change in the weather and you were never sure what to expect. Leaving the Azores to starboard when we were more than halfway it changed dramatically. It became really cold, so much so that you could not even go out on deck. As we approached Folkestone it got colder and colder and by the time we arrived it was freezing. My parents were there to meet me. It was lovely to see them and to be whisked off to their comfortable, warm Sussex home. We had much to catch up on; in particular they wanted to know all about Kjack who had been so kind to me after the crash but who was now probably going to carry me off to the States. I had not made too much of it as final plans had not yet been made. I assured them that they would meet him before and if I decided to go.

I stayed for a week with my parents and then went to London to stay with my sister Trisha, her husband John, and their two boys Ben and Billy. Great to see them and give them a rundown on life in Jamaica. I had to go and retrieve my trunk from the disembarkation point in Kent, so we borrowed a van from a friend and off we went to collect it. Once again I felt my heart in mouth, wondering what might happen. We were ushered in and shown the trunk plonked on the far side of a vast custom's warehouse. We were told to just go and pick it up as it had been cleared by customs. Thank God for that I thought. With help we loaded it into the van and set off gleefully back to London where my sister had arranged a glorious homecoming party. We had a wonderful night with good old friends, all pleased to see that I was still alive and that I was happy to be sharing a little Jamaican magic with them.

Now I needed to find a flat and start making some money. The Pavitts had returned from Jamaica at the same time and were living in Barons Court. They offered me their basement flat on a temporary basis while I got myself together. It was a convenient place to be, near to the station and easy to get into town. They were kind and fun to be with for a short time. I remember having yet another party for family and friends who were all pleased to see I was well after my car crash. Once again I had to make a new start and decided that as I knew the rag trade best I should stick with it. I decided to design a modest range of clothes and accessories to sell to smaller boutiques, so I started on another summer collection. The first thing I needed was a sewing machine, so I bought the best I could afford and made up samples including a few bikinis. I still had a good selection of cloth available: it was something I had collected over the years. I also made some enquiries through friends about flats and discovered that an old associate from the sixties had a spare room in his flat in Iverna Court - a most convenient location as it was near Kensington High Street.

David Sheffield, the owner, and I agreed terms amicably. I had one of the bedrooms and use of the rest of the premises. I moved in and set myself up in his front room with my machine, clearing everything away at night when he returned from work. David had been the manager of Sibylla's discotheque, where I had had my first fashion show in 1966. It was interesting that I should end up sharing a flat with him; he had been such a part of my life when we had the shows at Sibylla's. He was just starting a new life working with 'futures' in the city and later he became a millionaire.

I gathered together the samples I had made - including at least two bikinis - packed them in a suitcase and started to do the rounds. I aimed for South Kensington and the Kings Road. One of the first places I visited was a shop called 'Brother Sun', whose clothes and accessories were made in their own fantastic provencal cotton. They liked what they saw and placed an immediate order, which meant I was in business! It was for sixty bikinis and a dozen sundresses to go with them. I felt I could make these up myself and set off home to get started. They supplied all the cloth so I did not have many expenses apart from cottons and paper for the patterns. For the first time I cut and graded my own garments.

In the past at the Chelsea boutique and in Jamaica, I had had pattern makers and sample makers to do that hard work. Now what I was making was quite simple and did not require great expertise, such as a jacket would. So within a couple of months of returning home I had started out on a new track which I did not want to become too successful as there was every possibility that I was going to the States in a few months.

I quickly made up the first order and delivered it safely to 'Brother Sun'. To my surprise and joy within a week they called and asked for a hundred more bikinis. Again, I decided to make them up myself because as soon as outworkers are involved there is an additional expense and the price would have had to have gone up. I managed to get them finished but my hands and fingers were in tatters by the end as there was a lot of hand finishing. By this time I was getting really tired of the work; it was a lonely and rather repetitive task as I was working from home. One evening when I was having a glass of wine in a bar with a friend I asked the owner Andrew Henderson if he needed any assistance and luckily he needed help behind the bar and with some cooking, so he offered me a job.

I worked at 'Ruskies' wine bar about four nights a week for the next few months. It was called 'Ruskies' because it was opposite the Russian Embassy in the Bayswater Road. It was convenient for me, being just a short bus journey from my Iverna Court flat. It got me out and created a social life for me and I made some new friends. I learned two important things at this job: the first was a knowledge of wine as Andrew was an expert, and the second was how to indulge in a mean game of backgammon. If there were no customers Andrew and I would have a game. Once the bar was set up and ready to go there would often be an hour before anybody came in. We played often and became seriously good at it. The contest might last a whole night as we served customers in between moves.

Soon after I started he was invited on a trip to Spain to visit the Torres Vineyard near Barcelona and he asked me to join him. Andrew had been approached by Miguel Torres to be his agent. The Torres label was not well known in London though we did sell it in the wine bar. Charming Miguel met us from the airport and we stayed with him in his beautiful home. He wined and dined us in some of the most amazing restaurants all over Catalonia where we enjoyed many memorable feasts. The thing that impressed me most were the vineyards. Row upon row of immaculate vines, all meticulously kept.

At the end of our visit he took us out to a splendid restaurant in Barcelona with a flamenco cabaret. It was during this meal that he told Andrew he would like him to be his UK agent. I was pleased for him and thought that I had helped bring a positive outcome from our visit. Andrew had told Miguel that I was his assistant and in many respects I was, though I must admit that I did not remain working there for long. We flew back to England happy with the result which would remain in place for some years. He went back to his wife in Surrey and I went back to Iverna Court. He was a married man and I was absolutely not going to get involved because Kjack was arriving soon to take me on holiday to Ireland. Kjack had called me from the States many times since my return and we planned to visit the Emerald Isle together because his family was of Irish extraction. He wanted to tour the country and have a look at his father's heritage. So we rented a car and booked it on to the ferry in preparation for a nostalgic trip. I met him from the airport and we drove straight down to my parents. It was important for them to meet him and hopefully to like him as there was a strong chance he would become my second husband and part of the family. We stayed for the weekend and then set off for Holyhead and Ireland.

It was fun to be with him again: we had much to catch up on as we had not seen each other for a few months. Somehow we always managed to have a good laugh. He found my turn of phrase amusing, mainly because of my accent and my rather quirky sense of humour. I found him practical and organised as well as being a caring man. He had been really superb when I was ill in Jamaica and after my car crash. The truth was, though, we were different characters. I was an artist and he was a businessman with high ambitions for the future of his company, Paramount Coin - regretfully, not something I was drawn to. It soon became apparent that he would be based in Dayton, Ohio and not travelling as much as he had been.

We arrived safely in Dublin and drove straight to Wicklow. We had not made any bookings, the idea being to drive and see where we ended up, although we did have a vague plan as to where we would like to go. There did not seem to be any relatives to visit, I was glad to hear. If there were, he certainly did not want to do that. He basically wanted to get a feel for the place, and the interesting thing was that we both thought it had some similarity to Jamaica. This was because it was so green and beautiful and on the whole the people were warm and friendly even though in theory we were in the middle of the 'Troubles'. Next we drove to Wexford and Waterford with me doing the navigating and Kjack doing most of the driving. It is always a tricky situation to be responsible for the route-finding as it can cause all kinds of problems but I made sure I did a good job as my life would not have been worth living if I had screwed up. It was a special time of getting to know each other better, and I think for both of us trying to decide if we did want to live together. Luckily for me, with Kjack the sex was always good with his 'Chevy Chase Specials'. He was quite uninhibited which surprised me a little as he had been brought up Catholic in Washington DC.

So from a passionate night in Waterford we drove towards Cork. On the way I remember stopping at a pub for a beer and a sandwich. There were a crowd of what appeared to be farmers at the bar; probably they were working with pigs because they smelt terrible. Quickly finishing our drinks we tumbled out, with Kjack practically gagging. 'Gee Susie, did you smell that - how can people go out stinking like they haven't showered in a year?' He was disgusted, being a chap who often washed twice a day - so human cleanliness was near to his heart. I never forgot this reaction.

We drove on through Cork, taking a right to visit Blarney Castle as I wanted to kiss the Blarney Stone for luck and for 'the gift of the gab'. We arrived in the late afternoon and climbed up to the roof of Blarney Castle from where there was a wonderful view. I suffer from vertigo and cannot stand up too well in this situation so I wanted to get it over with quite quickly. We had to queue awhile and then two strong chaps hold onto you as you bend backwards to kiss the stone, then you make a wish. I was in love with Kjack and decided I wanted to go to the States to be with him so I wished for a successful outcome to the visit. Thanks to the kiss - in a few months I was packing my bags for America.

We had a joint in the grounds of the castle, before setting off for Killarney where we spent the night. The next day, after a delicious breakfast, we headed for Limerick where there was a family connection, though we did not exactly go looking for it but we stayed overnight there. The following day we drove straight to Dublin where we spent our last night before catching the boat to Wales. We had been together for the best part of a week and most of the time it had been really good so we started to plan my next move.

He had various schemes in place for some work-related travel so we decided that probably the best time for me to arrive would be November 1975. I asked him if I could bring a dog. Thankfully he agreed and I began to look for a dog. I decided to go to Cruft's which took place in Earls Court. Once there I had a wonderful day walking around talking to participants and their animals. The best temperament seemed to be the English Pointer. They were friendly and calm in comparison to many of the other breeds. I had a marvellous conversation with one of the breeders, who just happened to have a litter of liver-coloured puppies for sale. I told her I wanted a bitch and she had three in the litter. She said, "Would you like to come to my home in Surrey and choose one?" When the show was over I went and chose Zelda, who remained with me for the next twelve years.

I continued to work at 'Ruskies' for Andrew and to make up orders for 'Brother Sun'. The two jobs went well together and paid my bills, but it meant I would not have much capital when I arrived in the US. This did not worry me as I knew Kjack had a good income and as soon as we got married I would be able to get a green card and start work myself. It did not exactly occur like that but this was what I imagined was on the agenda. I began packing and decided to send some things ahead by boat, which included my precious sewing machine which I'd converted for American electricity.

It is interesting how things happen in your life because the next catastrophic event almost prevented me from going to the States. I went to a party at my sister's and met up with my first boyfriend Jack Bond. He was now a successful director and had some great films and television programmes to his name, including the classic movie Salvador Dali in New York. We had seen each other before but this time it was different: we had so much to talk about as I was preparing to go to America. He came back to my place and without hesitation we made love. It was very special because although we had spent all of our young years courting, we had never actually done the deed. Almost immediately I realised I was pregnant, as I soon started to feel different.

What timing! All of my life I had been longing to have a baby. It had been particularly difficult for me to conceive as I had only one Fallopian tube, a result of my ectopic pregnancy. It was a terrible time for me to consider a family. I could not go to America with another man's child inside me so I decided to have a termination. It was relatively easy to organise. Through my private doctor I arranged to go into Chelsea Women's Hospital for the operation. Almost from the moment of conception I had been feeling ill with morning sickness but as soon as it was done, I felt my normal self again.

The saddest thing of all was that I did not grieve for the baby. I thought there would be time later for having a family. My grief came much later when I realised I would not be able to have any children. I imagined that I would be able to have a child later in life but it slowly dawned on me as I aged that I had passed my time to conceive. That dreadful deed of mine is the greatest regret of my entire life, made worse by the fact that I found out they were twins. I have tried to make up for it with my work with children as an art therapist but it is definitely not the same as having your own.

Within weeks of the abortion I was leaving for the States and had to make our travel arrangements. This involved booking the flight for myself and the dog, getting a substantial kennel made, and having Zelda vaccinated for rabies and anything else appropriate. With all the necessary paperwork done I decided to collect the dog from the breeder with only a few days to go before leaving. David was not very pleased to have a puppy in the flat as she was not entirely house-trained. I did my best with newspaper but it was hard to train her as we were a few flights up from the garden. The best thing was to leave her overnight in the kitchen.

Having had a farewell drinks party at 'Ruskies', Andrew drove me to the airport the following day. I seemed to have little with me for such a big step. I had one case, my hand baggage, and the kennel with the puppy in it. She was still small but not too young to know something traumatic was happening. I gave her some tranquillizers from the vet this time. I checked her in, then passed her on to the airport staff. The journey was long but straight-forward. Thankfully there were no dramas en route as there had been to Jamaica. I went through to the baggage collection and there she was just sitting up in her kennel with a bemused look. I collected her and my bag and as I approached the arrivals barrier' I saw Kjack waiting to collect us. So started the next exciting phase of my life.

CHAPTER THIRTEEN
LIFE IN DAYTON OHIO WITH KJACK

Hotel California

My first impression of Washington was how vast everything was. The buildings, the cars, even the people seemed to be bigger than in London. By now Zelda was out of her kennel and sitting on my knee as we sped in Kjack's car through the city to stay with his friends once again, before we set off for Dayton Ohio. We spent a few days with them doing some sight-seeing. He took me to meet his family. As Catholics, I am sure they did not approve of the fact that I had come all this way from England to live with their son. We certainly wanted to be sure of each other before tying the knot. I did not feel he was particularly close to them; they were kind and welcoming but not very warm, unlike my own loving family.

Staying with Chuck and Sheila was always fun. She had two daughters from her first marriage so it was a happy household. I can remember wrapping up Christmas presents which Chuck had bought for them and I could not believe how many there were. He had also selected beautiful paper and dried flowers with loads of ribbon and tinsel so the place was like an Aladdin's cave. I had a field day preparing them as exotically as I could for their first Christmas together. Later on they would get married and have two more children of their own.

After some days in Washington we set off north and west for Dayton. Zelda was excited to be on the move, having disgraced herself a few times. It had been a bit of a problem because she was still young and not exactly house-trained so I was quite relieved when we finally set off for Ohio in the car. Chuck gave me a big hug goodbye and I will never forget the way he said 'Good luck' as if I was really going to need it. He was quite right; unbeknown to me Kjack had a terrible temper!

He was living in The Meadows of Catalpa, a housing development of condominiums made especially for young people going places. It had a club house and tennis courts and in theory was rather exclusive; everybody seemed thrilled to be living there. It was well taken care of with manicured lawns and safely organised paths to walk the dog. There were a number of other pets there so I soon got to know people on my strolls around the place. For everyday exercise it was fine to just wander around the estate. For a good walk I would have to take the car.

The house was a typical bachelor's pad without many feminine touches so I soon set about changing a few things, buying colourful cushions and some material for new curtains, hopefully without offending him. The one thing he did not like doing was spending money on the place because in his opinion he had smartened it up already for my arrival. Thankfully the things I had sent in advance had arrived, the important one being my sewing machine. Thus I was able to set to work making the new additions. It did not take long to make the house feel as if I belonged there too.

To my horror though there did not seem to be much in the kitchen in the way of utensils and saucepans. One weekend, we had a blast in one of the shopping malls and found some cooking equipment, enabling me to prepare a few delicious meals. The one thing he did have was an enormous fridge: full of beer, in preparation for football nights when all his mates would come to watch the game. Not exactly my favourite evening, the room full of young men drinking nonstop and shouting at the television. Since we met, Kjack had called me Susie, so suddenly with all these new friends I became very aware of my new name. Our life together soon developed into a routine of my driving Kjack to work, at the ungodly hour of 8.00 am and then driving home for a leisurely breakfast. Luckily, I had the dog to fill my time so we would go for walks and do the shopping. Once, coming home from the local farm store I was stopped by the police and they asked me what I was doing. They were amazed to hear I had walked to do my shopping. 'Be careful,' they said. On the whole people drove everywhere and it was unusual to see somebody walking on the highway with a dog. I continued to do it though because it was pleasant exercise for Zelda and an opportunity to buy some excellent locally grown produce.

In a strange way I felt more 'married' to Kjack than I had when I was with my husband Nicky. We had one car - so I drove him to work and collected him. During the day I would do household chores like shopping, dry cleaning and repairs: not to mention the garden. Quite early on in this idyllic spell Bo came to live with us. He had completed his time in prison in Kingston, Jamaica and needed a bolt hole while he got his life together. There were long discussions into the night about his adventures inside. He was a tall beautiful man and soon had the inmates' respect. He taught them basketball which he was rather good at; in return they gave him ganja.

He stayed only for a few months. It was great to travel into town accompanied by these two all American guys. We would go out to eat, to the pictures and to shop, it all being a bit of a novelty for Bo as he had been locked up for three years. He was looking for work, for somewhere to live, and for a girlfriend. It would not be long before he had all three, though the job was not exactly what he wanted. He had always hoped to be a sports presenter and contacted television stations with no luck, eventually ending up selling insurance.

The frustrating thing for me was not working because I was unable to without a green card. Getting married would have been the solution but neither of us was in a hurry. Since selling my London shop I had wanted to open another. Jamaica had not worked out for various reasons so now I wanted to open a boutique in Dayton. Looking into it was a good exercise for me as it was badly needed, all the shops were so American, not stylish. It would be good to introduce a European look selling clothes from London, Paris and Milan and I knew which suppliers to approach. The name I chose for the shop was 'Cream of the Crop' which I thought had a nice ring to it.

I soon realised I was on a very sticky wicket. I started looking at properties which I thought were in the right place to open, but they were hugely expensive. I approached banks and because I had no collateral and was not married to Kjack, they were not interested. I was too much of a risk for the kind of money needed. In the Sixties I had started with £10,000 with help from friends and the Midland Bank. In Dayton in the Seventies, I needed to raise five times that amount. Kjack was not enthusiastic about investing his hard-earned cash in a project that would eat up his money. In the end I realised it was just a dream - but I did at least check it out before abandoning it.

Compensation for the disappointment from this excursion was a new second-hand car. I did have some say in it and persuaded him to buy a beautiful BMW Bavaria. It was the most powerful car I had ever driven and what a pleasure it was to drive. He was generous with his motors in as much there was never any problem with my driving whatever one we had. I spent many exciting hours powering it up and down the highways. By this time I had decided if I was not going to work, I needed another horse to occupy my days and therefore started to look for one. I found a bay gelding in the local paper, needing a good home, for a reasonable amount of money. He was stabled in Yellow Springs near Antioch. He was called Caesar and his previous owner had had to give him up because she had been offered a job in California. He came with all his equipment, saddle, bridle and various blankets and brushes. He was a big horse, rather skittish, and was nervous of anything such as a police siren or a bird. It made for some exciting rides when we would be going along nicely, all of a sudden he would be spooked, then turn and dash in the other direction. Because he was a bit of a risk in open country, I started to train him to do dressage which was fun but limiting.

I would drive out to Yellow Springs about four times a week during my first summer in the States. I met various people while exercising my horse there, the most interesting being Richard Basch and his wife Meredith. He was managing director of a theatre called the Otrabanda Company which was based in the amphitheatre in Antioch College. The actors were from a group of young people who studied there. They were working on a play, New Burlington, about the life and death of an American village adapted for the stage by Ken Jenkins from the book by John Baskin.

They were full of enthusiasm for the project and could not stop talking about it. They somehow had found out about my background in design and to my delight invited me to do the costumes. I accepted their offer and after much discussion and reading the script, I set to work on my machine. There were only a dozen in the cast so it did not take too long to make up the outfits. I made endless dungarees and colourful skirts with blouses and scarves to go with them. There was a limited budget so I was paid a token payment. It was great fun to be involved in the production which I had found on my own initiative. Kjack came to the opening, he enjoyed it but I think he found the whole thing rather bizarre. 'My God, Susie, what was that about?' he asked.

He was an interesting man with many contradictions in his personality. He was kind and caring when you were not well and had obviously been brought up properly by his parents. But he did not understand women at all, partly, I think, because he had grown up in a household without a sister. In the past he had enjoyed the company of men sharing manly interests such as drinking and sport, especially football. None of this was really my scene, so it was a relief for me to find some artistic friends even though they were in Yellow Springs. Kjack had a terrible temper, so I always had to do my best not to set him off about something because he could be violent when provoked.

In times of trouble I do tend to look to the church for a little help so I decided to start attending one which described itself as a 'Free Church'. The service was similar to the Anglican liturgy with hymns and a sermon and some good intercessions. On my first visit, I remember being embarrassed because I put only coins into the collection plate for all to see. I always made sure I had a ten dollar bill after that. The assembly had an excellent choir and on finding out that I could sing they invited me to join. The building was very modern and had recently been constructed. The choir were tiered up facing the congregation which for me was unusual. Above all it was well attended and I enjoyed my time there. Kjack, as a Catholic, did not cross the threshold.

Despite these difficulties we settled into a reasonably comfortable family life. My frustration continued to be that officially I could not work without the famous green card. It was important to keep busy and my next idea was to help out in the office of the Meadows of Catalpa, where we were living. After some discussion they asked me to be the Public Relations Officer to promote various events that were arranged in-house and to come up with some ideas for the future myself. It required that I write a monthly newsletter which was interesting. Because of my work restrictions - they did not exactly pay me but I was given a budget for the newsletter and each monthly occasion.

It was a good arrangement and continued for some time. I enjoyed it, it kept me busy and made me feel part of the community. In the end I knew more people living at the Meadows than Kjack. I also dreamed up some exciting ideas such as a fashion show, a pizza night and a tennis tournament. The latter was probably my most successful event. I managed to invite the Gullickson twins to play in the tournament and one of them won it. All of these events were publicised in the local press and required making and designing posters and producing tickets. This was all comparatively easy for me to accomplish because I had done quite a lot in the publicity department for my own business.

Each year I was in the States, Kjack agreed to go to England for a holiday. I was homesick for the family and missing out on my brother's and sister's children growing up. The first time we went was for Christmas - always a special time for my family - I remember we stayed in London for a few days: he had arranged some business meetings there, so we stayed in a hotel at the company's expense, leaving us time to do our shopping. For the rest of the visit, we stayed with my parents, who were now living at the seaside in Aldwick near Chichester. We had a good few days with them and it was lovely to be able to give rather extravagant presents. I remember getting my sister's boys a game called 'Battleships' (which they loved) from Hamleys.

We flew back to Dayton, having left the dog in kennels. I did not like to do this but it was the only way. The horse I had offered to a friend while I was away. She eventually bought him from me, as it became increasingly difficult to get out to Yellow Springs to exercise him. It was not too easy to ride out into the countryside as you can do so freely in the UK. Now I decided to concentrate on promoting events at the Meadows and to start preparation on what would be my first book which I had called 'The Vital Balance'.

It was about combining a healthy organic diet with exercise and meditation. Along with recipes and basic movement for maintaining an energetic lifestyle and at the same time achieving spiritual well-being. I set to work researching the healing qualities of various herbs, fruits and vegetables along with the importance of a balanced diet. I was rather naive at the start and had no idea that I had entered an absolute minefield of information and contradictions. I planned it to be in three parts, starting with an introduction and then the food section. Followed by one on exercise and another on meditation.

When I got my job as the public relations officer at the Meadows of Catalpa, we had invested in a typewriter. I taught myself to type when I compiled the Meadows' newsletter and so when I began to write my first book, it was another opportunity to practise my keyboard skills. Each day I would bash out a few hundred words and, if Kjack was in the right mood, I would ask him to proof read it. On the whole it went quite well but there were many occasions when he would laugh out loud at my spelling or something I had said. I tried not to let it affect me, or put me off my stride - but somehow it always did. The whole experience was a learning curve for me, firstly writing the book and secondly researching and getting the correct information - trying to create something informative yet a good read. In those days it all had to be done by personally researching everything available on the subject. In retrospect probably the bit I enjoyed the most was testing all the recipes because they all had to be original and tried out before publishing.

Unbeknown to me at the time, this would become my main project during my stay in the States. It would be ongoing throughout my days there and took up an enormous amount of hours. Towards the end of my stay, I approached various companies as to the possibility of publishing it. But they mostly came back: 'You are not qualified to write such a book' which indeed I was not, but I got together an enormous amount of information which is still useful to me to this day.

Although it was understood that we would get married - strangely it was never discussed. I eventually went off the boil about it as he probably did too. There would be rows about silly things, usually money. Kjack did indeed have a terrible temper. The worst thing for me was that because of the pressure of his job, the good sex we had always enjoyed went out the window. He was always too tired after work and it eventually came down to once a week at weekends which just did not suit me. All the romance and spontaneity went out of the relationship and it became rather routine.

At least he went off happily every day so I could write, and there was plenty of time to cool down if we had had a row. I found myself looking forward to our vacations when we would get back to the way we were. And there were many wonderful trips during our time together which usually involved an enormous amount of driving. An early memorable trip was to Canada for the Montreal Olympics in 1976 where we went to all the equestrian events; another the following year was a tour through the northern states of America. He was on the whole quite generous when we travelled always in some style, but he could be tight sometimes.

Probably the best fun we had was when we decided to go back to Jamaica in 1978. It was still pretty chaotic there with the tourist trade badly affected by violence and Gun Court. We wanted to visit Rock House in Negril to celebrate St Patrick's Day with his mates. It was owned by Gilly Byles, an old friend of both of ours from days at The Blue Hole Polo Club. We were able to book it with a phone call from the States. We reserved four of the chalets with the use of the main dining area as well. Many of Kjack's friends were Irish and had been celebrating St Patrick's Day together for a long time. We were four couples including Chuck, Sheila and Bo with his girlfriend CJ. I knew I had to be prepared for some serious drinking with this group, not to mention the dope which would be available.

Each couple had their own chalet situated on the rocks at the far end of the long, beautiful Negril Beach. This was before it was developed so there were no huge hotels as there are now. During our week each couple would take turns to produce a meal and, of course, we would also go out to eat as well. One day, walking on the beach, we were offered some magic mushrooms. We bought a whole basketful for just a few dollars. They are similar looking to other edible fungi but rather bluish and famous in Negril for their hallucinogenic qualities.

We rushed back to Rock House to prepare them and decided on a big fry-up consisting of bacon, eggs, sausages and mushrooms with baked beans. This was washed down with a tea we had made from brewing the stalks and smaller mushrooms together. We had boiled it for about half an hour and let it steep awhile. We then started to celebrated St Patrick's day with this rather delicious brunch and the very powerful drink. This was still the morning and the beginning of our festivities, in the evening one of the other couples was producing an Irish stew. A few of us were completely out of it for most of the day. I remember Bo standing for hours naked preparing to jump about twenty feet into the sea from the rocks. We all eventually made it into the water below and I had the most sensational naked swim I have ever had. I hasten to add that Rock House was a very private place with nobody else able to witness our antics unless they were in a boat.

That evening some old friends joined us for dinner. They were not quite sure what was going on but after a few drinks all was well and we had a cracking time catching up on some of the more outrageous stories of life in Jamaica and telling Irish jokes. It was certainly one of those days and nights to remember, from which we spent most of the following one recovering. Just as well, because we were leaving soon so for me there was the packing and cleaning up to do in our beautiful chalet. The final thing which I wanted to do was to visit Toggles, my bearded collie, whom I had left behind and we had planned to see on our way to the airport.

We piled into the two cars and set off from Negril for Montego Bay Airport. I had explained to Kjack that I really wanted to see Toggles. It was slightly out of our way, up into the bush near Round Hill. We were running a little late so he said I could not go. I started getting upset and insisted I had to go to see him as it had been planned. A row followed and I began crying; he was furious and my tears made it even worse: the whole thing escalated into a huge drama. Eventually Bo, who was with us in the car with his girlfriend said, 'For Christ's sake, Kjack, let her see the damn dog!' We did get to see Toggles and I spent a few minutes with him which was great, but I had made a fool of myself over it in front of Kjack's friends and I knew he would never let me forget it.

It is interesting how you remember what you were wearing when you blot your copybook. I was in jeans and an apple-green tee-shirt with blue and white stripes at the neck and on the sleeves. It was messed up after rolling around with the dog in the grass so I had changed it at the airport. I was pretty subdued all the way home and I could feel that Kjack was not pleased with me. I had brought out his terrible temper and had managed to embarrass everybody. Although his friends were quite aware of what Kjack could be like, as this was not the first time they had witnessed it. All was rather quiet as we drove back to Dayton and I was thinking 'Do I really need this; should I be thinking of marriage with this man?' The answer came back, 'Probably not' but 'What to do about it?' was the burning question. We soon returned to the daily routine of my driving him to the office, writing during the day, walking the dog and then collecting him. The next event on the horizon was Thanksgiving, so I suggested to Kjack that I do it in our home as we had had a considerable amount of hospitality from friends during my time there. I enjoyed cooking for a party and decided to really go for it. It had to be turkey and all the trimmings with a pumpkin pie. I ordered a free-range bird from a farm and set to work.

Whilst I was in Dayton I had visited a number of antique markets, mostly at weekends, and had made a collection of long-stem glasses.

I decided to use these for the occasion. Some were old but none were particularly valuable. The table looked great the centrepiece being a pumpkin with various fruit and flowers. I served the turkey cold with a potato salad, a Waldorf salad, a green salad, and one with beetroot and corn. When they arrived, I gave them their drinks in my special, rather unusual glasses. Looking at the table they remarked 'Gee Susie, did you prepare all this from scratch?'

Almost from the moment they came in I realized I had done it wrong. Later I found out that most Thanksgiving dinners were hot meals, like our Christmas lunch. Kjack had not told me this and just thought my idea of having a cold meal would be fine. In the end - of course - it did work because everything, especially the turkey and stuffing, was delicious. The next test was the pumpkin pie. Needless to say, it was the first time I had made one. I followed a recipe but did not use enough spice; there should have been a lot more cinnamon and allspice to make it really spicy. The party was memorable for these reasons and because a couple of my precious glasses were broken. No wonder they tended not to entertain at home but preferred to take you out to a restaurant instead; in future we would do the same.

For Christmas 1978, we were invited by his family to the Chevy Chase district of Washington DC. This was a privilege for us to be able to stay under the same roof but still at the time - not being married to each other. I believe it was not really discussed with his parents because we both had doubts about it and they would never interfere. Kjack was earning good money, and for the first time in my life I was dependent on a man. Deep down he did not like that at all although, of course, this situation would change if we married. He also had quite a lot of investments which I did not really know about and he preferred to keep it that way.

We had an enjoyable, if rather formal time and it is always interesting for me to see how other people celebrate Christmas. There were drinks and nibbles first then the giving of presents and then quite late in the afternoon the meal. I was impressed with the serving of just a turkey breast but it did mean there were no wings or legs to nibble on, which I usually enjoy. Also there was dish of cooked sweet potato with browned marshmallow on top which I had never had before. Absolutely delicious. But no roast potatoes and no plum pudding or mince pies. So I did feel there was something missing; they were warm and generous to me: especially his father, We returned to Dayton with my having warmed slightly to his family, more so than I had felt on previous visits.

There then proceeded to be a very cold winter with temperatures well below 20 degrees. It was almost impossible to walk the dog. Many of the roads were blocked though some were cleared, enabling Kjack to go to work a relatively short drive away. I did not venture out much except to exercise the dog having wrapped her first in two of my sweaters. Somewhere amongst my things I have a certificate saying I survived the blizzard of 1979. The cold weather made it a good time to get down to some serious writing which I did. The following spring it was decided I would go to the UK alone to see my family for my annual visit.

We both needed a break from each other after a difficult winter with me being stuck in the house writing, and Kjack working hard. It was at about this point he was promoted to vice president of his company. He was thrilled as I was for him but my thought was, 'Do I really want to stay in Dayton, Ohio?' Doubts about this latest piece of information made me pleased to be going home to spend time with my friends. I stayed for a month and moved between them and my parents who were now getting on in age. It was during this period I decided I did not want to marry him or remain in the States. I decided to try to persuade Kjack to come to Europe. He was a talented and able man who would do an excellent job anywhere in the world.

It was good to see him again but by now I had already decided that I wanted to return to the UK for Christmas. We discussed the possibility of his leaving Ohio and coming to the UK but he had an excellent job in Dayton and for the moment was determined he was not going anywhere. We went out to dinner and over deep-fried potato skins I told him I missed my family, and that I wanted to go home later in the year. The only sign of emotion was that his eyelids flickered repeatedly, before he eventually replied, 'Why don't you go back sooner, at the end of the summer?' If he had begged me to stay and marry him, I probably would have, but he was much too proud a man for that.

I continued to develop my book, trying to get it to a state that I was reasonably happy with. I had also done some black-and-white drawings for it, hoping they would make a good impression. I had tried a few publishers in the States without success but none in the UK. So I set my sights on that market for when I returned. Our last few months together were reasonably happy without any rows. Life continued in the same routine. I tidied up all my loose ends there and started packing again, sending some things by boat ahead of me as I had done when I came out.

Our final week together was sad. I think we both regretted it had not worked out. At last we were having some good sex again but it was too late now to change what had been set in motion. I don't think men realise how important the sexual side of a relationship is, especially when you are young, because as soon as that has diminished everything seems to fall apart. Well, that is how it was for me this time around. By now my forties were approaching fast and it would take a few more years before the sexual side of a partnership was not so important. In that particular period it was.

It was with a heavy heart that I boarded the plane for Heathrow. Kjack took me to the airport with Zelda in her cage. I had made special arrangements for her to be collected from the terminal for her quarantine in nearby Langley. I think I detected a tear in his eye when we finally said our goodbyes. I certainly had a good weep in the departure lounge as I waited for my plane. I realised that matters of the heart need to be worked on constantly. Neither of us had made the effort required to make a success of it. Importantly, we meant a lot to each other and had spent some exciting years together.

My parents met me at the airport; the next phase of my life began.

Top left:
Grandpop and Gran

Right:
Sue's Parents Wedding Day
26 November 1938

Below:
Baby Sue and Daddy

Top:
Sue and Trisha in the 40s

Left:
Sue ready to go to boarding school; with Mummy, Trisha and Honey

Right:
Daddy in riding gear with Sue's brother Simon

Below Left:
Brother John

Below Right:
Brother Simon

Top Left:
Sue's First Love - Jack Bond

Top Right:
Shaun Noble

Below:
Sue and Richard Nevil on Gozo

Right:
Sue - Chelsea Art School

Below:
Mark and Sue in the Kings Road

Top Left:
Captain
Gianandrea Fazio

Top Right:
Trisha in Malta
in the Early 1960s

Below:
Sue with
Jon Bradshaw
in Rome

Nicky Head

Top Left:
Sue and Nicky Get Married
9 July 1966

Top Right:
Sue and Nicky leave
Carlton Towers Hotel

Below:
Best Man John Bell
and the Bridesmaids

Jeremy Brett

Top Right:
Mary, Gale and Sue in the
Boutique wearing
'Sue Locke' designs

Below Left and Right:
Fooling around
at the Boutique

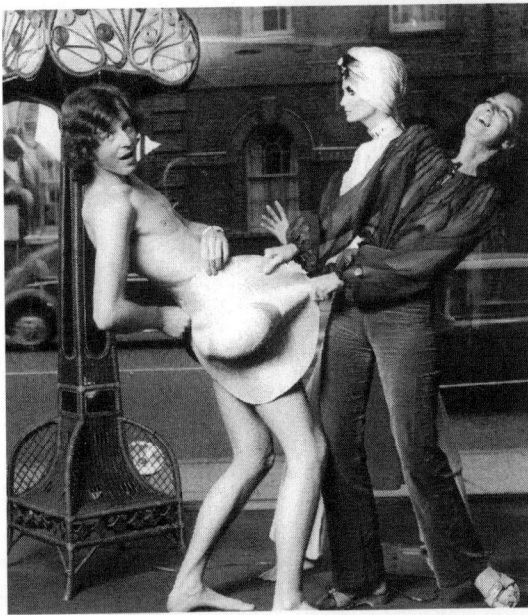

Top Left & Right:
Photo shoot with Patrick Lichfield

Below Left:
Sue with Michael Fish

Below Right:
Sue in Lebanon

Top:
Trisha with Ben, Billy, Tonia and Christian

Right:
Daddy and Sue, Mummy holding Paphos, and Toggles

Left to Right: Honey, Teal, Mark, Sophie with Jack, Toggles, Flora and Teal, and Badger the Cat

Top Left:
Kjack

Top Right:
Sue and Kjack
in Jamaica

Middle & Right:
'Coffee & Spice'
Delicatessen
in Barnes

Top Left:
Alihan Zangiv

Top Right:
Sue, Margaret and Glen in the Urals - Russia

Left:
Mummy and Daddy in Breinton

Below Right:
Simon, Trisha, Sue and John at 'Shieldbrook'

Top Left:
Sue in Majorca

Top Right:
John Warren and Isobel

Below Left:
Zoltan

Below Right:
Sue's godchildren - Anna Rose and Blathnet

Top Left:
Trisha, Sue and Mummy at the Wedding at Breinton - 26 September 1998

Top:
'Shieldbrook' Kings Caple

Below:
Sue and Oliver at 'Shieldbrook'

Top Left:
Traian, Gabriel and Mychaela

Top Right:
Sue and Lindsey in France

Right:
Harry

Below:
'Biography' group meeting in Sue's studio

Clockwise from Top Left:
Harry Franklin, Jenny Pickford,
Peter King, David England

CHAPTER FOURTEEN
STARTING OVER AGAIN IN LONDON

Suzanne

It was good to get out of the airport and to be on the way back to Aldwick in Sussex where my parents had lived for the past ten years. The dog had been safely collected and taken to the kennels in Langley where she would be in quarantine for the next six months. I had said that I would visit her when I had a car and would let them know when I was coming. I had heard that it is a beneficial idea to do this as often as possible, thus keeping the bond between you in excellent shape. My plan was to stay with my family for a couple of weeks and then find employment along with a flat in London and of course the necessary transport.

My father took The Daily Telegraph and with the help of the 'Situations Vacant' page I immediately started looking for a job with a car. I replied to a few and the one I was thrilled to get an interview with was S.T.A.G.S. This was the sales and marketing department of Scottish and Grampian Television. I had applied for the advertised position of marketing executive which came with a vehicle and a salary of £4,000. I thought this would suit me fine while I was finding my way back into London life and it would enable me to visit my dog, as planned, in Langley just beyond Heathrow airport.

Within a few weeks of my return from the States I found myself boarding a train at Bognor station for an interview in London with

Jonathan Stone, a director of the company. It was my first meeting of this type for a long time and things had changed over the years. For a start, he was a pompous ass and quite a bit younger than me and, to my surprise, he was actually flirting with me. My thought was 'Heavens, does he want me to sleep with him?' I was not somebody who flirts with the manager to get the job. It certainly might have helped if I had wanted to move up in the company but that was not the plan.

To my relief, I had chatted my way into being offered the position. I felt I was qualified to be a marketing executive for them as I had done mine and Ruth Claridge's promotion. Basically, I was selling airtime for Scottish and Grampian Television and for that matter some advertising on radio. They operated in the name of S.T.A.G.S. I had come back from the States in September: by November I had a job and soon found a nicely furnished flat.

I had stayed with my sister initially when I arrived in London but it did not take me long to find an apartment, which was advertised in the Evening Standard. I had called the number in the paper and went to see it immediately. It was in Netherton Grove, a cul-de-sac off the Fulham Road, and was the top floor of a three-storey house which had been the nurses' home for St Stephens Hospital opposite. The best thing about it was that the landlord agreed to my having the dog (Zelda was still in quarantine). By the time we left a few years later though, he was happy to see the back of us. As the landlord complained, Zelda made an awful noise dashing up and down the stairs; sadly this was true.

The office was in Davies Street and it was with some trepidation that I arrived for my first day. I certainly felt like the new girl but I was also one of the eldest and could not believe how young everybody was there. The weeks always started with a meeting around a huge table in the boardroom. Apart from my fellow marketing executives I met company co-workers there. I then was asked to come into Jonathon's office to be given the sections which would be my responsibility. They were recruitment, transport and, thankfully, fashion. At the same time he gave me the keys to a Ford Maxi which was my transport for a while, thus fulfilling my important ambition of getting a car to visit Zelda.

There were four other executives on the marketing floor. We each had our own desk and stacks of directories containing the names and addresses of all the companies we were meant to contact. You spent your day calling all those appropriate to your specific categories and made appointments to see the advertising director, the purpose being to try to sell them airtime in the Scottish and Grampian area. The chap sitting next to me was a young graduate from Lancashire called Andrew and he was the one who showed me the ropes. The others were very snooty and left me to my own devices.

Strangely enough, my first success in more ways than one was with recruitment. As my father and brother were in the Navy I had some knowledge of procedures so my first appointment resulted in a sale from the Royal Navy. It was wonderful to go to the board meeting the following week and tell them how I had clinched the deal. I was familiar with naval expressions and knew where the ships were, and that young men were needed in Scotland for recruitment - I had found this out from my brother.

My next success was with the Metropolitan Police. When I contacted the recruitment officer Inspector Ralph Wilkinson he said that week he would be at Olympia for the International Horse Show. He suggested I meet him there in the mobile recruitment unit which they had set up there. I was delighted to do so as it meant I could see some of the events. I arrived early and watched several performances - the amusing one being a kind of obstacle race between the show jumpers and the police. It involved the debagging of the law-team and the winner wore yellow boxer shorts! Little did I realise that this was the very man I was meeting for my interview later.

I arrived at the Police Mobile Unit in time for my appointment, knocked on the door, and was asked to come in. There was the chap in the yellow boxer shorts, still not dressed properly in his uniform. It was an awkward moment but we both laughed and he said he would not be a minute. In no time I was discussing possible recruitment for the Metropolitan Police force in Scotland over a cup of coffee. All went well and for the first time in my life I found myself being attracted to a policeman.

Ralph was a charming and delightful man with a James Bond twinkle in his blue eyes. He agreed to the Met advertising in Scotland but said I would have to come to his office at Paddington Green station to do the paperwork as he did not have it with him there so we made another appointment for the following week. He then politely offered to walk me to my car which was parked behind Olympia. He took my arm as we crossed the road and I felt an electric buzz go through my entire body. The next thing I knew we were beside my car and he was looking straight into my eyes and kissing me on the mouth, in uniform. Wow! This was a first!

I seemed to fly to Chelsea in the car and could not believe that this had happened to me with a policeman. I knew then that we would probably have an affair but where would it end? He called me at home and invited me to stay on after my forthcoming meeting with him. There was going to be a Christmas party and an awards ceremony. I accepted and arrived dressed up accordingly. We did the paperwork and then he took me in to meet his colleges. It was strangely like a naval cocktail affair with drinks and nibbles taking place at the police station, a high security station for terrorists. I actually had a delightful evening being chatted up by various policemen. It did seem unreal to me and I had to pinch myself. Was this really happening?

It turned out that he was leaving the department of recruitment and moving to other duties. He had been in the job for five years and was receiving an award for his work. He was in especially good spirits and everybody was congratulating him and wishing him well for the future. While all this was going on I was taken to one side and asked if I would be interested in training as a police officer. In other words join the Met! They seemed to think I would make an excellent policewomen! I declined and said I had just started a new job that I was enjoying, which was true. It was one of the most bizarre evenings but it did give me a good laugh.

After the party we had planned to go out for dinner but I said I had some food at home. Therefore Ralph followed me back to Netherton Grove as we both had separate cars. We kissed on the doorstep and then flew up the stairs to the top floor where, without much hesitation, we started taking our clothes off. He was still in uniform but I did notice how carefully he put it down, laying the belt on the top. The whole uniform bit was quite a turn-on which rather surprised me. He was a wonderful lover and we spent a beautiful night getting to know each other.

The next morning we had a leisurely breakfast in bed. It was not far from the kitchen to the bedroom. Being the weekend, there was time for some good conversation. I told him about my time in the States and that I was still recovering from the breakdown of that relationship. He was suffering from the aftermath of a divorce; his ex-wife and their children were in Cornwall. We were both in need of some tender loving care so that is what we decided to give each other in the following few months.

One important thing he taught me was just how dangerous drugs could be. He had spent a lot of his working life dealing with the consequences of their abuse. He had especially coped with dealers and the prostitutes who were invariably in their hold. I had used drugs socially, and thought I was in control, not taking them as a prop or an excuse for living. I had seen what it could do to some of my friends though, one of whom had spent time inside in Jamaica. It was an enormous eye-opener for me and from then on I was more careful.

We continued to see each other on a regular basis; it was just what we both needed. He was not too demanding and I think I could honestly say we were in lust with each other as opposed to being in love. It was too early for either of us to have had a serious relationship. Eventually in the following spring he was posted to Northern Ireland for special duties. It was at the time of the Troubles so I was rather terrified for him; but he kept in touch regularly though it was never the same after he started to work there. Before he left for Ireland we had a special farewell dinner and he gave me a Metropolitan Police Medal celebrating one hundred years of the force: 1879-1979. It is still in my jewellery box.

Six months after my return from the States I went to collect Zelda from the kennels in Langley. I had visited her regularly at weekends. I would go and sit with her in her kennel as we were not allowed to walk the dogs. At one point I was so cold there with her that I demanded some extra heating. They fitted a large special light bulb which supplied some heat for her during the winter. On the day I collected her I had decided to take her to Richmond Park. She was the same as ever and had a wonderful time running around in the bracken and enjoying her new-found freedom.

Life continued at S.T.A.G.S. and I soon realised that one of my favourite categories was Fashion. I knew about it and there was more money available for advertising so they were usually open to my call and would make appointments for me to come and see them, which was half the battle. I discovered that Boots had some fashion and children's clothes available in their larger stores. I decided that they would be a possible client and found out that the company to approach was Barbara Attenborough PR Ltd who handled all their publicity. They were literally round the corner from my office and I could walk there for the appointment.

I arrived there in good time with the schedules and prices. Their advertising company and the directors of Barbara Attenborough were there along with the appropriate PR executive. This was probably one of my most high-powered meetings which lasted a long time, and I remember having some delicious Danish open sandwiches for lunch half-way through. I was as efficient as I possibly could be because I realized they could be an excellent client. By the end of the session I had secured airtime for my company and surprisingly had made an impression on Barbara Attenborough because a few months later they would head-hunt me to join them. I agreed to do so on condition that they would keep up the leasing of my company car, which by then had been upgraded to a brand new Ford Capri. To my delight I started working for them in the autumn of 1980.

In the meantime Kjack had kept in touch and we would speak on the phone regularly. He was delighted that I had found a job and that I was enjoying it. Also that Zelda was now out of quarantine and settled into her London life. As I had some holiday due to me we decided to motor through Europe down to Portugal in the Maxi, which I was still driving. I had found a place called Casa Grande in Burgau on the Algarve. It was a privately owned villa/hotel which was advertised in the paper and sounded perfect. He duly arrived at Heathrow and I went to meet him. We drove back to my place for a reunion and then later in the day went down to my parents, taking Zelda with us. She was going to stay with them whilst we set off for Portugal from Dover the following morning. I had pre-booked the Calais ferry, with a long journey ahead of us through France and Spain.

Luckily, he did most of the motoring as he was used to driving on the right side of the road. I remember we had a terrible time getting through Paris but eventually got on the correct route. As in Ireland, we did not have any reserved accommodation: we just drove and stayed somewhere when we were tired. It is always wonderful to arrive in a small auberge in France, find a comfortable room and know that you will have the most superb dinner. I ordered fresh river trout and was amazed to get two. It was fun to be travelling with Kjack again; he was a good laugh and amusing company on the road. The hotel was showing Les Vacances de Monsieur Hulot on the television; this we watched. It was one of my favourite films; then we fell into bed exhausted from a long hard day's travelling.

We crossed the Spanish border and headed for Madrid. Before going into the city proper we turned towards the Portuguese border and Badajaz. We were then on the road to Lisbon where we had decided to spend one night. Our stay at Casa Grande was starting on the Monday so we had the weekend for exploring. We just had the evening and the morning to have a brief look at the capital. It certainly had a feeling of grandeur about it though you sensed it had seen better days. This was the early eighties so I am sure much has been done in restoration since our visit.

Mid-morning we set off south through acres of cork trees towards the Algarve and, finally, Burgau. Casa Grande was easy to find as it was the only grand house in the village, set back from the sea but actually on the main road. It was owned by Sally Vincent who had started off years before with a beach-bar at Burgau. Along with her husband they had had a great success with it and when Casa Grande came on the market some time later, they were able to buy it with the proceeds. After a couple of years of building work they had transformed the private house into a small hotel but by the time it was ready for paying quests the husband had left. The plans for a swimming pool went on hold and Sally put her expertise into the restaurant. Her cuisine was really delicious: every night we had something different and almost did not want to go anywhere else to eat. The best night was a Portuguese evening with Fada music and songs. The food was wonderful starting with a fish soup followed by her speciality - rabbit stew.

They were a memorable few days, in particular star-gazing for falling stars, which are in abundance at that time of year. One day Sally directed us to a beach where we could swim and sunbathe in the nude. We took a delicious picnic, supplied by her, along with a bottle of wine. There we enjoyed our day, swimming and making love in a cove in absolute privacy without anybody seemingly for miles. This was in August 1980 and we had been separated for nearly a year. It was good to be together again. We had regrets and thought maybe we still loved each other. Should we get together again? But the truth was I did not want to go back to the States and he did not want to give up his excellent job to come and live with me in Europe.

Having discussed all this at some length over our last romantic night together, the following day we set off for Calais via Seville and Valencia. It was a great drive through acres of vineyards and oranges groves. All went well until we managed to hit a pothole at speed, ending up with a puncture and a twisted wheel. As we had stopped just outside Valencia we decided to stay there for the night and made arrangements for the wheel to be mended. It would be too dangerous to drive all that way to the UK without a good spare wheel. Finally, we headed for France and the Pyrenees in the late morning and stayed somewhere in the mountains en route for our last night together before aiming for the channel port.

It was such a relief to arrive at the queue waiting to get onto the ferry. In due course we boarded and had a pleasant time on deck before arriving at Dover. We then set off for Aldwick along the south coast which is always further than you think. We were both exhausted and happy to get there; I had done the last bit of the driving. Zelda was pleased to see us as were my parents. We stayed with them and then drove back to London. After a night together in my flat I took Kjack to the airport to catch his plane to the States. I returned thoughtfully to Chelsea. It had been a good time with not many rows, and I sincerely hoped we would remain friends and occasionally go on exotic holidays in the future.

I soon got into the rhythm of things at work and found I was going further and further afield for my meetings. Often they would take up the best part of a day with my driving to Somerset or to Norfolk. The Maxi was fine but a bit slow and uneconomic with the petrol so I applied for another car which seemed to be the normal thing to do. To my surprise I got it and was actually asked to choose which one I would like and what was my favoured colour. I fancied a gold Capri; it was approved and turned out to be an early Christmas present from the company.

The one rather disconcerting thing about working there was that I was made to feel very aware of my age. I was forty but I liked to think I did not look it. Almost everybody was younger than me. The advertising world seemed to be a young person's game. Often in the dreaded meetings I was made to feel uncomfortable and, of course, I had not responded to Jonathan's flirtation or anybody else's for that matter. Although I had not been there for much more than a year - I was beginning to have itchy feet. It was around this time that Barbara Attenborough made an approach about my coming to join their team of PR consultants, working for Boots.

I was delighted to accept and Jonathan was not that opposed to my leaving; he knew I was replaceable and he might have more luck with the next executive. As mentioned, I had just received a new company car so I was keen to take it with me. Consequently Barbara Attenborough agreed to the leasing arrangement from the company. So in the late autumn of 1980 I cleared my desk at S.T.A.G.S and almost walked across the road to my new position as a public relations consultant.

I was looking forward to working for Barbara Attenborough. There was such a good atmosphere in the office - with six executives all handling a different aspect of Boots' business. Once a month, the men in suits from Nottingham would come down for a meeting to discuss the latest advertising campaign with us. We worked closely with them. My category was fashion and I was delighted to try to get to grips with this as it was one area which needed attention. As the summer season was approaching, my aim was to get a new swimwear collection in place.

I approached Zandra Rhodes to design some beachwear for Boots. She was a friend from my boutique days and we had done shows together. Eventually the day came when I would present the collection to the men in suits from Nottingham. Zandra and I had had a number of meetings; she was more than capable of designing something fun and had come up with some good ideas. I emphasised that as I was representing Boots, the designs should not be too outrageous. They were certainly colourful and eye-catching - exactly the kind of thing I would enjoy wearing on the beach.

The great day arrived. There had been a business discussion first followed by the Danish open sandwiches. After this Zandra arrived to make her presentation. I will never forget the look on the faces of the three sales directors as she walked in the door. Always dressed rather outrageously, she wore a short skirt and matching boots, but the icing on the cake was the pink hair with a black fringe all the way round the bottom with orange ping-pong-ball earrings! I thought she looked great but I don't think they had seen anything like it before. She made her presentation of matching swimwear, beach wraps, bag and hats in various designs and colours, which I thought were marvellous and, in fact, just what Boots needed.

However, the designs were not taken up. The same rather boring swimwear, beach towels and hats appeared that summer as usual. It took them a long time to jazz up the swimwear department. They did a good job on the children's wear but this was after my time. They did an excellent line in hats and scarves with matching gloves, good value and easy to place in a newspaper or magazine. These items were part of my responsibility, and putting them in with an appropriate paragraph and photograph was relatively easy to do. I spent my working day pursuing these kinds of opportunities.

It was an exciting office to be working in; there was constant activity with fashion editors, photographers and journalists coming in. Our aim was to ask clients for a lunchtime meeting, they were popular amongst us and were usually preferred. Also things could be negotiated or a shoot arranged easily over an informal lunch rather than a lengthy formal one in the client's office.

My job with S.T.A.G.S. had been sound preparation for work with Barbara Attenborough, the main difference being that we were all working for one company, all aiming to achieve publicity in the press for Boots. We had some good initiatives building up to the festive season followed by a great office party to celebrate our achievements. They had some great items especially gifts and toiletries. Our big line was that you could get everything you needed in Boots, except the food!

That Christmas I decided to visit my old friends Paul and Susie Orssich. He had been the photographer in my boutique in the sixties and married Susie who had modelled for him. They had bought a large rambling farmhouse in Minorca and spent the last couple of years doing it up beautifully. Paul had also developed the land for growing soft fruit. He thoroughly researched the business possibilities first before planting his fruit. Now everything was ready to accept visitors and I was thrilled to be invited.

Minorca is a beautiful island to visit for a holiday and a number of my friends had chosen to live there and had bought homes. Paul moved to the island in the late sixties when the Labour government started to demand enormous tax rates. He originally bought a converted farmhouse in San Luis where I had been a number of times in previous summers. This would be the first time that I visited him in the winter. The weather was usually warm in comparison to our winters but there could be terrible winds and even the occasional hurricane.

I arrived to a howling wind and was practically blown off the airline steps. Paul was there to meet me with his Mini Moke and dog walking to heel. The house was not far from the airport so we were soon there, to be greeted by Susie and a welcome glass of wine with tapas. These nibbles always miraculously appeared whenever you had some wine. Paul, now specialising as a soft fruit farmer, supplied all the local hotels and restaurants with the most delicious raspberries and strawberries. The season lasted much longer there. He proceeded to show me his well-attended fields and the results of his hard work which he had completed on the property. Susie with the help of their young son Alexis, had done most of the decorating of the inside of the house; it was warm and welcoming and full of character.

We had a typical Minorcan supper of cold cuts with various cheeses washed down with plenty of local wine. The next day the girls intended to shop for the final Christmas preparations. Paul decided to climb the hill behind their property and set off with Alexis to find a suitable tree for the festivities. Hours later they came back with a good specimen. We spent the rest of the day decorating the house with the selected larch and other evergreens. The turkey was duly stuffed and the Christmas pudding which I had brought, soaked in brandy. We were all ready for a splendid festival but the weather was really blowing up a storm.

It howled all night and poured with rain. The commotion was beginning to develop into a force-8 gale. Hurricane Charlie had arrived on the island with a vengeance. We were determined not to let it spoil our celebrations so we carried on preparing things with the wind blowing around our ears. The big question was would the electricity stay on or would there be a power cut. We went out to check the property and see that everything was secured. All was fine basically because we were in a valley and somewhat protected; other areas in the north of the island would later be devastated.

We had our Christmas in the traditional way despite the inclement weather. We started with champagne and tapas followed by presents and luckily for me everybody was well pleased with them. I had brought Paul a diving watch which he seemed thrilled with, as he was keen on diving and wind surfing. We all helped to get the turkey on the table along with some tasty seasonal vegetables. The pudding came in alight and smelling fantastic. I had to admit to not making it. I had bought it in Harrods Food Hall where they were excellent. We played a Barbara Streisand and Barry Gibb record constantly, along with the usual carols.

The following day the radio news was pretty bad about the hurricane. Property had been damaged and the sea front in Binni Becker decimated. Being nosey-parkers, we decided to drive to the area and went for a walk to observe the outcome for ourselves. There were great slabs of the seafront and the road pushed onto the beach, and the beautiful palm trees were uprooted and strewn across our path. Roofs had been taken off some of the houses and doors were hanging on their hinges. It was a terrible sight to behold, like a war zone, and amazing what devastation had been caused literally overnight. There seemed to be thousands of pounds worth of damage done in a single night.

We returned with heavy hearts and were glad that our part of the island had been spared. The weather improved for my last few days of the holiday and I was able to visit friends. In particular I wanted to see Annette who at one point I had planned on going into business with in her boutique, Gemini, situated in Mahon the capital. I had decided against it because Nicky, my ex, chose to moor his boat Sea Victory in the magnificent harbour and I thought it would be too close for comfort. Nettie had also memorably visited me in Jamaica, staying with me and then moving in with Kasimir for a few days. She was also good friends with Paul and Susie so there was much for us to catch up on with my having been in the States.

All too soon it was time to go home. I think I managed one cold swim and a meal in my favourite restaurant in Fornels. Paul drove me to the airport for my flight and as soon as I was home, went to collect the dog from my parents. I stayed to celebrate New Year with them. I was soon back in London and returning to work in the normal way. Almost the first person I saw was Daisy, a girl of about ten who happened to live next door. She loved my dog and always wanted to hold her lead. I asked her in for a soft drink and said it would be a good idea if I could meet her mother.

We arranged for them both to come to supper one day after work. I made a quiche and salad because I was mainly vegetarian. Marika worked as a background artist for Dick Williams who had a very fine animation studio in Soho. Here started a long but rather fraught friendship which lasted for more than twenty years. She told me how she was in the process of buying her basement flat which at that time was owned by the council. She had also started a relationship with one of the young animators at the company and it was all rather exciting as to what would happen.

In the following months she bought the flat at a good price. This was during Thatcher's premiership and we were being encouraged to buy our own places. Also her relationship with Clive had developed and he came to live in the flat. Life continued happily for a while with my driving to Barbara Attenborough to work until one day I was called into the office and told that I was going to be made redundant. Apparently, as I was the last to be employed I would have to be the first to go. It was incredibly quick with my being told on a Thursday and having to leave on the Friday. It shocked everybody but especially me, that Barbara Attenborough

PR were having their budget cut by Boots. The thing that I wanted and asked for was the car - and they agreed that I could keep it.

Never one to be unemployed for long, I made a few phone calls and decided to become a freelance cook. In those days it was relatively easy to join a cooking agency and do directors' lunches and prepare food for other events such as dinner parties and special occasions. I called 'Blues' to make an appointment for an interview; all I had to do was convince them I could cook and be responsible with the clients' money. I thought I could do all of that and soon I was on the books and preparing directors' lunches.

Every Monday you called the office and got your bookings for the week. I seemed to be flying all over London arranging meals for film companies, advertising agencies and banks. My favourite company to cook for was Scottish Widows in the City. I especially liked working there because you did your purchasing at Leadenhall Market, the most fabulous place in the world to shop. The other reason I liked it was because you could not help but overhear the conversation the directors had over lunch about investments they were making. I decided they would be an excellent company in which to invest what little money I had and one day, after getting their lunch for them, I took out an endowment plan.

A memorable event I catered for at this time celebrated the marriage of HRH Prince Charles and Lady Diana Spencer. The party was in a house on Kensington High Street just opposite Hyde Park. There was going to be music and fireworks in the park and everybody was invited. The guests had champagne and nibbles in the house before going over for the festivities. There were more than fifty people to do canapés for and I spent the whole day making them. Everybody was so excited: it was a very happy occasion. They finished the food quickly then rushed across to observe the spectacle. I cleared up everything as soon as I possibly could and went to join them and the heaving throngs there. I shall never forget the thousands milling about the Serpentine and the wonderful fireworks which followed. It was a special day with everybody in high spirits for the happy couple and, thankfully, to my knowledge nobody was hurt.

The next celebration was for the actual wedding itself on July 29 1981. There were street parties everywhere with flags and bunting decorating the streets. Most people watched it on television and had a get together afterwards. I went to my sister's and, with our various friends and family, we had a tremendous celebration all day long. The dress had somehow been kept secret and it was truly magnificent; she looked so young and vulnerable, just beautiful. The nation really had taken her into their hearts. The early Thatcher years were difficult so it was just what we needed.

At about this time I rekindled a friendship with an early boyfriend. His name was Bim Davies and we had met at the schools 'seven-a-side' when we were teenagers. Later I would meet him for lunch when we were both in advertising. I discovered he was living just around the corner with his second wife Marianne who was an interior designer. I went round to their place for dinner and saw for myself what kind of things she was doing which included making and decorating a delightful patio at the back of their home. That evening she asked me to design some cushions for her, which had to be custom-made to match the sofa and the curtains of her client. I agreed, they were patchwork made of sample lengths and looked great.

By now, Bim was employed by the International Coffee Organisation as the marketing director. It sounded a fascinating company to work for. Their whole purpose was to promote coffee and everything connected with it. They are, I think, largely responsible for the culture in this country now for drinking the beverage. In the early eighties tea was by far the more popular drink. He was earning a fantastic salary and, more importantly, had a good pension plan or provident fund as it was called. I jokingly said, 'If they need a cook, let me know'. Sure enough, a few months later he contacted me and said would I like to come for an interview for the job. The bizarre thing for me was that he conducted it along with another colleague.

The post advertised had been for a home economist and involved testing and creating recipes using coffee. A new purpose-built London Coffee Information Centre had been created with the most amazing up-to-date equipment. It had a demonstration studio/kitchen where we showed a promotional film about coffee production and then demonstrate how to make coffee-marinated mushrooms or a coffee-and-walnut cake. I felt qualified for the job and was delighted to accept their offer. As well as the cooking - which I loved - there was another side to my job where I had to put on exhibitions which were primarily for promoting coffee sales.

I started in the spring of 1982 with a salary of £16,000 the most money I had ever earned. The best thing was as a professional, I was entitled to the famous provident fund where the company paid two-thirds into a pension fund and the employee paid the remaining third. This turned out to be a real bonus. As well as all this I had a space in the car park and was able to drive to work. The Coffee Centre was in Berners Street which was near to where Marika and Clive were working at Dick Williams. Most mornings they would come with me in my gold Capri and I would drop them in Soho.

It was exciting starting what was to be a new project for London. Everybody in the organisation had their own ideas as to which was the best way to go forward and then everything had to be passed by Mr Beltrolle, the president of the organisation. The first and most important thing for me was to get staff to man the place. They would demonstrate how to make the best coffee and would entertain the press and clients who were visiting. My immediate boss was Bim - though now I had to call him Barry as that was his proper name. We would share a secretary Linda, with him obviously taking precedence.

After initial teething problems of getting things to run smoothly we soon developed a routine which worked. We had two receptionists meeting and greeting people and a coffee expert, Mary Banks, who became very knowledgeable about it. The organisation would get a sack of the best beans from all the producing countries in the world, of which there are dozens. We would select and roast the coffee for the day and surprisingly quickly one would be able to differentiate between one from Costa Rica and one from Brazil, for example.

Part of my job was to arrange for various clients to visit the Coffee Centre to discover what we were actually doing there. This could be the food editor of a magazine when I would demonstrate how to use coffee in an unusual way for a recipe and then offer them lunch from the well-equipped kitchen. On one occasion, I cooked a salmon in orange juice followed by a coffee mousse. I had been running late and everything was hurriedly put together. I thought the salmon was undercooked and that the mousse was not set enough but my guest raved about these dishes. From then onwards I always only just cooked a salmon, and any other fish for that matter.

One of the best things that came out of my job was a publishing deal. Cookery books were all the rage and Octopus were doing a series called 100 recipes of Pasta, Beef, Fish etc. I managed to persuade them it would be a good idea to include in this series a book of coffee recipes and also one of vegetable recipes, the latter coming from the one I had been working on in the States and had not yet found a publisher. They agreed and both were published soon after each other in the early eighties. The coffee book was part of my work for the Centre but they paid me separately for the vegetable one.

For the coffee book I decided to invite a friend to help out. She was very good at cakes, which have always been something that I was not particularly efficient at. We decided to do fifty recipes each, this was a challenge for me along with everything else I was supposed to undertake at the Centre. She was obviously paid handsomely for her efforts. We had endless meetings and testing of recipes until finally we had the right mix. The bit I enjoyed the most was the photography. I had worked with photographers many times but never with food. It was terrific to direct the shoot and watch the food stylist do her magic and discover some of the tricks of the trade. I still have a large photograph of a coffee-marinated leg of ham decorated with coffee beans from this shoot on my kitchen wall.

Finally, the book was ready and published by Octopus. We had a launch party at the Centre, inviting everybody from the press, magazines and the coffee world. It was an interesting evening for me as the hostess, because by this time I realized that my friend was rather jealous of my position. It was a prestigious job with an excellent salary and she was probably more qualified than I was for the role. She also knew some of the journalists and had invited them herself. But I overheard her suggesting that she had my job and found her interviewing people in my office which I was not pleased about. Thankfully, the evening was soon over, as was our relationship. It did take the glitz off the proceedings and left me completely dumbfounded that somebody could do such a thing.

Running alongside the preparations for the book and its launch were the various exhibitions which had to be arranged, agreed, and set up. The first one was simply called Coffee Paraphernalia. It involved getting together as many items as possible connected to the sale and drinking of the beverage. We hired, begged, borrowed and managed with the help of colleagues to amass an enormous amount of old grinders, pots, packaging and memorabilia from years gone by up to the present day. These were displayed in the reception area for a few months where they would remain for people visiting the Centre to view at their leisure. This exhibition was later shown in Harrogate at 'Betty's Tea Shop' which I helped to set up there.

There were two other events I was involved with while I was there: a John Leach Pottery Exhibition and one of Coffee Tables. I had seen John's pottery in the Craft and Potters' Association, a shop next door to Cranks in Soho where I would go regularly for lunch. Also, on a visit to my friend Marika's cottage, which she was renting in Wiltshire, I had visited John's pottery in the village of Muchelney. While there, I asked him if he would be prepared to make some special coffee pots for the Centre which could be sold with the rest of his work. He agreed and all I had to do was get Mr Beltrolle and Barry to agree. We had a meeting where everyone decided it was a grand idea and John's first London exhibition was in the making.

It opened in the summer of 1983 with a private view. As I had always had a great interest in pottery, I made certain all the right people were invited for his first London show. For example one of the celebrities who came was David Attenborough who is known for his pottery collection - and he was one of the first to buy. John was the grandson of the great Bernard Leach and there were three generations of Leaches at the private view. During that evening they agreed they would like to have an exhibition at the Centre sometime in the future, a real coup. At the time it had never been done and I felt honoured that they all agreed to contribute to such an event. Needless to say when I discussed it in the next meeting, it was turned down because we had just had a pottery exhibition. They never realized that they had spurned a historical event.

It was at about this time that I received the dreaded phone call from the States. Kjack had called, starting the conversation with 'Susie, are you sitting down?' He was calling to tell me he had met somebody else and was getting married. She was a hairdresser and lived at the Meadows of Catalpa and they had met at the clubhouse. She obviously did not feel the claustrophobia I felt living in Dayton, Ohio. He brought her to the UK later so that I could meet her. She was charming, just right for him and his life as a numismatist. I was sad that I had lost his friendship which I always valued and strangely enough, I hardly heard from him again. It was a sad ending to what had been rather an exciting liaison.

After hearing that news, the first thing I decided to do was to try and get a mortgage and buy a flat, probably in Barnes where I was born. I went to the Halifax Building Society in Putney and somehow managed to persuade them to give me a 100% mortgage. Thatcher's government was all for home ownership and the rates were reasonable. I thought it was about time I had my own place and stop wasting money on rent. I also felt that I was earning a good wage and could afford to buy. Everything was arranged quickly and I gave in my notice at the flat, packed up my few possessions and moved into a first floor-flat on Castlenau in Barnes.

This also made me aware that the time had come for me to make a new start. It takes me ages to recover from a broken relationship; with the call from Kjack and my new flat something had shifted. I started to get the next exhibition together the Coffee Table Exhibition. Strangely, I had this strong intuition that I would connect to one of the table designers. It was planned to open the exhibition in the spring, and I invited about a dozen makers to contribute. It was amazing just how different each table was - all shapes and sizes, each one surprisingly and unintentionally made in different woods and materials.

The prices also varied enormously, ranging from £500 to £9,000. We were nearing the moment when I would need to prepare the catalogue and arrange the private-view invitations - but still no sign of my imagined special friend. Until, that is, I saw a newspaper article promoting two young designers working in a warehouse on the Thames. They both sounded as if they were doing interesting stuff so I called them to tell them about the exhibition. They invited me to come and see some of their work, so a few days later with trepidation I set off to the East End to find their studio.

I found their place at Butler's Wharf with difficulty, was ushered in, and was shown some marvellous pieces, none of which you could actually call a coffee table (which frankly was not the kind of thing either of them would make). One of them, John Warren, showed me a design which he was working on incorporating a backgammon board, into a tabletop with fine veneer work, which I thought could be adapted to be used as a coffee table. His design was in the early stages, so John said he would finalise matters and come and show it to me as soon as he had finished. I said it would be great for the exhibition but that there was not much time left as we were opening in a month.

Leaving with butterflies in my tummy, I thought 'This is the man, but will he make the table up in time?' About a week later he arrived in a flurry of papers at my office to show me the completed design. It was a beautifully designed backgammon board with an indication of the coloured veneers he would use. The only problem was, would he be able to make the table up for the private view which now was less than three weeks away? He assured me he would be ready. He was the last person to place his table and, of course, it was one of the most interesting tables in the exhibition. So started a long-term relationship that continues today.

The private view was a great success, with people in the furnishing business, the press and the magazines there, basically, I think, to see what it was we were actually doing at the Centre. I did the hostess bit and chatted to most quests but ended up deep in conversation with John. It turned out that he was an oarsman and came to row at his club Tideway, on the Thames near Barnes, where I was living. Apparently, he rowed every Saturday morning. The preview was on a Thursday night, so we arranged that he would come over to my place after training and that we would go for a walk in Richmond Park with the dog and take a picnic. The day arrived and we set off in his car for the Park, which was about twenty minutes away. Having parked we then went for a long walk, taking our food and a rug.

In the early days of a relationship there is so much to get to know about each other; we did not stop talking or walking for hours. It was a beautiful summer's day and everything seemed to be perfect. I could not believe that I had actually predicted this would happen and it just seemed to be rolling out in front of me. We had both just broken up from long-term partners though mine was further in the past; his was quite fresh and we were still hurting and vulnerable. Then we talked about our work, Though I was happy at the Coffee Centre, I really missed my productive creative side and wanted to get back to doing my own art, rather then putting on exhibitions of other people's output. He was absorbed making special one-off designs for clients and was thinking about becoming more commercial.

Eventually, hot and exhausted, we found a suitably remote spot to have our picnic. Spreading the rug out carefully, we literally fell into each other's arms. We kissed passionately and it felt to me rather like coming home to a wonderful reunion with a kindred spirit. We then made beautiful tender love under the drifting clouds as they passing overhead. It was very special and romantic. I think we both felt something enormous had happened. I certainly did. Afterwards, we opened the bottle of wine and toasted our friendship and then proceeded to have our delicious picnic. I remember being worried about the dog when this was going on, but she had stayed nearby and when the food came out was there wanting her share.

We ambled back to the car. Luckily we had gone in a huge circle so it was not too far away. We then drove home to Barnes. I had brought some fresh fish for us so after a leisurely bath together we had supper and listened to music. Thankfully, we discovered we had the same tastes: Fleetwood Mac and Van Morrison. We continued our conversation and now I was telling him I was considering leaving the Coffee Centre to open a delicatessen specialising in selling a superb selection of coffee. He stayed the night and the next morning he was rowing again at Tideway and I went for my regular ride in Richmond Park, which I had been doing since I got back from the States. Someone asked me how I had grazed my chin. I said I had fallen over, but it had been the stubble of John's beard!

For the next few weeks I would be walking on air with that wonderful feeling of new-found love. I can't say that John really felt the same about me but he came most weekends partly because he was rowing regularly at Tideway and he knew there was always a good meal after his great work-out. It was a gentle time of getting to know each other. I was aware that I was quite a bit older than him but he did not seem to mind. I liked to think that I did not look my age then.

Life at the Centre was in the process of change. Norman, the architect who had designed the building, had decided to come back from Portugal where he had been living. Consequently it turned out that my job would be changing somewhat. Norman who had set up the first exhibition (about the production of coffee from berry to cup) wanted to take on the responsibility again. As this was a major and interesting part of my job I felt that it would leave me in the kitchen as it were. I also had some guilt about the enormous salaries we had while the coffee producers still earned so little. Hence my discussion with John about my possible departure from the Centre and the opening of a delicatessen. With his encouragement that was exactly what I decided to do and soon, to my parents' horror, I was giving in my notice.

CHAPTER FIFTEEN
'COFFEE AND SPICE' DELICATESSAN

Lady in red

During my spell at the Centre I had become really knowledgeable about coffee and knew the types I would like to sell. I also had got to know the suppliers and decided on one near to the Centre so in my last few weeks I went there and discussed my plans. What I did was to buy a different coffee of theirs every week for my own personal use so that I could make a considered choice. There was a great deal to do though before it would be delivered but my selection of coffee was of prime importance. During the months leading up to my giving in my notice I had seen an old electricity shop in Castlenau slowly running down its stock because they were closing. It was just the place for my delicatessen, although not in the best location in Barnes. Luckily, I left the Coffee Centre with a big cheque from the Provident Fund. It was enough to get me started and to start my new venture.

The owner, Mrs Redman, had another electrical shop in Barnes High Street so I was able to go and talk to her about my interest in her other premises. She put me in touch with her solicitor and estate agent so that a deal could be negotiated. It was the most reasonable on the market at the time. I looked at a few other places but they were expensive in comparison. The reason it was not too pricey was because there was an enormous amount of work to be done to the place before we could open. It had been an electricity shop for years. It was filthy and I remember the back yard being full of old TV sets and broken irons. This area eventually became a garden where our customers could have coffee and cake in the summer months.

I employed a local architect to draw up plans for the shop and then set about organising the building work. The front would be the delicatessen and in the back would be a restaurant where people could have lunch or coffee. We also had to put in a new loo and a kitchen area for washing up. The only things we kept from the old shop were the window and the door, which happened to have a nice Art Nouveau handle. Meanwhile I designed a logo for the delicatessen, naming it 'Coffee and Spice'. The design was an oval shape with the name in the middle linked by a coffee bean. I was planning to sell a number of 'dry goods' such as sugar, sultanas, currents, lentils, and broad beans needing bags. I arranged for a printer to produce letterheads, paper bags for the goods, and a small carrier for purchases. It was all printed in tan with our logo on a cream paper and looked most professional. I was pleased with the result and felt proud whenever I handed clients a bag of goodies.

The building work was progressing well; it was a great relief when the new tiled floor went down and we could begin to think about putting in fridges and fittings. I found two wonderful old counters in an antique shop and was able to find two second-hand fridges for the cheese and meats quite reasonably. I was dreading the rewiring of the place and this delayed us somewhat. Having given instructions where all the points should be, I decided it was a good time to take off to France with John for a short break and also to find some French suppliers of things like goats' cheese, olives and wine. As in the early days, I was planning to sell wine as well.

We headed for the holiday home of a friend in Riberac in the Dordogne. Driving my gold Capri, we took the ferry from Dover to Calais and set off south through Paris and the Loire valley and on towards the river Dronne. Here you can see the eleventh-century church looking down on to the old market town of Riberac. It was a relief to arrive safely and collect the key from the main farmhouse to our smaller tithe cottage situated in a cherry orchard. The first thing John did on arrival was to go and pick a huge bowl of cherries. We unpacked, took a short walk around the property, and then went into town for a meal.

It was John's first visit to France. He was entranced and amazed by everything. It was the early eighties and in those days things seemed cheaper there than in the UK especially, wine, cheese and eating out. We ate out most days and, because we chose to dine in unpretentious restaurants it was always reasonable and delicious. We shopped in the local market and visited local sites such as Chateau de Teinteillac, Bergerac and Perigueux. We often made a picnic for lunch, would drive to a suitable spot, go for a walk, and then have our meal under a tree. Occasionally we would swim in the river which was usually cold but always refreshing. We developed a taste for making love in the open-air. It was wonderful after a cold swim to snuggle up and lie together for a while hoping nobody would appear. On one occasion, in the middle of everything, we heard somebody approaching and had to sit up quickly. They would not have minded; we were in France after all.

We visited various chateaux in the area and tasted wine and bought plenty of goats' cheese. All of these proprietors were possible suppliers for the shop so I bought a few samples to take back, but of course space was limited with our bags filling most of the boot. On our return there was only room for one case of wine a beautiful mellow red which we bought in the Medoc region, having spent the night on the beach nearby. I seem to remember we were both bitten terribly by midges that night - the first time we had been bitten whilst touring in France. With John doing most of the driving, we just about made it to the ferry in time. It was an uneventful crossing to Dover and we were soon back in Barnes, having collected the dog from my parents en route, finally arriving exhausted.

After a good night's sleep, I went to see how matters had progressed in my absence. Some work had been done on the electrics but there was still more to do. I commissioned some shelving units to be made for all the produce such as jams, honey, and tracklements. The shelving units were made by another friend, all in wood without the use of nails. He had worked as a boatbuilder and knew a few secrets; these are still going strong decades later as bookshelves. I then started to order some of the goods we would be selling and which could begin to go on display. One of my favourite early suppliers was Whole Earth which happened to be owned by a friend of Marikas. She had moved to Wiltshire and I did not see so much of them.

September was busy, putting last minute touches to the shop and getting all the stock ordered in time. I remember going to collect the twelve made-to-order copper coffee hoppers, which I had copied from one of the old fashioned-hoppers we had shown in the Coffee Paraphernalia Exhibition. It was an exciting time and everything was coming together beautifully. All we needed was a little burst of publicity in the paper, which I organised.

In the middle of all this and before we actually opened, I had to go into hospital to have some vascular surgery done on the birthmark on my head. My period was late and I thought I might be pregnant so I arranged with the anaesthetist for a special anaesthetic so as not to harm the baby. I related this to John when he came to visit me in hospital and he replied with the memorable line 'But I don't want you to have my baby'. This did not go down well with me. He had arrived with a bag of cherries which he proceeded to eat; frankly I did not have the stomach for them anyway. It was with some relief that I was able to tell him a few weeks later that I was not pregnant. In hospital one does have time to think and I suppose I finally realized it was silly of me to expect a committed relationship from him after all, I was older than he was and had a new business to run.

Within days I was out of hospital and making arrangements for the 'Coffee and Spice' opening. The coffee I had ordered arrived smelling absolutely gorgeous and I placed it, ceremoniously, in the smart new hoppers I had had made. In the same week the spice selection arrived and they went into the spice rack. Slowly we were getting there, with new produce being delivered every day.

It was John's birthday in October so I had planned the opening party for the shop to coincide with his special day. The place looked fabulous with the shelves groaning with interesting products ranging from a selection of organic jams and honey to special pasta from Italy. The large display fridges were full of a wonderful selection of cheese and cold meats. In those days you could have both in the same fridge - though I kept them in separate areas. A special fridge was all ready for the freshly-prepared sandwiches, which became our big seller.

On the big day I had invited the local press and a selection of our potential clients whose names I had gathered from friends. It was a memorable occasion with masses of delicious eats placed strategically around the shop, mainly made from the produce we sold. A number of rather well known people came and proceeded to eat their way through the food. A selection of coffee was available for tasting but the more popular drink was a couple of good wines I had selected from the vintners close by. I also remember getting a beautiful bouquet of flowers from the florist which made me realise my neighbours were kind. There were two people helping me that day - one was Nici Graham and the other a delightful girl from Ghana called Abby who had answered an advertisement I had placed in the local paper. She continued to work with me in the shop until we closed.

Nici was a friend from the sixties whom I had met up with again at a party at my sister's. I mentioned I was opening a delicatessen in Barnes and as she lived in nearby Mortlake, she said she would be interested in working there. She gave me her number. I called her and she became our first manageress. We soon developed a system of duties: Nici would open the shop; I would collect the granary baps, along with some white ones which were for the lunchtime rush. In the meantime Nici would prepare the fillings, the most popular being tuna and sweet corn, followed closely by egg mayonnaise, then ham and cheese or Brie and tomato; in the beginning the sandwiches sold for 95p - the price rising with inflation. I made soup and quiches for lunch, which people could either eat in or take away. Abby arrived at about 4 o'clock to help during the afternoon and clear up at the end of the day.

When you have a shop of any kind you are certainly tied and you need to be there most of the time. From the beginning it was nonstop, especially at lunchtime, with often a long queue waiting for our now-famous sandwiches. The produce went well but truthfully could have sold better; I suppose in comparison to supermarket prices the goods were expensive but they were all special. I will never forget our first Christmas. The shop was full to bursting with seasonal products including fresh geese which had arrived by train from a friend who bred them in the country. On that first Christmas Eve we did more than £2000 of business. This was our best ever day in my years of trading at 'Coffee and Spice' - never to be repeated.

Our staff Christmas party was held at my flat. We were eight in number including John and Witham, Nici's fiancée, with Abby and other staff who had helped during our first months. It was memorable for two reasons: firstly, I decided to cook one of the geese, a new experience for me (and I had no idea there was so little meat on them. Luckily Witham was a really good carver and managed to provide enough for eight people.) Secondly, a goose produces an enormous amount of fat and I had drained it into a bowl for later use. Zelda, my dog, decided it was just too tasty to ignore and ate the lot. Apart from those anxieties it was a marvellous meal. We toasted the shop and during conversation I told John I had designed it, using a lot of natural wood surfaces, because of him. He said he would have done it completely differently and I was absolutely speechless.

Our first winter was difficult and sales were not as good as they had been leading up to Christmas. The electricity and telephone bills were coming in, as well as those from our suppliers. I needed help from the bank to get through these months and with this in mind I had a meeting with the manager to arrange an overdraft facility. In those days it was relatively easy to do this. He was charming and friendly and after telling me all about his amateur dramatics escapades soon agreed to what I wanted as long as I put my flat down as collateral. I immediately agreed and the deal was signed and sealed. Naively I did not realise what danger I was letting myself in for.

John was still around and came to the shop on a regular basis, usually when he was rowing and therefore in need of sustenance. He had progressed with his designs and had started to specialise in more complex veneer work as we had discussed in those early days. I suggested we put on an exhibition to show his new designs and set about finding a suitable venue. The 'Orangery' in Holland Park was reasonable and nicely situated with good parking facilities and they also offered the possibility of doing your own catering. So in the summer of 1985 we arranged an exhibition of John's work there. It was a great show and well attended at the private view with one or two sales; there was no problem with my doing the catering from the shop. What I was not prepared for was that John arrived with a new lady on his arm which really took the wind out of my sails. And she was absolutely beautiful. We were not seeing so much of each other now with the shop. I might have thought there could well be somebody else but in these kinds of situation you do not like to think about things like that. I always saw John as a catalyst in my life in as much as he made me look at myself and see what I could do differently. He encouraged me to see my cushy job at the Coffee Centre for what it was and I soon realised I was much happier working for myself. But above all I had not enjoyed exploiting the coffee producers who were still getting paid peanuts while the fat cats in London were creaming off enormous bonuses and that included me. Imagine being able to leave the Centre after a relatively short time and open 'Coffee and Spice' with the proceeds of my Provident Fund. So I was happy that he had brought this awareness to light and made me change the direction of my life.

Feeling on my own again, and becoming aware that the shop was struggling somewhat, I set about thinking how I could bring in more income. The first thing I decided to do was advertise our outside-catering facility and at the same time got a friend to produce and supply some ready-made meals. We bought a box freezer and filled it with fish pie, shepherd's pie, steak and kidney pie, not to mention apple crumble and bakewell tarts, which became our best sellers. They were homemade, way before ready meals were available.

The other sad thing was my darling Zelda died, which was devastating. After a sad month, I needed something to perk me up a bit. I decided to go on a wine-tasting holiday in Italy to have a serious look at the Chianti Classico district, which was an area I knew I would enjoy visiting. The purpose of the trip would be to look at the possibility of selling wine. Once again I went to the bank and arranged for a further loan to enable me to go wine researching. By this time I had got to know the manager Mr Needham and the sub-manager Charles Overde quite well. The later often called me to tell me the latest situation and would let me know if funds were needed. So with a further overdraft arranged and the shop covered by Nici and Abby, I went to Italy for a much-needed break.

I flew to Pisa and stayed in my first hotel. I was quite anxious because I had never been on holiday on my own before, but there was an interesting mix of people all knowledgeable about wine and food, so we had plenty in common. I was the only one with a delicatessen there on a business mission. But increasingly I was thinking we could not afford the outlay of a good stock of wine and the expense of getting the necessary licences to operate as an off-licence. Typical me, I was feeling sorry for myself so the first thing I thought about was to get away from it all on the pretext that I was on a wine-buying trip. Luckily, I decided not to be irresponsible and buy wine which had been my original intention. I would just have a look at and make a note of possible suppliers. And that is exactly what I did.

The following morning we boarded our minibus which would take us to the various vineyards selected for our visit. The first was a Chianti specialist and we were invited to have lunch which was beautifully laid outside on a long table. We had the most delicious meal consisting of four courses starting with antipasti and then homemade pasta, grilled chicken and a dessert. Later we would have a wine tasting from the various appropriate barrels. I think what surprised me most was how young the wine was we were drinking. There were many other fantastic vineyards which we visited. They all went to a great deal of trouble to make us feel welcome.

Being away from the business gave me a chance to have a long look at what was going wrong. The problem and the shame of it all was that we were at the busy end of Castlenau. The buses and the traffic were fairly motoring along when they got to us, and therefore it was only the local people who came to us for their supplies. Meanwhile the overdraft was getting bigger and there seemed little chance of ever reducing it substantially. I was holding on by the skin of my teeth. I decided to try to relax and enjoy my time tasting wine, to savour the landscape and the conversation, but not to buy or order anything with the business in its present state.

On returning from my holiday all was well except for the pile of post. I had left Nici, who had recently married, in charge with help from Pinky on sandwiches. Abby came in as usual in the afternoon.

Now she had finished college and had a job in the local library but was still coming to us for the last couple of hours to help clean-up. Life continued at Coffee and Spice with my trying various new products, but basically the routine was pretty mundane. There was a moment when I asked myself 'Do I really want to do this?' The truth was I missed John, though he still dropped by when he was rowing - but less frequently. More importantly, I missed having a creative input in my life so I decided I must do some painting or go nuts.

I discovered a life class in Wimbledon which happened on a Friday. There was just a group of lady artists, without a teacher, who had arranged to hire a model for the day, we would split the costs for her and the venue. This suited me fine and it began to be something I looked forward to. The granary baps were now being delivered to us, Nici was still running the shop and we would always get an extra person to help out with the sandwiches, still our best seller. At about this time Mary Lyas joined us. She restored antiques three days a week, the other three days she came to work for us. I had met her through her sister who organised the painting group.

One of the aspects of running a business is having to arrange the PAYE for the staff and for myself as I was getting a small salary. I was quite organised in the beginning and would pay monthly but as things got difficult financially it was one thing that went out the window. Eventually, I got a summons from the tax office and that was extremely difficult as it was the last thing I wanted to spend money on. I arranged to pay it off monthly again, taking the outstanding amount into account. It was at about this time I had a row with Nici. She was late coming in one day and when she arrived she was obviously hung-over from the night before. I was furious with her and, after a few cross words, asked her to leave. She got her things together and as she walked out of the door I could not resist saying, 'And please do not come back again'.

It did, of course, mean I would have to find someone else because we needed a manageress. Vicky came to the rescue. She was the daughter of Mr Worthington who owned the flower shop. It was she who had brought me the beautiful bouquet when we opened. She loved the place but her father was keen for her to help him. So with the promise that she would assist with flower arrangements when necessary she came to run things. She was a character- punctual and reliable, and she lived nearby in Castlenau.

Next door to us was Calpe Cars, a minicab company. They would come in on a regular basis for coffee and sandwiches. They were always joking around and chatting us up. I went out briefly with one of the drivers but more importantly it was during her time with us that Vicky encountered her future husband. She was in the process of a divorce from her brutish Hungarian spouse and met her charming partner-to-be during her time with us as he was one of our regulars from the company. They fell madly in love and would marry just before the shop closed. They remain happily married and continue to live in Barnes.

During the later part of the 'Coffee and Spice' era, the dreaded letter from the bank arrived saying they were going to foreclose on the debt. By now the overdraft had got out of hand. The bank manager had let me have almost everything I'd asked for. What happened was that he had been sacked for being too lenient with customers like myself, and the bank were calling in all the money they could. It meant I either had to sell 'Coffee and Spice' or my flat. I chose, perhaps rashly, to sell the flat. I knew it had doubled in value and would be a lot easier to sell than a struggling delicatessen. In theory though I did not have much alternative as it all had to happen quickly.

I put it on the market and it was sold in a month. The problem for me was where to live because it was important I stayed in Barnes and I would obviously have to rent somewhere reasonable. At these kinds of moments I would go and see a clairvoyant and one of the things that came out of the session was that I would find a flat near to where I was already. Sure enough, within the week somebody came into the shop for coffee. In conversation I said I was looking to rent something and she apparently owned a house, divided into flats, in Castlenau just opposite my old place which was perfect. The flat was the ballroom of the original house which had been made into a bed-sitter with a small kitchen and the use of a bathroom. It was pure luck and cost only £50 a week, which was reasonable. I literally moved across the road. I remember taking my curtains down from my own flat and bringing them to my new one and hanging them the very same day, making it immediately feel like my place. The next thing I did was to clean and polish the beautiful parquet floor and the Art Nouveau central light. It was a wonderful space which, strangely enough, I almost preferred to my own flat as there was a garden. I settled in quickly. There was a fire which I lit to keep warm of an evening: just as well because the central heating was not up to much.

Life continued at 'Coffee and Spice' with Vicky coming in most days and if she did not, somebody else would help out on the sandwiches. Every day we had to make up about a hundred or so; it would keep one of us busy most of the morning. Things were still difficult with the bank: I had a small overdraft but was not allowed to exceed it so I would have to go regularly to pay in cash to keep things covered.

I remember once chatting to Charles who was usually helpful and we happened to talk about rowing. I offered to lend him a book called True Blue by Daniel Topolski which the auther had given to me. He was a friend from the sixties and was the Oxford coach for the Boat Race. I suggested Charles come for dinner to collect the book, and we made a date. My new place was five minutes from the bank so when he had finished work on the designated day, he knocked on my door and I proceeded to make dinner for us. He had brought a good bottle of red wine. We had a few drinks and soon got chatty. We had known each other a while from the bank so it was enjoyable to find out a few personal details about each other. After we had dinner I made some of our famous Java coffee, and just off the top of my head I said 'I wonder what you look like without your suit and tie on!' In fact, I had wondered what he would look like in jeans - but in no time he had taken all his clothes off and was in the bed. It was not what I had expected but it was a wonderful spontaneous gesture from somebody who I thought was not often in such a position. We tentatively made love, and then he fell asleep beside me - and stayed the night. We had an early breakfast before he left for work. It certainly firmed up our friendship and over the coming months and years he would be a good ally, always helping me out with a phone call if it was necessary for me to come to the bank and pay in cash to cover a cheque. You certainly do not get that kind of personal treatment now; you are lucky if you actually get a human being at the end of a phone.

On one occasion, waiting for the bus to go back to the shop after paying in what was required, I saw our dustmen coming along in their lorry. They stopped for a chat and offered me a lift up the road. To the absolute astonishment of everybody in the bus queue, I got in with a giggle, and drove off with them in a smelly flourish. Our dustmen had become good friends; they stayed for a coffee and a sandwich when they collected our rubbish. They were flirtatious and full of jokes; we always had a laugh.

'Coffee and Spice' continued to be a hive of activity, especially at lunchtime. There was also a steady flow of people who would come in for coffee and cakes. Often I would find myself sitting and chatting to somebody in need of someone to talk to and it was at this time that I realized I was quite good at just listening, and coming out, hopefully, with something appropriate at the end of their outpouring. There were two special people who came in on a regular basis. One was Andrew Kazamia. He was an actor/ writer who lived in a flat opposite. At the time he was in the middle of writing a script. He would later go on to star in London's Burning but at this point he was a struggling thespian. He was always entertaining over a cup of coffee. He had a lovely girlfriend, Fran, who came in and whom he later married.

The other chap who visited us regularly was Alex Gard, a council surveyor who worked on the local estate. In the beginning he would come in at the end of his day often with his mates and chat up whoever might be in the shop. He had the touch of the Irish about him and a twinkle in his eye. His favourite line was 'How's the craic?' I thought what a thing to say but he did not mean that crack! Over a period of a couple of years I would get to know him well and enjoy his banter. He was, in fact, married but they had terrible rows; she was always on the verge of leaving him and eventually did.

The next dramatic thing to happen was that my landlady decided she was going to put the house on the market. It was a wonderful old Edwardian property which had once been a splendid family home but now converted into various flats, mine being one of the biggest. I loved it there as I was responsible for the huge garden and had made my first forays into gardening, the most interesting plant being marijuana which I had planted amongst my tomatoes. Thankfully, I had recently harvested them and dried them thoroughly in the oven. She was, of course, sitting on a fortune: some of those houses went for a million. But hers was on the market for £250,000 - a very reasonable price as it needed a lot of work doing on it.

On one of my evenings with Charles, we got to discussing the possibility of buying the property and doing it up together. We were quite serious about it and went into it thoroughly. I would sell 'Coffee and Spice' and the money from the sale would be my contribution. As far as I could make out he had private means and was even related to the French royal family. But he was secretive about his history and never quite divulged everything. I believe his ancestors came over to England at the time of the French Revolution.

Of course, the property would have cost an enormous amount of money to do up properly. It would have had to have been gutted, rewired and replumbed and have had central heating put in. It would have been exciting to have overseen the work but between us we did not have the funds. In the end it was bought by a local hairdresser and her husband so it was in good hands. I watched the building work progressing over the months that followed and often thought how different my life would have been had Charles and I committed ourselves to the house. I might even have married him which would have been something else entirely! The immediate problem for me was to find somewhere else to live. During that time I was having regular shiatsu treatment from a friend in Baron's Court and she was still living at home with her mother. They had a self-contained flat on the top floor of their house which I could rent, and that is what I did. By now I was fighting a losing battle with 'Coffee and Spice'; it was never going to develop into the business I had hoped for.

Once again I found myself in a position where I had to start thinking about my future. The shop could not continue as it was, with my already reducing the stock to avoid the expense of filling the shelves. I had continued with my life-class in Wimbledon and realised what a great relief it was for me to spend the day drawing and painting. I used to look forward to Fridays: it was my therapy for the week. I began to realise that it was a life-saver for me, and if it helped me then it would help anybody else suffering from stress. I slowly thought that I would like to train as an Art Therapist and started to look for possible places to do such a training. This was the end of the eighties and Art Therapy was just beginning to be recognised and there were only a few places where it was practised, and therefore difficult to find training courses. Some of these required either nursing a or psychiatric background, neither of which I had.

I therefore put the shop on the market. It was sad that it had not been financially successful: it certainly had been an interesting way of life; but I am good at cutting my losses and getting on with the next phase of my life. Though it took much longer to sell the delicatessen than I had imagined, eventually, after almost a year, an Italian restaurant called San Remo bought it. They had to wait ages to get planning permission to change the use to a premises which could remain open until midnight. By the time it was sold and I had received the £40,000 they agreed to pay for it, I was immensely relieved. Most of this money went on paying off debts connected with the business - suppliers, rent and council tax, leaving just enough for me to take up my plan to do an Anthroposophical Art Therapy training at Tobias School of Art in East Grinstead. It was finally all over - to my great relief.

I arranged to go for an interview there and had long discussions about my life and previous work. I told them why I was interested in Art Therapy training and explained the benefit it had been to me. I told them of my Chelsea course and thought that as I had already done some art it would be an advantage. I discovered years later that it had been rather a hindrance. I was asked if I knew anything about Rudolf Steiner and replied that I'd heard about Waldorf education and about his views on reincarnation. I have believed in this theory for most of my life so this was not news to me, but I did not know a great deal about the man himself. It was recommended that I read his life story and I was given his biography to take away with me. I enjoyed it and found it most inspirational.

To be truthful I never realised what I was letting myself in for, but I had a strong feeling that this was what I needed to do with my life. I was at a kind of crossroads. Should I continue to try to make money out of my cooking skills or should I do something a little more useful to humanity? The training was a means to use my creative talent which I had missed so much. At the interview I was invited to come and stay in the hostel for a week and experience The

First Goetheanum Workshop in which everybody on the Peredur campus would participate. I thought it would be a good way to discover more about the school and to meet some of the students.

I was made welcome and was amazed by how many of them came from abroad. The majority of students were already participating in one of the three courses available on campus. Some were art students, others were eurythmists, and some were from the Speech School. It was a refreshing mix of men and women of all ages from all over the world. It was great to be standing at an easel again and painting throughout the day with some good conversation in between. We ate in the Granary, which served really delicious vegetarian food.

During that week I became immersed in learning about Rudolf Steiner - the architect, designer, sculptor and psychologist, none of which I had fully appreciated before. I discovered that the first Goetheanum was once the most beautiful building in Dornach. He, with his colleagues, had been responsible for every aspect of the design. It was dramatically destroyed by fire in 1924 when the Anthroposophical Society had just been inaugurated. I felt after that week that the fire had destroyed a part of Rudolph Steiner himself. He had worked so hard with craftsmen and women from all over the world. The windows and the frescos on the ceiling had to be seen to be believed and I had this wonderful opportunity to reproduce them. We painted in what was known as the top studio where I met Mary Anne. She invited me to share her home, Burnt House Cottage in Forest Row for the following school year.

The next thing to celebrate was my fiftieth birthday. We did it in some style at a friend's house in Castlenau. It was a black and white party and as it was in July we were able to celebrate in the garden. I did my usual buffet lunch with the help of others from the shop. It had a large baked salmon as the centrepiece and a huge bowl of strawberries with meringues. I had a new friend now called Tahzeen who was a Kurdish sultan escaping the wrath of Saddam

Hussein. He had been a regular customer towards the end of Coffee and Spice. He kindly offered to pay for a jazz band which played for the occasion. My parents came and all my old mates were there including Marika, Nici, Clive, John and Charles. It felt like the end of an era but there were still a few things to tidy up before it was over.

Whenever I am preparing for a big change in my direction, I am drawn back to the church to give me strength for the journey. In Barnes, I went to St Mary's where my parents were married and I was christened. It was lovely and had recently been modernised, and had a welcoming warm atmosphere. It was family-orientated and many young people attending. I usually went on my own to pray and sing. I always loved the hymns which I believe takes me back to a previous lifetime when I was a nun. This life gave me my distaste for incense which makes me gag as I probably experienced too much of it in that incarnation.

Although I was going to spend termtime in Sussex, I felt I still needed a place in Barnes. When I paid off the shop rent to Mrs Redman, I asked her about a flat which she owned above the estate agents on the corner of the High Street. She agreed to my taking it on and gave me a new rent-book paying £50 per week, which was what I could afford. Again, it was in a bad state so I spent the summer having an enjoyable time painting it and getting a few necessary bits of furniture. I had also decided on another dog, I just did not feel quite right without one. Her name was Teal - also a pointer - and I took her to college with me as I had taken Brubeck when I was at Chelsea Art School.

Thankfully, 'Coffee and Spice' was now behind me. I had been able to sell off the counters and the fridges to another delicatessen opening in Barnes. They had a restaurant as well so I felt they had a better chance of survival. It was at the top end of the High Street, consequently in a better position than mine, which had been at the end of Castlenau - a very fast thoroughfare.

From time to time, there is a family event which brings a little joy into our lives. Before I started my training, my younger brother John married beautiful Maria. They had worked together at the Prudential. He had just been made redundant from that company, so their marriage was the happy occasion that we all needed. This was his second marriage and we were all so delighted that he had recovered from a sad divorce and met up with the delightful Maria.

I was excited, to think that at the age of fifty I was to be a student again, setting off on another extraordinary journey of discovery. My greatest fear, of course, was: 'Would I be the eldest in my year?'

Before I left for Sussex I decided to let one of the rooms in my flat to a lodger. Piers came through a friend; this suited me fine because he would be there during the week and spend the weekend with his girlfriend, and I usually came home to Barnes on Friday for the weekend.

On the evening before departure for Forest Row and my training, John Warren came for supper to wish me well. He brought his beautiful new lady Nicola with him, whom he eventually married. We had a memorable evening with scrummy fish pie and champagne - to wish us luck in our new ventures. I still thought I had John to thank for my present life.

CHAPTER SIXTEEN
TOBIAS SCHOOL OF ART

Speed bonnie boat like a bird on the wing

The Capri was still going well, so I bundled the dog and a large suitcase into the car and set off for Forest Row. Burnt House Cottage was named after it was supposedly torched in the Civil War because King Charles I was thought to be hiding there. The house was certainly old and some would say haunted. I felt a strange presence but it did not worry me, though some people would not stay overnight. I arrived a few days early so that I could unpack and settle both myself and the dog into our new life before starting my course. Mary Anne was there to greet us. She was in her second year, a year ahead of me but we still did a number of things together - attending lectures and eating in the Granary for example.

I had a good-sized bedroom upstairs and Juliet, Mary Anne's daughter, had the other bedroom. She was at Michael Hall, the Waldorf School in Forest Row, and could walk across the fields each day. Mary Anne had the sitting room which doubled as a studio and bedroom. She particularly liked it for the wonderful sunsets which streamed through the window; they were inspirational. We shared the kitchen, the bathroom, the cooking, and the rent. On the whole it worked out well. I was delighted for the dog to be in the country with plenty of space. I think Mary Anne and Juliet enjoyed having us there. Most weekends I returned to London and sometimes Mary Anne went back to the Round House, her marital home. Before doing the training she had worked with hospital patients, arranging several exhibitions of their paintings; now she wanted to become qualified to enable her to develop her work in art therapy.

The initial day of term arrived and with some excitement, I set off for East Grinstead. The first-year studio was the top one where I had worked in the workshop. I climbed the stairs to discover a group of twenty students - a large intake. Our teacher was an interesting lady of about my age called Celia Wyatt. We started by forming a circle and spent some time introducing ourselves and saying what we expected from the course and how we had learnt of Anthroposophy. I was the eldest and one of the few unfamiliar with the Steiner philosophy. They were all ages and many different nationalities.

After the introductions Celia gave a short talk about what to expect that term and how for most of the first-year we would be working 'wet on wet'. This was a new technique for me and it certainly took some time to master it. Basically, for this first year we would be working with Goethe's Colour Theory and everything we did as far as I was concerned was a preparation for the therapy year. It was important to get to know and understand the quality and the individuality of the colours you were working with and their effects on the human being. Colour obviously affects us all differently; but there are some standard reactions which we worked with. At this early stage the exercises we were doing would affect you, so by processing them yourself you were able to, for example, appreciate the difference between the experience of red to that of working with blue.

The year was divided into various modules with Celia teaching us most of the time, but visiting staff also came in for particular sessions. One lecture I remember especially was given by Anne

Stockton; before she began, she gave a short history of the School which she had started ten years earlier, with her husband. It was interesting to hear how it had been named Tobias. She had been on the phone in the process of arranging a bank loan. The manager asked the name of the School for the paperwork. It did not have a name as such then, but a Bible was open in front of her at the story of Tobias and the Angel, so she immediately used that. It really suited the intention and philosophy of the School.

As usual I was on a tight budget, so decided to complement the little I had with a job as an auxiliary nurse in the local hospital. They were desperately needed in the early nineties. With only a Pre-Nursing Course to my name I was employed by the Queen Victoria Hospital for three nights a week, which suited me fine. I was fitted up with a new white uniform with an auxiliary's badge pinned on it. It was scary arriving and not being sure where you would be working. I would go where I was needed; it could be the casualty department or a ward. When I arrived the staff nurse in charge had to teach me the process of resuscitation, especially in the cancer ward.

This hospital had the Guinea Pig Club museum in one of the buildings, honouring the great reconstructive plastic surgeon Archibald McIndoe. His patients were pilots who had been terribly burned in World War II - a fitting memorial to them. I enjoyed every minute of my first year at Tobias and made some good friends. I was drawn to two English girls, both much younger than me and for a time we were known as 'The Three Graces.' One was a nurse called Veronica and the other, the youngest in the class, was named Lisa. We spent a lot of time together and went to lectures at Emerson, an anthroposophical college in Forest Row, and occasionally out to the pub. During this time I decided to become vegetarian, and to abstain from alcohol and men - an unusual decision for me, but I had been quite badly hurt by John and by Charles for completely different reasons. When I get involved with a man, my better judgement seems to fly out the window - so I thought I might well be better off without, for a while anyway, and concentrate on my training.

I was drawn to Lisa because she had lost both her mother and her brother at an early age. As a youngster, I had always dreaded that something might happen to Mummy, so when I heard her story I was immediately sympathetic. I felt protective towards her and still do; she stayed in touch and lives near to me now. We joined the choir at the school and on a Tuesday lunchtime would have a good sing.

I went to London most weekends and also for Christmas and Easter. Piers was well settled into my studio flat but luckily we were hardly ever there together. I would see my sister and my old friends Marika and Clive though I had a strange feeling that they did not entirely approve of my being at art school again. They had both been to art school and I think they were envious of my being back in that enlivening environment. This time the course was completely different with much more emphasis on the spiritual, healing process which colour can bring to the human being.

Any organisation connected to Rudolf Steiner makes a special celebration of the festivals. They are deeply connected to the Christian faith. At Christmas the buildings and especially the Granary would be decorated with greenery from the garden in preparation for the annual Fayre. It was a fundraising event for the campus and usually in aid of a particular cause such as a new roof. My first experience of it was pure magic, with children dressed in costume with make-up and masks. There were many stalls selling cakes, cards, pottery and handmade silk scarves, not to mention jewellery of all shapes and sizes.

On one of my visits to Emerson for a lecture I met a special lady from Estonia named Ene. She was doing the Waldorf teacher's training there in order to bring the Steiner Impulse to her native country and later to Russia. She was younger than me but looked ten years older because she did not have any teeth. This was due to poor dental care received during the hard times of the Russian occupation, and due to her fear of dentists, some of whom had been particularly brutal. I decided that I had to do something about this so I introduced her to my own private dentist in London, a New Zealander called John Zinzan. I explained that she was a student with very little money; regrettably, nor could I help her out financially. Over a period of the next few months she went to London for treatment. When he looked into her mouth he had never seen anything like it, he told me later. I have no idea what he charged but it certainly was a much reduced price for a complete set of dentures. She was a transformed person and never forgot the 'Doctor' as she called him. They always asked after each other whenever I saw them.

This small act firmed up our friendship and in the summer of my first year, Ene asked if I would come to Estonia and go on to Russia to teach painting on a Waldorf Teacher Training programme she was organising. Having never been to either place, I was delighted to accept. I joined a small group of teachers from Emerson whom Ene had selected. I was in fact the only student but I had some teaching experience from my days at Dulwich College. The problem was: How were we going to raise the money to go? There would be travel and accommodation expenses and the cost of setting up the training programmes in both countries. I offered to organise a fundraising event which was held in the theatre at Michael Hall School at the end of the summer term.

I was in my element inviting people to perform and trying to arrange an interesting show. I was amazed how everybody I asked accepted the offer to perform just for the good cause. We opened with a performance from The Eurythmy Group at Peredur. It was followed by a scene from the Rose Theatre Group and some singing from Mary Anne, who had been a professional in her youth and had the most beautiful voice. There were other performances from the Speech School and some music from a trio which played together - a wonderful eclectic mix of friends and performers. Posters and tickets were made in-house with little expense.

The great occasion arrived. It was a wonderful July day which also happened to be about the time of my birthday. So with Mary Anne's agreement, I had a lunch party before the show inviting most of the performers, friends, and the family as well. It was quite something with the usual great selection of food to which others also contributed. My parents and my sister came along with some of my favourite people such as John, and his fiancée Nicola. The show and the whole day were a great success, being the result of a lot of hard work. I was so grateful for everybody's contribution and had really enjoyed getting it together. We managed to raise more than £2,000 which was just about enough for air fares, train tickets, accommodation and food in Estonia and in Russia.

It was a proud moment when I handed the money over to Ene who, along with some extra funds from Emerson, made the necessary arrangements. At the end of July Margaret, Glen, Sally and I gathered at Heathrow airport to fly to Tallinn. We were met by Ene at the airport. She took us to her home where we would be based for the first week of teaching in a local Estonian school. I had brought all the brushes, palettes, paints and sponges required along with a large baking tray in which to wet the paper.

Having completed a successful course in the capital we set off for Moscow and then on to Yekaterinburg. We travelled on a sleeper and I shall never forget the Russian Border Guards coming on board and shouting loudly for our passports. Thank goodness Ene was nearby to translate for us. It was a scary moment for us all. Eventually, we arrived in Moscow and, after hanging about at the station for ages we finally boarded our Yekaterinburg train. There was constant hot tea on tap from a samovar at the end of the coach; this was most welcome. Having had a couple of days of travelling, we finally arrived at our destination. Luckily going by train in Russia is relatively inexpensive. One of the head teachers connected to the training, Tatiana, was there to meet us with her husband Misha. They would soon become firm friends.

We were taken to a local student hostel where we stayed for our time there. It involved our taking a bus to The Palace of The Young Pioneers where the course was held. People were curious about us because we were virtually the first foreigners they had seen; before Glasnost, Yekaterinburg had been a closed city. One day on the bus we started singing, partly to practise a song but also because we were nervous. The other passengers could not believe it! The Palace had once been a rich merchant's house and was directly opposite the spot where the tsar and his family had been murdered. The royal Winter Palace had long since been demolished, but we saw a small wooden shrine where fresh flowers were laid every day. It was very moving to go over and see what people had written and left in memory of their royal family. Now there is a much more suitable memorial to them which stands on the same spot but, when we were present the shrine almost looked as if it had been erected by somebody overnight. The Palace was huge and especially for the youngsters. My room, called the Pushkin, was covered in beautiful murals illustrating his work.

My classes were an introduction to the kind of painting favoured by Waldorf Education and I basically used the exercises I had done in my first year with Celia. In other words the classes were based on Goethe's Colour Theory. All of the compositions were in 'wet-on-wet' and the instructions were given in English through an interpreter. I was amazed at how they all painted with such vitality and joy. They could understand me because in their schooldays, they had all had to study another language and many of them had chosen to study English. The eurythmist, Glen, would proceed in the same way and also Sally, the kindergarten teacher. Ene was the only one working in Russian.

One day, having completed my lesson, I was coming down to the staff room when I heard the most amazing singing. I peeped through the door towards where it was coming from and found a full-sized theatre where a group of musicians were rehearsing. I thought I would stay and listen for a while. It was a magical experience, all in Russian, of course, the singer had a beautiful voice. I then went to join the rest of the staff for lunch, which usually consisted of sandwiches and cakes. After about ten minutes the same singer joined us and came straight over to me as he recognised that I had been listening to him. Like many Russians he could speak excellent English and in no time we were having an animated conversation.

His name was Alihan Zangive and he was a friend of Tatiana, teaching English at her school. He was an Honoured Artist of Russia and gave regular concerts with his band. On this occasion, unbeknown to us, he had been invited to sing to the guests from England and soon he picked up his guitar to sing. It was brilliant, like having a private concert, but the embarrassing thing was that most of the songs were directed to me. I did not know where to put myself. I was thrilled on the one hand but felt strange being singled out. By then though we had already started talking about his coming to England to give a concert - this is what he wanted to do above anything else. When I got home, after some difficulty over his visa, we arranged for him to come to the UK to sing. He arrived in November to give a beautiful concert at the same Michael Hall School theatre.

The trip had been memorable in many ways. I had met interesting Estonians, Latvians, Lithuanians and Russians, both men and women. They were all teachers, some head-teachers, wanting to be introduced to Steiner Education and to bring it into their curriculum. For the first time the school system in Russia had eased up a bit and they could introduce something new. I had particularly liked my translator, Luda. On another visit to Estonia I stayed with Luda in her tiny flat.

At the end of the training we always gave a performance in celebration of our hard work. On this occasion, for the first time, I read a poem for Glen to perform to. It was Solzhenitsyn's 'Longing of the Earth for Spring'. I enjoyed doing it, and this became something I did regularly for eurythmy performances. The travelling on these trips was always hard work. Again, it was a long train journey back to Moscow. From there, we flew back to Heathrow where Eric, Glen's boyfriend, came to meet us. We were all extremely tired but I could tell that things were not quite right between them. Sure enough, in our absence, he had got involved with my friend Lisa. Eventually, they would end up together but it made it difficult for me as I was friendly with them both. So in the second year the Three Graces were somewhat disbanded.

It was good to spend time in London before starting my next term. I had to find somewhere else to live because Mary Anne had decided not to continue at Burnt House Farm - the landlady had put up the rent. For the next term, I found a room in a small cottage, which had been advertised in a local paper. It was owned by a charming lady in Rusthall, a village outside Tunbridge Wells. It was further to drive but ideal for Teal as Ashdown Forest was nearby. Sometimes I would leave Teal with my landlady who was a dog-lover and happy to walk her. I often found I had the house to myself when my landlady spent time at her daughter's. Basically, she wanted somebody there because she had been burgled before.

With a new home organised, I was looking forward to the next phase of my training. It was all about going more deeply into the colour: 'painting out of the colour' it is called, which for me as a traditional artist was a new way of allowing the pigments to move across the paper. From the start I knew I was going to have difficulty achieving what I wanted from this type of endeavour. What I eventually discovered was the healing quality of working in this way, but not before some frustrating moments with my new teacher. He was a German called Claus, much younger than me and rather arrogant. I think I unnerved him somewhat as I would ask him questions, none of which he seemed able to answer. It was only at the end of the year with him that we reached some kind of understanding.

The interesting thing about an anthroposophical training is that you have a long hard look at yourself. Before you can work with other people you have to sort out your own problems. It is something you become aware of in the first year but in the second you have to come face to face with your dragons. You see all your faults blazing out at you and thankfully you also recognise your good points. I have always been a reasonably confident person and believed in my ability to get things done, but had no idea how intolerant of others I could be. It became pretty obvious that I lacked patience and humility with people less able than myself. This was the first difficult task I had to tackle. I tried to be a little more considerate of others and to be more patient with those students who were always late or asking unnecessary questions.

In the middle of all this I was attempting to make the necessary arrangements for Alihan to come to the UK and give a series of concerts. Firstly, I had to write a number of letters requesting permission for a visa for him. Eventually, everything was sorted and I went to meet him at Heathrow. It was great to see him arriving with his guitar and a big smile across his face. Secondly, the booking arrangements had to be made for the first concert, which was to be held once again at Michael Hall School. It was an enormous theatre and quite difficult to fill. I did my best but it was only about half full so it was not the success I had anticipated. He consequently did not make much money after the booking fee had been paid. This was rather a shame as he was now my responsibility and like any man had a huge appetite and needed feeding!

He arrived with a six-month visa. The plan was to do a series of concerts and perhaps make a recording as I knew of a studio near to my delicatessen in Barnes. After my return from Russia there had been a few letters exchanged between us and it was obvious he really wanted to try his chances in the West. He was so enthusiastic about coming I found it hard to tell him that breaking into the music business was extremely difficult, but I certainly agreed to do what I could for him: after all, he did have the most amazing voice. I arranged three concerts, the first at Michael Hall, the second at Rudolf Steiner House, and the third at my local church in Barnes.

The initial concert was at the end of November, when the turnout had been disappointing, and I have to say it was the same in the other venues. It was partly because I was on a limited budget; I could not afford to spend money on advertising and publicity. At least I managed to get posters out, inexpensively. There were other things to worry about as well. Luckily, my landlady was away and he could stay at the cottage. But I still had a couple of weeks of college to do so it meant leaving him there on his own. I remember he habitually went for walks in Ashdown Forest with the dog. One day, as he was spouting off Shakespeare to the trees (as was his wont), a chap came along and congratulated him. He was astonished to find out he was Russian; then the stranger beat a hasty retreat!

Sometimes he came with me to the Art School and contributed his songs to the end-of-term gathering, which was a treat for us all. He did have the most enormous repertoire and seldom repeated songs but then, of course, they were in Russian, which I could not understand. He also did the same thing at the Christmas Fayre, another magical morning I had helped to arrange, getting all the stalls and events organised. It was a real traditional atmosphere with minced pies and mulled wine, I was happy to share this with Alihan, a little taste of an English festive season for him.

After the end-of-term celebrations we headed back for Barnes. Although we had been quite passionate in our embraces on meeting up again, we had never actually slept together. Now there was no stopping us, and we were soon in bed; I really had tried to avoid it because he was married, but I was so hopeless when I got involved emotionally with somebody. It did not take much for me to change my mind. Inevitably, I was on the road to a broken heart. He was delighted to be in my bed, having kept him at arm's length for some time.

As usual I would be joining my family for Christmas. That year my brother Simon was doing the honours, and we all spent Christmas Day with his family in Alverstoke. My parents had to be persuaded to allow me to bring Alihan. They were always hesitant to accept a newcomer into the fold but I emphasised that if he did not come, neither would I. With some difficulty it was resolved. We stayed for a few days, before going to my brother's home for the day. Alihan had taught me a Russian song which I sang with him to the gathering. He was delighted to meet everyone, performing to them at the drop of a hat. I think they were all suitably impressed by his huge presence and magnificent voice.

We came back to Barnes and started to prepare for the next two concerts which would be in London. It was cold and they were not well attended. He was disappointed, but we made up for it by booking at Glentham Studios for him to record some of his songs on tape. It was quite a thrill to be there for the recording with him as he did the tracks. Strangely enough, it was the only time I saw that he was nervous. He was so used to singing to huge crowds in Russia that almost nothing fazed him, but he seemed to find recording much more nerve-wracking.

Frankly, I had not expected him to stay in the country so long. It had been delightful though I was somewhat relieved when the phone call came from his manager requesting him to return to his band or else they would get another singer. He certainly did not want that so he decided he must return. I helped him arrange his flight and a few days later, I would be bidding him a tearful farewell at Heathrow. At least he went home with a good recording in his bag.

I soon returned to college where I tried to concentrate on my painting but my head was full of Russian songs, especially the one I had learned to sing with Alihan. In truth though, I had not expected anything from him so I had to treat it as a passing flight of fancy. I am sure that is all it was for him as well. Things might have been different if the great career break had happened. It was a special time for both of us though made more difficult by the fact that I had so little spare money. He had arrived with virtually nothing, yet he managed to make a few pounds busking at South Kensington Tube station. He would come back with his pockets full of one pound and twenty pence coins and we would go off for an Indian meal to celebrate. After he went back to Russia, he called me a few times just to check that I was alright. I was expecting to return there again in the summer, so I hoped to see him then.

I returned to the cottage in Rusthall with Teal and eventually settled down to some serious painting at college. I was getting on a little better now with Claus, finally realising that he did not know the answers to my questions. Ultimately you had to find the solutions for yourself after hours of working and wrestling with the dilemma that troubled you. The great excitement of that term was the decision for the whole class to go to Italy.

Throughout the training we had regular art history lectures, often on the spiritual aspect of Renaissance painters such as Giotto, Leonardo da Vinci and Michelangelo. It was a tradition that second-year students visited Italy, and we were delighted to have it confirmed we could go to where we could study the original works of these great artists. My problem was getting enough money saved in order to go. It fascinated me just how little you could live on and still be able to put something aside. My plan was to work an extra shift at the hospital and so I saved enough for this life-changing trip.

We went to Italy in the Easter break in April 1993. Claus was the only teacher to come with us and I thought he was brave to take a dozen students on a foreign trip. We caught a plane from Gatwick to Pisa and then took a very crowded train to Florence. At this point we almost lost one of our party; Dragisa was always the last to arrive for anything and on this occasion she just jumped on board as the doors were closing. We arrived at night and made our way on foot from the station to the Hotel Azzi. It was in the artist's district yet within walking distance of most of the places we would be visiting.

It was great to be back in Florence again. I associate it with two romantic visits in the sixties which I had loved. The first was with Gianandrea, my Italian love, and the second was with Robert Hughes, the art critic. They had both taken me to the Uffizi Gallery. On this occasion, though, I was able to do some drawing; on previous visits I had felt much too intimidated to do any sketching. As soon as we had chosen our dormitories, and unpacked, we set off in groups to find something to eat.

After a quick breakfast we made our way to the Church of San Miniato, a glorious Romanesque building covered extravagantly in black and white marble. It was full of paintings and sculpture with many religious symbols which were so typical of the period. It was ornate and symmetrical in its architecture and a real gem of its kind. We broke up for lunch, arranging to meet at the Baptistery later. This is where in the old days all Christians of Florence, such as Botticelli and Michelangelo would have been baptised. Now the Baptistery is a huge tourist attraction - because of its magnificent doors. The south door was designed by Pisano and the north door by Ghiberti who jointly won a competition with Brunelleschi, who conceded the job to him. The doors are an absolute marvel, beautifully modelled - a sight to behold.

Next we walked to the Santa Croce Museum, where we saw the Cimabue crucifix, which had been damaged by flooding in the sixties. It is surprising that it is still possible to see some of the terrible damage done to the art in Florence when the River Arno rose so destructively. There was much to look at in this museum so I stayed and did some drawing. Later we walked to the Pazzi Chapel which had the most wonderful acoustic and those of us who sang could not resist a song or two.

Some of us decided to eat in that night to save money. So on the way back to the hotel we bought wine, some typical local cheeses, and some crunchy bread for supper on the hotel terrace. It was great to discuss our plans as art therapists and what had drawn us towards Tobias in particular, over any other course available. At that time I wanted to work in the prison service, because I felt inmates were badly neglected in the education department with little or no access to therapy.

The following day we made our way to the Uffizi, walking past the Baptistery and taking all the beauty around us into our souls. We were able to get in for free because we had a special letter, as we were art students. Claus had told us that it is a good idea to start at the top and come down slowly. So this is what we did; but what a climb! I was exhausted and had to sit for a few moments before I set off on my journey of discovery. We actually spent three days here, and it is without doubt my favourite museum. I spent time drawing all my special favourite paintings and sculptures. I still have my Italian sketchbook to remind me of those remarkable days.

Later, we went to the Carmina Chapel to see the Massacio frescos, which had been recently restored. They were absolutely beautiful and I would have liked to have spent longer here but we had a designated timeframe. One of my favourites here was Massacio's Adam and Eve Leaving the Garden. It was one of his later frescos; as he died at the age of twenty seven one wondered what else would have come from his brush had he lived. After this we went to the

Academia to see Michelangelo's work. It was fantastic to see the real 'David' and to be able to draw it. Almost as impressive were the 'Slaves' which are supposedly a series of unfinished carvings by his hand. Everywhere I went I made sure that I got a good selection of cards as a memento of our visit, and took photos.

On our last day in Florence we went to the Basilica of Santa Maria where Fra Angelico had lived and worked. It had a very peaceful atmosphere and thankfully fewer people. There was the wonderful 'Annunciation' fresco on the wall, greeting us as we came up the stairs to visit the various painted cells. I spent some time meditating on the sacred feeling of monastic life in those bygone days, with my friend Annukka, a student from Finland, before we headed back to our hotel to pack in preparation for the following day. We had an early train to Assisi where we visited the Basilica of St Francis. This was before the earthquake so everything was in pretty good order. We had a couple of hours inside and then we met up at the west door. We were rather battling with the crowds; but it was worth it. To see the Giotto and the Cimabue Frescos was a dream come true. The Upper Basilica has the story of Christ's life in all its glory painted by Giotto and his students. Sadly, it was badly damaged in the earthquake, so I was pleased to have seen it intact. The crowning glory for me was St Francis Feeding the Birds by Giotto, of which I bought a print.

We rushed to catch our train to Rome where we were going to spend a few days at the Vatican. I had arranged to meet up with an old friend there and spend a few days with him before flying back to Gatwick. Our hotel was some distance from the papal palace so we took a bus and joined the queue in the normal way. Once again, we could get in on the magic letter. It was reasonable to use my student card, which I did when I came back later.

After a few days, the rest of the group returned home and I stayed on with Michael. He collected me in his car and took me on a sight-seeing tour around the city, ending up at his tiny flat in the Campo dei Fiori. I had known him since the fifties when we were at school and we had kept in touch. He was now a writer and made ends meet by teaching English. He had a girlfriend in Rome, so some of our time would be spent with her and her children. Mostly he would be working during the day and I would visit churches and fountains, but my great interest was the Vatican. It had so much to see there and I went often to have a good look at everything. I was particularly drawn to the Sistine Chapel: it was simply amazing. The first time I had seen the Chapel was in the Sixties with Gianandrea; then it had been really dirty and dark. Now it had recently been restored so that it looked as good as in the time Michelangelo painted it. The fact that he painted it at all is remarkable as he was a sculptor and he only reluctantly accepted the commission from Pope Julius because he was a difficult person to refuse. The Pope had originally asked for the vaulted ceiling to be covered with portraits of the twelve Apostles, but Michelangelo decided otherwise; he thought it needed something grander and decided on the creation of the universe.

He designed his vision on paper first with nine main frescos running lengthwise down the centre of the vaulted expanse. This was then transferred to the ceiling through the prick-and-blow method. Which is pricking with a pin round the outline of the drawing then blowing and pressing powdered charcoal through the paper directly onto the surface above. He built a movable wooden scaffold to enable him to do the work and be close to the painting; sometimes he would stand to work, but other times, if he were working on the detail of a face, for example, he would lie flat on his back. The whole procedure was most arduous and took him four and a half years to complete - by which time he was exhausted.

He started work in the summer of 1508 with the help of six assistants. They helped with the mixing of the plaster, grinding paint and with applying some of the colour. As he worked with wet plaster, the colour had to be put on very quickly. There was no time for mistakes, because the dry, hard paint would have to be chipped away and started again. Michelangelo made few errors but by the time he reached the end of his task, he was working alone. He had so many disagreements with his assistants, that he sacked them because he thought they 'lacked inspiration'.

During the time it took to complete the work, there were many confrontations with Pope Julius. The Pope would climb on to the scaffold to check progress and ask 'When will it be finished'? Michelangelo would reply 'When it is ready'. The artist would go for months without being paid when papal funds ran out. The process made him quite demented and people thought he was going mad. He cut a colourful figure as he dashed through the streets of Rome with his head down, clothed in filthy rags, covered with paint, his hair and beard matted with plaster. The Sistine Chapel paintings were finally completed in the Autumn of 1512.

With great anticipation, the scaffolding and covers were removed to display this amazing work of art. Pope Julius and his court came to see the finished ceiling on All Saints Eve and the following day there was a service of dedication - a long celebratory mass with all those attending looking up in absolute wonder at Michelangelo's great achievement. He did not attend the mass; he could not wait to get back to his sculpture which he felt he had severely neglected over the time it had taken to complete the Sistine ceiling. Finally, it was finished and we humble people, five hundred years later are able to see one of the wonders of the world. I decided to draw most of it and also took some photographs, ending up with a stiff neck after only a few days!

It was enjoyable to spend evenings with Michael and his girlfriend. They showed me some of their favourite places; I remember a very nice restaurant on a marina near Rome. Eventually my Italian trip was over. It had been such a pleasure to try to speak the language again, and Michael said to me, 'Where did you learn the lingo with that Southern accent?' Well, it certainly worked for me when I was buying food in the markets of Florence and Rome. I flew back to Gatwick, collected my car, and went to stay for a few days with my parents, who had been looking after the dog as usual.

Almost immediately I returned to college for the summer term. Everybody was pleased to be back, with buzzing conversations about our Continental trip. The first task we were given was to prepare, during the term, a lecture about a favourite artist, whose work we had admired in either Florence, Assisi, or Rome. It was to be a half an hour's presentation with slides. I desperately wanted to talk about Michelangelo but somebody else had selected him before I could get my oar in. So I asked for Leonardo da Vinci, the artist I had greatly admired all my life and whom I immediately set about researching. I enjoyed reading up as much as I could about him and needless to say, I found many books about Leonardo - including the one by Robert Hughes.

We continued to produce full imperial-size paintings with whatever topic of the day was given. During this term we had to paint the seasons, each having a slightly different palette of colours. It was always a favourite of mine which I would continue to use in art therapy later, but on these occasions it would be done 'wet-on-wet' whereas ours were 'dry', where the paper is stretched and the colour painted directly on to dry paper. All work done in the second year was in theory a preparation for the therapy year, when all our work would have a healing aspect.

I continued to live in the cottage in Rusthall and regularly found myself there alone as my landlady often went away with her daughter. I felt fine on my own and would go for long walks in Ashdown Forest or across the common with the dog. One day, when I was doing my shopping at the village supermarket, a rather strange thing happened. Not for the first time I had one of those interesting premonitions. I was standing in the queue to pay for my purchases and waiting in front of me was a grubby, smelly man: I suddenly had this weird feeling. I have mentioned before that I can remember past lives and this was an occasion when one of them was confirmed to me. The man had a strong smell about him of flour, sweat, and yeast. He was a baker from across the road and had a filthy white apron on and gave off an almost sweet odour. I responded instinctively to this - I recognised it from all those years before when I had been a baker. It made the hairs stand up on the back of my neck and on my arms. I did not say or do anything, just returned to the house with a feeling of satisfaction - a life I already knew about had been confirmed to me.

When I had any spare time, I spent it preparing my Leonardo project. My birthday was coming up soon, so I had asked my sister to photograph and make slides for me from a good book I had on the artist. She knew and worked with photographers so it was relatively easy for her to organise. She was now a successful set decorator and had dressed a number of films and television programmes. She was really doing well and often used her two sons - Ben and Billy - to help her. They would go on to have success in the film business too. One is an art director, the other an assistant director. She presented me with the slides for my birthday and I was able to use them for my show. The only thing I had to do was get over my nervousness at speaking in public, because I had to give my talk to the whole school - not just my own class. The way I overcame this fear was to force myself to speak out at our meetings on Friday mornings.

The big day arrived and I stepped up to talk on Leonardo da Vinci. I started with a slide of the familiar picture of the old bearded man, and announced that this was in fact his father not the artist himself, as many believe. I was able to show a number of portraits of him where it was obvious he had a straight nose not the hook nose in the drawing of the old man. Importantly, there was an early portrait of him done by his master Verrocchio. It was his sculpture of David which Leonardo had modelled for. There were also self-portraits.

His mother gave birth to Leonardo, illegitimately in 1452, in a small village called Anchiano, just outside Vinci. Caterina, his mother would later marry a local man Piero del Vacca, they would bring him up for the first four years of his life. His father, a notary and a well respected man in the area, acknowledged the birth by being present at his baptism. He married himself some- time later, living with his wife in Vinci. When he was four Leonardo moved in with his father and his wife. Although his father, Albriera di Giovanni Amadori would marry four times and have eleven other children; at this early stage he was brought up as an only child, as his first two wives were childless.

At a young age, Leonardo developed remarkable skills and spent most of his time drawing with crayons and observing nature, which he loved. After a limited primary education, it was normal for boys to be apprenticed to a local workshop and his father arranged for him to attend Verrochio's studio to develop his skills. Leonardo joined the studio when he was thirteen and stayed for some considerable time. Starting with cleaning brushes and grinding the pigments, he later became a capable assistant to the Master. It is recognised that he assisted Verrochio on the 'Baptism of Christ' and it was during the execution of this painting that the Master threw down his brush in frustration and in recognition of Leonardo's skill, declared that he was going to give up painting for sculpture. It is true that from that time on Verrochio concentrated on sculpture.

I will not relate my whole lecture here, it was a special subject for me and I really enjoyed researching it - Leonardo was the first painter I became familiar with through my parents' book. Also, my friend Robert Hughes had written a memorable volume about the artist's life. In the Seventies, Robert had taken me to Vinci to the museum there, where we saw displays of models of Leonardo's inventions. It is extraordinary that Leonardo is such a legend, because there are only about a dozen paintings which are actually attributed to him. In his lifetime - Leonardo was considered to be divine, and it was thought that his work brought healing to those who viewed it.

The end of our second year was approaching and we had to make a presentation of our own work to the teachers and talk about what we had learned. It was with a feeling of achievement that I covered the floor, spreading my paintings out for them to see. I had struggled with the fact that I could easily do a tree, a horse, or a figure. But this was not what we were meant to be doing here. The whole point of this technique was that we were painting out of the colour. By using careful transitions, something materialised, be it an angel or a cloud.

So finally, by the end of my time with Claus, things had moved on. In the beginning he would come up behind me and just say 'Transitions, transitions, transitions'! I would labour away, easing out the colour. By the end of the year, I was pleased that they had improved but still left a lot to be desired. I had also learned how the different colours truly affected the human being, an exciting discovery for me; others who had painted in the Steiner way all their lives knew these things and managed the whole process better than me. This was the 'hindrance' I spoke of and became aware of from my previous rather rigid training at Chelsea.

I had been asked again to teach painting for the Russian Waldorf Teacher Training in Yekaterinburg. This time I did not help with raising the funds to go. It was supplied by an organisation called The Godparents. We flew to Tallinn first and did a week there, before setting off on the long train journey to Moscow and on to Yekaterinburg, being met at the station by our friends from the previous year. Tatiana had already started her school with some Steiner influences, especially in the arts and crafts. Alihan taught English there, and I was looking forward to seeing him again. He had called me a few times since he had returned.

We were working in part of The University of Yekaterinburg, an imposing building where President Yeltzin had studied. He had been a successful mayor here and had gone on to gain high office. It was the man himself who had made Alihan an Honoured Artist of Russia after my friend had performed for him. We stayed in a student hostel a short walk away, but getting there was like battling over an obstacle course. They were in the process of changing all the pipes for the gas and water system; huge new pipes were lying stacked up in the road beside enormous smelly holes which had to be jumped across. There did not seem to be any Health and Safety regulations in Russia at that time. We were working in the Science Wing and my particular lab did not have any running water. It was on the second floor and I had to walk down masses of stairs, across the campus to the toilets in the main building to get it - and then carry it back. Luckily I did have some help. Almost all water was cut off everywhere due to the work going on laying the new pipes. It was a real labour of love getting water, boards, paints, and brushes ready for my students. It was great when they finally arrived and I saw their smiling faces.

This trip was particularly difficult to cope with, mainly because of the water situation. In the hostel there was a trickle for a shower but no hot water. We also ate in the student hostel where all the food seemed to be white with, to our delight, an occasional splash of beetroot. To top it off one day, when we had the afternoon free, we ventured out with friends to walk in the streets, and found a small market on the side of the road with people selling bananas and berries. I bought some fruit as there was none to speak of at the hostel. In the process of taking my money out of my bag and putting it back, my wallet was cleverly nicked.

It was not before I arrived back at our accommodation that I realised it was missing. Thankfully my air ticket and passport were not in it, just all my cash, about £50. I was advised to contact the police. If I claimed on my travel insurance, I needed proof that it had happened. Luda, my interpreter, did the necessary phone call and eventually they arrived to interview me. Two burly officers came in the room I was sharing with three others, and started asking questions. 'Mother's name, father's name, where do they live? My name, where was I born, where did I go to school and what happened?' It was hilarious and I did not take it seriously, but I got the necessary paper.

The incredible thing about the whole episode was that over the next few days everybody in our group came and gave me a few dollars. We were advised to use dollars because this was what everybody wanted. In the end I had more than I had lost. I could not believe how generous everybody had been because it is horrible to be abroad without money. Sharing is part of the anthroposophical way of life and there have been many occasions when I have been helped. Similarly, I like to think I have helped as many people as I could. The next surprise was that three of us, who had come on the first trip, were invited to stay on for an extra week at a chalet on a lake for a short break.

We arranged for our return tickets to be changed and when the course was over we got on a train with our friends and were taken to a secret location. We were met by a teacher's husband who worked in this 'forbidden city' and had the holiday home as a perk for his job. No foreigners were allowed in this place, so it was all rather clandestine and exciting travelling in a car through the city to the lake. We were dropped off at the chalet and the plan was that the family would arrive daily with food for us and we would cook whatever they brought.

There were three of us and we were all rather exhausted and sad. Margaret and myself, both teaching painting to different groups, had really suffered with the water problem and Margaret's mother had recently died. I was miserable because Alihan had not been in Yekaterinburg: at the time of our visit he was away on tour with his band. I received a message from him via Tatiana, so not surprisingly I shed a few tears over him. Glen, the eurythmist in our group, was suffering because Eric had left her for my friend Lisa. They had been together a while and were on the point of marriage. She was miserable and still tearful that it had not worked out.

It was, however, a strangely uplifting week; we had wonderful conversations about our respective lives. Glen and Margaret were both teachers at Emerson College and had been there for some time. I was soon to go into my therapy year to complete my training. Every day we swam in what I called the radioactive lake as it shimmered with shiny colours. Our friends arrived at about lunchtime with food which either had been cooked or we needed to heat. It was mainly vegetarian with some fish. We took it in turns to do produce a meal and interesting concoctions appeared on the table. The best thing was the walks around the beautiful lake and forest.

The week was quickly over and we were whisked away (having not seen a soul except our friends) back to Yekaterinburg to catch our train to the capital. There always seemed to be much hanging about to do at Moscow airport, and nothing much to buy. Thankfully, we arrived at Heathrow in one piece after what had been yet another considerable adventure, which, in my case, had cost little because my stolen money had thankfully been replaced by friends. It amazed me how I seemed to be travelling more than ever at a time in my life when I had few funds. My next problem was how I was going to pay my rent and final fees for my third year.

I approached my parents with trepidation I did not like to borrow money from anybody, especially them. My father, not surprisingly, said no. I then asked the 'Godparents', an organisation for this kind of emergency. They helped students, often in their final year, to finish their courses. It was to be an interest free loan basically for my fees, and paid back after I had started working as an art therapist. I had to do the usual grovelling to a board of people, one of whom had come to Russia with us. I showed some of my work and explained why it was important for me to finish my course. I told them I had set my heart on practising in the Prison Service and explained how it was an area that had been sadly neglected and where I thought enormous benefit could come. I mentioned that I had been in touch with Ford Prison and asked about a possible placement. Thankfully, they agreed to my loan and I went out with my head held high. I decided to find the cheapest option as far as accommodation was concerned, by renting a room in the student's hostel, as long as I was able to have the dog with me. They said it would be fine and so I settled in for my third year.

By now our number had been reduced to twelve, including a couple of newcomers arriving from Camphill, another Steiner establishment where Art Therapy was practised. This year we would have a number of different teachers, all therapists either in the UK or in Germany. It was always fascinating to hear about their techniques and what sort of success they were having. Our main teacher was Gill David, a gentle soul and a fine painter, whose speciality was fairy stories. Some of our original group had not continued into the Therapy year and would continue to paint, Lisa and Veronica amongst them. We still had an extraordinary cross section of students from France, Finland, Israel, Switzerland and Croatia.

On one occasion, the week we were engaged in painting the Epochs with Gill, I foolishly managed to have a head-on crash in the Capri. The car was a right-off but I came through it relatively unharmed apart from severe bruising across my breast. I missed only one day of painting and was back doing the Greek Epoch the following day. Interestingly, it was a very pale painting for me, due to the shock. I repeated it later in the term. What came out of it was that Gill wanted to sell her car and as she was prepared to have me pay what I had when I could, I agreed to buy it, so I was not long without a vehicle.

The year was divided into nine modules. Almost every one was with a new teacher. This was certainly a challenge, partly because it took a while to get to know them; then some you liked, and others were more difficult. There was one German teacher, who will remain nameless, who taught us slanted black and white drawing. I was never keen on charcoal drawing, especially negative drawing. The teacher liked it to be done just so, and would come round and say in a loud voice 'No, no, no!' when I was not doing it correctly. She was not one of my favourites, and I am afraid she knew it.

Once again I was invited to Estonia to continue teaching on the Waldorf Teacher Training Course. This time we would just stay in Tallinn as it was the middle of winter, not a time to be travelling in Russia. To my amazement a number of them came to Estonia from Russia - they were so keen to get their certificates. Some were also planning to come and study further at Emerson College. The memorable thing for me about this trip was that my case did not arrive with me. I had to do a very basic shop in Tallinn to have some spare underwear and made do with what I was wearing. I was pleased to get back to Heathrow and discover my bag waiting for me in 'Lost Luggage'.

On returning to my rather small room at the hostel, I decided to do something about trying to earn more money. I was still at the hospital during termtime, but it did not bring in much. I had colleagues who worked for Hove Social Services where the pay was better. I applied to them and got the job as a care assistant. There are a number of residences in Hove for youngsters with learning difficulties. For the next two terms I would go there, usually three times a week. It involved driving to Hove, which took about half an hour and doing my shift which included putting clients to bed, having bathed and fed them. Then driving back again. Sometimes I did a sleepover, which I was not keen on doing.

During my last year at college I started attending a church called The Christian Community there was one in Forest Row and one in Hammersmith. It is always fascinating to me the similarities and the differences between Christian worship. This was very meditative and on the whole rather quiet. There was little singing or music, I missed that aspect of the Anglican service but I did enjoy the moments of reflection, especially in Hammersmith where Evelyn Caple was the priest in charge.

I soon settled into my work at college. This term there were modules where you would be painting with others on the same piece. I would find this difficult especially if somebody came and planted a dash of red over my green. But that was the point of the exercise, not to be precious about your work and to try to understand others' efforts. The best part of this term for me was doing the Platonic Solids with Inga. I particularly liked this module. First, you made your clay into a sphere. Having modelled the sphere sitting in a circle we would pass it around the circle, and experience all the different qualities of each sphere. At the same time longing for your own particular one to come back and recognising it immediately when it did.

Over a few weeks we modelled all of the five Platonic Solids: tetrahedron, hexahedron, octahedron, dodecahedron and icosahedron. They were difficult to do and required great strength of will. Also, if you became red in the face doing this it was an indication of high blood pressure; a couple amongst us suffered from this during this time and got treated for the complaint. Some of these models were good to use with patients. I loved working with clay and found it useful for 'grounding' certain conditions.

One of our visiting tutors was Rainer Beyer, a German art therapist at the Paracelsus Clinic in Bad Liebensell. This was an excellent anthroposophical clinic, specialising in an alternative approach to healing. He brought the spiritual aspect of The Seven Ages of Man to us. It was complicated and he had difficulty explaining with his hesitant English. I helped him with his pronunciation and some of his explanations and consequently made a good friend. At the end of his time with us, I asked him if I could do one of my placements with him and he agreed. So, Paracelsus was confirmed and was to be my first one in September.

Finally, we reached the last term of the therapy training. For me, the whole training had been a form of therapy. I had learned so much about myself. I had taken a long hard look at my qualities but also become familiar with my weaknesses, lack of patience being one of the worst. I had stuck with it because I really wanted to complete the course and become qualified. I was focused and determined to succeed at the work. During this term we had to confirm and arrange each of our placements to be completed in the following year before we could be fully qualified. My placements were to be: the first with Rainer Beyer at the Paracelsus Clinic, the second at Ford Prison, and the third at the Blackthorn Trust in Maidstone - under the watchful eye of Hazel Adams.

There was a custom of having a spectacular bonfire at the Peredur campus on St John's Night and a party to celebrate the students' graduation. Somehow I had reached this point. I would take part in the parade around the bonfire and collect my certificate confirming the completion of the three years. My actual diploma to practice would come after I had completed my placements. It was a special day with singing, dancing and tremendous eats. When the fire had burnt down considerably - all those who could - took a leap of faith over the fire. I just managed to do it, and so ended my time at Tobias. After the celebrations I returned to my small room in the hostel, packed my bags, picked up the dog and drove back to Barnes. And so ended my days as a student.

CHAPTER SEVENTEEN
PLACEMENTS - FORD PRISON & BLACKTHORN TRUST

Layla

In the summer of 1994 I was invited back to Russia to teach painting on the Waldorf Teacher Training course. By now, many of the participants had done sufficient modules to collect their certificates and had started to practise in their respective schools. As a number were ready by now, this was to be a special celebration for their graduation. The instruction took place in a nearby building and we ate at a workers' canteen. I stayed with my interpreter Luda, in her tiny flat which she shared with her son; he had been parked with his grandmother for the duration. I had to share Luda this time and sometimes had another interpreter, whose name was Elly. She visited me in the UK a few years later.

One weekend, I was invited by Tatiana and Misha to their holiday chalet by a lake. On the way there we bought beer at the side of the road in plastic bags which seemed very precarious but they actually survived the journey! Misha had built a smoker in his yard and there were rows of fish which looked like sardines tied to sticks waiting to be smoked. While the fire blazed away we had a few drinks, then ate the fish which Misha had prepared. On the following day he took me for a drive to the border where you could stand with one foot in Europe and the other in Asia. I did so rather ceremoniously.

Although these journeys to Russia were always satisfying and tremendously exciting, I felt that I had had a good stint and that this would be my last, but I hoped my Russian friends would visit me in England. For the moment, I had the more serious task of doing my placements and getting work that would see me through the pretty lean year ahead. When I returned to Barnes I decided I would get back into the cooking game; it was a way of earning in the evenings, enabling me to practise Art Therapy during the day. I wanted to walk to work, so I approached the 'Bull', a pub on the river which had a jazz club in a back room alongside the 'Stable Restaurant', literally in the old stable from when the place had been a coaching inn years ago. I had befriended the landlord and knew he always had a difficult time with staff, partly because he was so ruthless.

I thought it would be alright for a while, as it was not intended to be a major career change. We arranged that I would start as sous chef in October when I returned from Germany where I was going to do my first placement with Rainer Beyer. I was delighted to be working with Rainer. He was a gentle man and incredibly patient with me and everybody else for that matter. He would show me how he ran his studio and I would help him as much as I possibly could with the endeavours but also with his English, which he was keen to improve.

I flew from Heathrow to Stuttgart where Rainer met me at the airport. I had only driven through Germany on the autobahn before so it was wonderful to see the beautiful countryside which we drove through towards Bad Liebenzell and eventually on to Unterlengenhardt, where the Paracelsus Clinic was situated on the edge of the Black Forest. He signed me in and took me to my room where I would stay for the next few weeks. It was at the top of the building and intended for visiting doctors. After dropping my bag off, he took me to his home for a welcome supper with his family.

The next day he met me in the reception area and explained that every morning there would be a briefing for doctors, nurses and therapists. He introduced me at this meeting and as I knew this would be happening I had learned enough German to say how happy and privileged I felt to be doing my placement at the clinic, one of the most highly respected in Germany. They gave me a warm greeting, making me feel welcome and appreciated. Somehow, my nerves vanished and I realised I was in the right place to learn as much as I could from Rainer, at the same time giving fully of myself.

Afterwards we went straight to the art room. It was great to find a good-sized area, well lit, with a number of easels for the patients to use. Each would require a board with a stretched paper, the colours, a rag, two brushes and some water. There were also large tables for working with clay and for drawing on. Unusually, his patients painted dry with plant colour; the majority of Anthroposophical art therapists work 'wet-on-wet' with watercolour. My first task was to grind the pigment ready for the painting. I had worked a little in this medium before so I knew they had to be ground until smooth. They are combined with a special emulsifying liquid. Some, such as red, take time to reach the desired consistency so the whole morning of my first day was spent grinding colours - an exhausting task.

On the initial afternoon, having had a much-needed healthy lunch in the vegetarian restaurant, I spent my time stretching paper on to the boards. There were only a few patients in the art room painting. In the first few days I basically prepared everything and then would observe Rainer. Later, he would give me my own patients to work with. These were the first ones with whom I had had the challenge and the privilege - it was a special moment. I kept a journal of what I was doing with them which would contribute to my thesis to be presented when my placements had been completed. I was in my element helping Rainer, getting the easels ready and cleaning everything up at the end of the day.

One patient he gave me was a young man with liver cancer. During his spell with me he executed three paintings, coming most days. Sadly, whilst I was there, he died of his condition and in a way my painting with him helped him over the threshold. In the clinic was a chapel of rest where the patients would be laid out in preparation for their families to come and pay their respects. He was the first person I had seen dead, it was moving and sad that such a young man should die. I helped prepare him by covering him with a sheet and flowers. All of the team who had treated him were there with his next of kin for the eulogy and blessing. At the end I went over to his family and gave them the paintings he had done with me. They took them very humbly and said they would always treasure them.

My days with Rainer were filled with special people and interesting events. On one occasion I was with a group doing some clay modelling and, having told them how to proceed, decided to do a lemniscate myself. They are hard to do. I was pushing and shoving, trying to get it completed by the end of the afternoon. Rainer noticed that I was red in the face by my efforts and suggested he make an appointment for me to see one of the doctors. I happily accepted his proposal and I did have high blood pressure and Cardiodoran was prescribed which I continued to use for the next year.

On one of our days off, Rainer took me for a drive with his children to the Black Forest. We went to find some caves where there were skeletons of the biggest bear I had ever seen. He also took me to visit King Ludwig's fairytale winter palace in the depths of the Bavarian Forest. When he inherited the throne, Ludwig had this beautiful castle built so that he could escape to the Forest; he loved to get away from the city and his court. Every day he swam in the freezing waters of the lake a short distance away. Much later - although he was a good swimmer - he was drowned in this lake - along with his doctor. Ludwig loved Wagner's music and sponsored him. It is said that because of the king's friendship and support, Wagner is now so well-known and popular today.

My last week in Germany was spent painting with Gerald Wagner and his wife Elizabeth Coc. This famous couple came to give a workshop, basically a training session on the seasons, in plant colour. It would be a wonderful opportunity for me to familiarize myself with this medium and get some instruction from them. I was responsible for stretching all the boards, about forty of them; and mixing and grinding the plant colour in readiness for the workshop. It was a real labour of love and took me the best part of two days to complete, rewarded by a tremendous concert in the hall at Paracelsus and supper with Rainer and his family before the evening began.

An interesting cross section of people came to participate in the workshop. They had come from all over the world. Gerald Wagner was the most respected anthroposophical painter alive, and had a tremendous following. We all felt privileged that we were in the presence of the master. On the first day we were divided into two groups, one with Elizabeth and the other with Gerald. I was in Elizabeth's group but Gerald would come and visit all the students, regularly. When he came to see what I was doing he noticed how some of my colour work had become sticky and dense, which sometimes happens with this medium. He said, 'You must use the sponge!' Taking my sponge, he dabbed the offending paint away and said, 'Now, you have let in the light!' It was a revelation to me how he used that sponge, and now it is my best friend on those kind of 'sticky' occasions.

We produced a painting every day over five days. It was a challenge for me to work in this new medium, and was good to become aware of the different qualities of the colour. There is a translucent quality about it which can make the painting appear to shine. At the end of our time together, we presented our work and Gerald selected some paintings and explained why he had chosen them. This was useful to have the benefit of plant colour pointed out; in some respects it was obvious. One of the days, he chose one of mine - a small confirmation that I had mastered working with them. It was a wonderful experience to be working with other artists and therapists from all over the world.

September had been a special month for me - working with Rainer in the art room and getting to know his family. I was especially impressed by the way they cared for their patients who had died whilst at Paracelsus. There were others as well as my patient and if I was involved in any way I would be expected to attend; it was always very respectful and moving. I finished off my time there by preparing everything for the workshop and participating in it. It was satisfying to come home with a big roll of paintings under my arm. Then I had to make an attempt to get back to some kind of normality.

As soon as I returned I started working in the evenings at the 'Stable Restaurant'. My role was to cook the supper for the staff, having prepared all the vegetables beforehand. The chef was a stocky Moroccan, smelly, short and bad-tempered. If he had a lot of orders in at one time he could be quite unbearable. It was hard graft, often spending eight hours on your feet - ending up with your legs feeling like lead. Producing food under such pressure, I was on a very steep learning curve. The worst thing the chef did, rather too often, was to overcook a steak or a duck breast. Thankfully, the job did not last for long as I had a huge row with him and walked out in disgust.

My next placement was at H.M. Prison in Ford, Sussex. I had been in correspondence with the Governor and had a meeting with him. He showed me over the campus and appreciated my coming, because we are not paid to do these placements. On my first day, having been told to wear trousers so as not to upset the men - I was met at the gate and taken over to the education wing, to a chorus of whistles. Once safely inside the purpose-built building I met Frank, the young man who had been selected for me to work with. He was virtually blind in one eye due to a conker fight in his youth, and was recovering from drug addiction.

We worked together every day for a month and by the end of our time together he was a changed man. He literally altered before my eyes as we painted and talked together. He told me what he was in for and how he was trying to give up drugs because his addiction had got him into so much trouble. He had robbed a garage at gun point, bashed up a few people, and run off with the money. He had a young family to support and desperately wished to stay straight for them. I certainly wanted to help him because he was sincere and a charming individual whom I knew could change his life for the better. When working with somebody so intensely you have to make a plan, ideally to create about twenty paintings. Within these there is often one which facilitates 'the turning point' as I call it. For Frank, it was when he did his fire; it was amazing with really strong flames shooting upwards and at the same time the painting was well grounded with a substantial fire beneath the flames. In these few days the colour had rekindled his soul and awakened his spirit. We had made excellent progress. He also realized he was not colour blind after all, as he had thought.

It was a tremendously satisfying time. On the last day I made an exhibition of his work and invited the Governor and Education Officers to come and see it. They were impressed but also amazed at the difference in the man. From a shy person who had shuffled in to meet me, now came this upright, smiling individual, proud of what he had achieved. He was determined to continue to paint when he got 'outside'. On further discussion with the Governor, he said he would be delighted for me to come and work there. Within months, however, Michael Howard had taken the money out of the Education Budget for Prisons. I think one of the stupidest things a Home Secretary ever did and my plans for working with the Prison Service went up in smoke.

In Barnes again I decided to look for work as a care assistant, on the condition that I could do art therapy with the client. I joined an organisation called the Skylark Agency and started immediately to do the occasional shift. The work involved helping with dressing, washing, meals and shopping. Occasionally I would do a sleepover, helping with bedtime - which was when there could be all sorts of dramas, such as falling out of bed or having nightmares.

Once I was asked to look after a woman for a week. Her husband had been the main carer throughout her illness and he had been advised to have a rest. So I agreed to do it on condition that we painted everyday whilst he went to sunny Madeira on a short holiday. Before he left I went round to their house, which was just five minutes away from mine, to have a look at the layout and find out Jane's routine. They were a charming couple and had been together for years, during the last eight of which she had been ill and latterly confined to a wheelchair. Her husband did everything for her with some help from Social Services. There was a stair lift in the house - so I went round to practise helping her on to the seat and taking her off at the top of the stairs. A nurse came in the mornings to help with washing and dressing. Jane was a heavy women and not easy to move around but she had developed ways to help herself; between us we would be able to manage.

We soon developed a routine of breakfast in bed, getting up and dressing when the nurse arrived; then we'd go downstairs for painting. I had brought my equipment with me: a board, paper, brushes and my basket of pre-mixed colours. As I had five days to paint with her, I decided to do the ages of man starting with early childhood. Her first 'wet-in wet' painting was a landscape with a church in it and two children walking hand in hand to worship. She explained she was with her sister. Later, I would hear from the family that this couple were in fact atheists and did not go to church now. Finding this out, that first painting was most significant. We painted every morning, before perhaps going for a walk around the pond or doing some shopping. On a couple of occasions I took her to have lunch with neighbours, one of whom happened to be a doctor.

In conversation I told her about my recent trip to Italy and that for the first time I had been brave enough to fill a sketchbook with drawings. She wanted to see it, so I returned to my studio to get it. I showed it to her and we had an interesting conversation about some of the paintings I had drawn. They were mainly religious images and she seemed delighted with them. We had a light supper together, having been out to lunch, and she then asked to go to bed. I put her to bed tenderly, she had had quite a day. She was excited because her husband was coming back the next day. After watching something on television, I went to bed on the floor above. She usually called me with a bell during the night to help her on to the commode.

The following morning I woke, she had not called me. I thought it strange, put on my dressing gown and went down. She was lying on her side and had died during the night. I felt for a pulse but there was none and her body was cold. She looked beautiful and at peace. It was an awful and unexpected moment. I decided to go and have a shower to prepare myself and then go round to the doctor, whom we had seen the day before. It was still early in the morning as I rang their bell and told them the news. He said he would call the hotel to tell her husband, and I then called her doctor, the nurse, and the funeral director. The nurse was the first to arrive and tearfully we prepared to lay her out on the bed. I covered her in flowers as at Paracelsus.

I then called the funeral directors' and explained the situation. I did not want her moved until later in the day. I told the undertaker I was expecting her husband home in the afternoon from Madeira and wanted him to be able to say his goodbyes in their home. Her doctor arrived to sign the death certificate and it was only then that I discovered she had had eight previous heart attacks and that her death was almost expected. It was a small consolation because you do feel responsible when somebody dies in your care. When all the arrangements had been made, I gathered my things and went for a walk by the river and had a good weep. I returned to my place to tell my parents what had happened, and tried to relax.

Approaching their house to welcome her husband back was one of the hardest things I have ever done. All I could do was give him a big hug and hold him while we had a weep together; he then went upstairs to say his goodbyes. He came down, we had a cup of tea, and I showed him Jane's paintings. Soon after this the funeral directors arrived and took her body away. When I got home I called Evelyn Capel, priest at the Christian Community, and told her what had happened. She said, 'My dear, the painting helped her over the threshold.' I realised that it had moved something in her. Showing her the sketchbook had probably helped her on her way as well, and I felt a little better. Jane had been in pain and discomfort for some considerable time - now she was pain free, bless her.

I continued with my care work and also arranged to paint at Vera Gray House, an old people's home, in the area. Soon, it would be Christmas and time to welcome in the New Year. I went down to my parents as usual, for the celebrations, but I was feeling rather subdued due to Jane's death and cremation, where all the relatives had been present. I had explained our last week together many times and shown the family her paintings, one of which - a self-portrait - they had framed and put on the wall.

I now spent long weekends with my parents; they were both getting on in age but at the same time keeping fit and active. My mother was an excellent flower-arranger and belonged to a couple of clubs, and was the president of one of them. Occasionally I would accompany her to a meeting and watch a local demonstrator share some of the tricks of the trade, such as wiring long unstable flowers or pinning large leaves to show off the shine or the colour. Years later, I had a go myself at arranging flowers, and remembered some of the things I had learnt from my mother's many beautiful flower arrangements. It had been her way of showing her creative talent.

The following spring I went to Maidstone to do my final placement at the Blackthorn Trust. I would be assisting Hazel Adams with her patients and would also have some of my own. In theory, the Trust is a normal general practice but a special one as it incorporates a number of therapies into its treatments. Most importantly, it is an anthroposophical clinic. Hence, my reason for wanting to be there and by necessity discussing patients with a doctor. It would actually be the first and only time that I would do this with anthroposophical doctors, so it was an especially enlightening and rewarding experience.

As I would be there for two months I arranged to stay with a friend who lived in Nutley. My dog Teal came with me, and stayed with my friend during the day. I went to Maidstone in the morning and came back in time for supper. At the weekends I returned to London and visited various groups in the homes there. It was a pleasant relaxed time; I was given patients to work with, and I could discuss treatments and therapy with Hazel and the doctor concerned. The Trust had weekly meetings where you had the opportunity to go into detail about the patient with everybody who was working with them. This was a great practice and I was able to learn so much from everybody's input. I remained there for the spring of 1995, arriving just after Easter and staying until the end of May. In all I must have had about a dozen patients, some of whom would come back on a regular basis, others came for just a few visits. I decided to use Frans Marc's paintings, so when a patient was able - they would start by making a copy. This is an interesting way of working and can be particularly worthwhile. During my time there I had to keep a journal which I used to prepare for my presentation to Hazel at the end of my tenure. The best thing about being at the Blackthorn Trust was having Hazel's advice and support whilst working in this unusually special environment with anthroposophical doctors. After my time there, I set about writing my thesis discussing all of my placements with prisoners and with patients. When my thesis was completed, I would present it to the school.

On returning to London I began to work with Annie, a patient paralysed from the neck down in a fall and was in a wheelchair most of the time. She was in the Roehampton Brain Damage Unit and I visited her regularly there to paint with her. She could not hold the brush but I did get a response when I painted for her, her eyes would flicker in approval or she would shake her head, slightly, in disapproval of a colour for example. After I had been visiting her in the hospital for some time, I was asked to be her carer at their holiday cottage in West Wittering and also to help care for her in their Chelsea house. She had a devoted partner who would help me to lift and wash her. He tried hard to allow her to be at home occasionally.

One weekend in Sussex we invited some friends of theirs (who ran a marvellous clothes shop) for Sunday lunch. I had cooked a delicious shoulder of lamb with roast potatoes, parsnips and other vegetables, followed by a rhubarb crumble. As I had had the shop in the Kings Road in the sixties, I could not resist talking about those times. An animated conversation followed about the Rag Trade and about buying and making clothes. The friends were having difficulty getting stuff delivered in time from South America for the appropriate season. The best thing was that Annie, who was seated at the top of the table in her wheelchair, thoroughly enjoyed the conversation and was in her own way taking part.

The summer was going to be fun as I was going to teach at two interesting workshops. The first was to be in Kings Caple, Herefordshire and was called 'A Celtic Journey'. It was being organised by a group of parents from the Waldorf school in Much Dewchurch. I arrived with the dog and stayed above the stables; most of the others were in the main house at Poulstone Court. It was a wonderful week, visiting various churches such as the beautiful Norman Kilpeck Church, which has many extraordinary corbels of animals, faces and figures on the pillars, over arches and around the eaves, carved by medieval masons in the Herefordshire Romanesque style. We also visited local Arthurian sites - Merlin's Cave and Arthur's Stone.

Some afternoons were my painting time with the participants, when we followed the King's trail working with the Arthurian stories. Many had done some painting before but others were new to the 'wet-in-wet' technique. They enjoyed it and did some excellent work which we exhibited later. The week at Poulstone Court was a real journey of discovery for me. Herefordshire was glorious, and as we were leaving after the workshop I turned to Teal and said, 'We will be coming back here - you just wait and see'.

I had also been invited to teach on the annual Curative Eurythmy Course on the Peredur Campus. Staying for the period with my friend in Nutley, it would be something I would continue to do for the next few years; in fact - until the training stopped. It was the only curative course in English for eurythmists who had completed their artistic training and wanted to work with eurythmy in a healing way. They travelled from all over the world. I was once again in the same top studio at Tobias with about thirty students. The most difficult thing for me was remembering all of their names as they came from so many different countries.

Steiner had given two sequences for eurythmists to use in a curative way. Now that we would be painting these, they would be, forever emblazoned in their memories. One was known as the cancer sequence which is made up of O.E.M.L.I.B.D. The other was connected to asthma. Each part had three colours attributed to it by Steiner, and we painted one part a day. We started with the movement and the sound, connected to the consonant or vowel, before painting it. In the painting - one colour would be connected to the movement, another to the temperament and another to the character. It was a fascinating journey and was incredibly powerful. Each morning I would put all the paintings up from the day before, for the students to see.

At the end of the week, having come to a profound understanding of the sequence, we selected one painting from each day and displayed the whole thing. On the last day we performed it in the way that it should be used with patients. This teaching was one of the most inspiring and rewarding I have ever done, and I made many good friends in the process, some of whom are still in contact with me. This exercise is incredibly energising and uplifting, and I find it very good to use it with my own patients and for my own protective purposes.

When I returned home to Barnes, I discovered my diploma waiting for me. I was pleased that a stressful year had been worthwhile. My reward came in the form of Tobias; a friend's cat had had kittens so when they were ready I had one of them. Within weeks I collected him and named him Tobias. Now I had a dog called Teal and the kitten. After a few days of fear, the kitten warmed to the dog and even ended up suckling from her. For the moment Tobias was an indoor cat and quickly settled into our life. I have always liked to have my animals from babies, probably because I have none of my own; therefore each animal I have is precious.

Just as you feel everything is going along nicely there has to be a nasty surprise. This time it was that my landlady was going to sell the building where I had the top flat, or as I called it, my studio. In some respects it was good as I was a sitting tenant; whoever bought it would have to pay a fee to get rid of me. I decided to sit tight and see what happened. Being on a prime site in Barnes High Street it was soon snapped up by an estate agent, which again was lucky because they know the going rate for sitting tenants. I was delighted when they offered me £10,000 to leave, allowing me time to find somewhere else, the flat being the last floor in the building to be converted.

I continued to do my care work for Skylark and would have all kinds of patients to look after, including Annie. One in particular became a firm favourite. He had had a stroke and found it difficult to walk and talk. I would arrive early, having exercised the dog, get him up, wash and dress him, and sometimes give him a massage because his joints were stiff. I would then bring him down on the stair lift for breakfast, and take him to his chair for his coffee. He read the papers and when I had cleared up he would do some painting. His wife was pleased I was around because it gave her a break. I stayed there a few months and by the time I left, he was able to walk with sticks down to the pub for a pint and also to go swimming. With his strong will, he had made tremendous progress. I like to think the painting helped with his recovery because you can use certain exercises to strengthen the resolution.

In the meantime, I was looking in the paper for flats to rent, mainly in the Barnes area where I wanted to stay. Of course, everything would be terrible expensive there. I had been very lucky in the past, finding incredibly reasonably priced accommodation. By the New Year it had became increasingly apparent that the ones I liked were way beyond my means. There would be a deposit and a few months' rent to pay in advance. There would be nothing left of my little nest egg, especially as I was planning to pay back the 'Godparents'. One day, contemplating my future in the local coffee shop, I saw an advertisement in 'The Lady' - a cook/housekeeper was needed to look after a couple in Herefordshire. I had enjoyed myself at Poulstone Court and loved the countryside. I applied and wrote sending my CV to the couple who lived in Breinton, west of Hereford.

While I waited for a reply I decided to have another go with prison work. I called Holloway Women's Prison and arranged to do a day there and also approached Latchmere House, another near Richmond Park. The day at Holloway was fine, if a little harrowing, having to deal with some really tough women. It was a long drive there and hard to park. I decided on Latchmere House and agreed to do six sessions over a six-week period. I had a group of six men, all rather cheeky and difficult to control. There was one awful day when one chap took his palette and emptied all the colours on to the paper and mashed them around with his hands, and all the others followed suit. I am glad to say it was my last session and I did not apply for more. Thankfully, I soon received a reply from Eileen Sidders inviting me to come for an interview in Hereford.

It was Easter and I had agreed to look after my man with the stroke at their country home in the Cotswolds over the holiday. I decided to drive on from there for my Hereford interview with the Sidders. It was lovely driving through the beautiful countryside and felt this would suit me well. I felt I was finally ready to leave London. I arrived in good time, and had been told to look out for some stag's antlers on the gateposts of the house. I parked in front of a beautiful old residence and was soon greeted by Eileen, who was delightful. The special thing about the job for me was that it came with my own accommodation. I was shown this almost as soon as I arrived - the old gardener's cottage. After being shown this and the garden at the rear, we returned to the house through to the main kitchen to have lunch and discuss the detail.

There would be no pay as such but I had my home free. Most afternoons I would be able to work with my Art Therapy clients. I would cook every day, usually lunch and dinner. We would do the shopping between us, or sometimes it would be delivered. Occasionally, there would be guests and maybe a party - none of which sounded too daunting. Sometimes when Eileen was away, I would be expected to look after Douglas. Best of all - they agreed that I could bring Tobias and Teal, and that the gardener's cottage was quite separate from the main house.

Eileen had prepared a marvellous lunch of a lightly-cooked whole salmon with new potatoes, peas and salad with hot bread. My thought was, why have me if she can produce such delicious food, served with homemade mayonnaise? We women, do not like to have to produce tempting food every day, except of course if it is our job. We got on well. They were genuinely interested in my work in prisons and I told them some of my escapades. They both had a great sense of humour and seemed happy for me to try to get some clients as a therapist, and as the animals could come too I was well pleased! To my surprise they accepted me there and then, telling me there had been twelve other applicants. The one thing I would have to get used to was cooking on an Aga, which I had not done since I was a kid.

I drove back to London feeling as high as a kite. Just thinking about my proposed new life made me excited. I had loved Herefordshire on my first visit and now I would be able to explore it more fully and find out about the history of the area for myself. The money had come through from the estate agents so I was able to tidy up my financial affairs, with a little left over to live on. In the next few weeks I told everybody I was off to live in the country. I got rid of as much stuff as I could to charity shops, and packed my remaining things into boxes. I then hired a white van to bring the heavier furniture to Hereford, and one day in early May 1996 packed my Volvo, the one I had bought from Gill, and set off for Breinton. The dog and the cat in his carrier were on the front seat. With the cat howling all the way there, it was quite a difficult drive and I was relieved to arrive in one piece.

CHAPTER EIGHTEEN
MOVING WEST

May your little light shine

I announced my arrival at Breinton to Eileen and she suggested I unpack and get settled in. I went across later to cook supper for them. As it was the first one they invited me to eat with them. I had left the animals in the house with a cat-litter box for Tobias as I wanted to keep him in, to start with. When I got back the cat was missing. I thought he must have got out so I went around the garden calling for him, without success, I then called my parents to tell them I had arrived safely, but that the cat had vanished. In the middle of this call I heard him 'Meow'. The cat had been hiding up the chimney! With difficulty, I pulled him down; he was as black as soot. I then had to shampoo him; surprisingly he let me do so.

The first week Eileen showed me where the suppliers were and introduced the butcher and fishmonger. We did the shopping together but in future I would do this alone. That weekend they were going to a private view at The Tidal Wave Gallery in Hereford, and invited me to join them. It was a wonderful exhibition by Crispin Thornton-Jones with some huge landscape paintings and, contrastingly, smaller tender portraits. I met the artist and congratulated him on his excellent work and told him that I had just moved to the area and would be hoping to exhibit later. He assured me that Hereford was a good place for an artist to live and practise, though much of his work would be commissioned portraits in London. Later Crispin set up a successful gallery of his own in Hay-on-Wye.

Within days of arriving - I felt comfortable and happy to be in Breinton. The river was near and every morning I walked the dog along the bank, each time going a little further, and in the end I found a good circular walk. When I eventually let the cat out, Tobias also came as far as the river with us and then dashed back to the safety of the garden. My days involved shopping and cooking lunch and/or supper. Occasionally, Eileen and Douglas had guests to stay or held a dinner party. Then sometimes I would cook the meal, serve it and then join the gathering, which was nice for me as I knew few people in Herefordshire to start with. Sometimes the gatherings were more formal affairs, and then I would vanish, thankfully, to the kitchen and get on with the washing up.

Now I needed to find some work - my funds would not last long and I had to pay my own bills, such as the telephone. I had seen a rather grand old people's home, called The Weir, near to Breinton and decided to pop in and meet the manageress to see if there was anyone there who would be interested in art therapy. She said she thought she had somebody who would be interested, but would have to contact the family first. Within days I was being interviewed by her sons in their office in Hereford and they agreed that I could work with their mother once a week. We would continue to have monthly meetings to see how she was progressing. This relationship continued successfully for several years.

One of the first things I did was to visit Hereford Cathedral, dedicated to St Mary the Virgin and St Ethelbert the King. It is a beautiful building and has the most welcoming atmosphere of any such place I know. It was built in the twelfth century from Herefordshire pink limestone and has a warm glow about it especially when the sun is shining. The Norman arches in the nave greet you and the stained glass windows shine down on you. There are a number of modern pieces of art there including three John Piper tapestries. There is a beautiful corona above the high alter, made in metal with silver and gilt finishes. The sculptor, Simon Beer won a competition ahead of a number of applicants. It was put in place in 1992 as a memorial to Bishop John Eastaugh's episcopate.

The Lady Chapel is a wonderful place to sit and contemplate one's future, but my favourite spot is a small private chapel where you can stay for as long as you like. I visited this chapel regularly and offer up some of the awful things which have happened in my life. One of the worst experiences of my life was my abortion - and this is also my greatest regret. At the time I felt it was the wrong time for me to bring a child into the world and that I could have a baby later. But you cannot do that when a baby is conceived, they come for a reason. It was even more sad for me because I lost twins and never had any other children.

Before coming to Herefordshire, I had written to two organisations in the hope of finding some employment. The first was the Steiner School at Much Dewchurch, where they had indicated that they needed an art teacher for the older pupils. They interviewed me, and the discussion went very well. I remember laying out my work for them to see and having an animated conversation about anthroposophical education and art. They wrote and said they were delighted to meet me and were interested but, sadly, could not pay me. I had decided I had done enough voluntary work and was not going to do any more. Eventually I managed to gather some paid pupils from the school for art therapy. Similarly with St Michael's Hospice - they wanted me to paint with a group - unpaid.

I had hoped to organise some workshops to go to with Eileen. I found a woodcarving course and another one for pottery. Unfortunately, Eileen did not have the time to join me. The first group I joined was for woodcarving; I had done carving in both art schools and wanted to continue with it. My teacher Chris Pye was just the right person to get me going again. He suggested I begin by working in relief, because his students found it was good practice in using a number of different tools. I then moved on to a bigger and better relief, of an angel, and have since carved some quite large pieces out of lime, oak, and ash.

I had a few more art therapy clients at the Weir Nursing Home, where my main important contact was Anna Irwin. She worked there doing reflexology, and occasionally we would be present at the same time. On one occasion we discussed the possibility of opening a therapy clinic together in Hereford. The seed was planted then and a year or so later we did exactly that. We opened on the top floor above an estate agents in Bridge Street. It was an ambitious move but worth having a go as the rent was reasonable.

For the moment I was still struggling to get things together. Luckily for me Bibi, a friend from Barnes, happened to work in Hereford. She would come up most weeks and stay with me, usually for about three days. We made a B/B arrangement which also included an evening meal. It was a real life-saver for me at the time because I was still finding my way and badly needed a few more clients. Gradually they came and I was able to live comfortably albeit frugally. One of these clients still paints with me today.

Now I had time to do my own painting, and had the idea of arranging an exhibition of my work. I approached a gallery called the 'Mayor's Parlour' in Hereford. A few hundred years ago, the gallery had actually been the Mayor's parlour; it was a lovely bright airy space in Church Street. I rented the place for a week and set about getting various paintings framed. I held the exhibition in the summer of 1997 and it was a great success. Well - I sold a few paintings and invited many friends to come and see me there. It is important to sell something!

I was happy in Breinton. I enjoyed cooking for Eileen and I especially loved my garden. It gave me the opportunity to plant vegetables and flowers of my own choice and have my own supply of vegetables, although there were plenty available grown by George, the surly gardener. Douglas also worked there most days and I could always ask his advice. He was pleased to help and just watching him was instructive. He made a beautiful woodland garden while I was there, of which he was very proud. On my birthday, I had a party in the garden and invited my parents and a number of friends from London. One of these - Fiona - had arranged for everybody to give me woodcarving tools. She had suggested this and organised it herself, which touched me greatly. Finally, I had a magnificent set of tools which would last me a lifetime.

I often attended our local church, 'St. Michael and All Angels' with Douglas. Eileen was not keen to come so we went together. The vicar, Graham Sykes and his wife Clare became my good friends. They had decided to adopt a toddler called Sophie and soon after she arrived, they had asked me to look after her in church. Clare was working at another church in Tupsley, so she could not take Sophie herself. Graham wanted the little girl to have experience of attending church services from an early age and so I would take her up to the altar for a blessing during communion. Happily for all, this arrangement continued for some time.

In September I joined Mary Kenny's pottery class in Weobley. She is an excellent potter and an especially good teacher and I still attend these classes today. New people have joined us but basically we are still the same core group, always lunching at 'Jules' first. Again, Eileen decided not to come with me as she had become interested in playing bridge and seemed keen to do that. My first pottery effort was a pinched pot, where you start with a ball of clay and pinch it out until you have a lovely thin bowl with a curly edge. They are fun to do, and sometimes I ask a patient to make one of these. As I continued with Mary's class, I learnt how to throw pots and how to make quite large sculptures using the slabbing method.

I was regularly driving around the countryside and discovering many amazing churches and museums in the most unlikely places. Ludlow is an hour away and has a magnificent castle where they perform Shakespeare in the summer. Usually this is around my birthday, so that it has become a regular treat. You can take a picnic to have with friends beforehand and hope that it will not rain. I have sat and watched a performance, in the pouring rain, but in a way - it is all part of the fun. The cathedral is also a favourite place to take visitors to see the beautiful windows and hear the superb choir.

One day when Bibi was staying with me, we decided to meet in Hereford for a drink at the bar of the Green Dragon Hotel. We sometimes went out together when she was here. On this occasion, I was early; and sitting in the bar with a beer was a charming man with a natty beard. We started talking. We had had quite a conversation by the time Bibi arrived and I had told him I could not stay long as I had to get back to run the jam stall at the Breinton fete. I had invited him to come, not thinking for a moment he would. Bibi and I finished our drinks and I left for Breinton. Many local people had offered produce for the fete, held in our garden - to raise funds for the church.

Oliver, the man with the natty beard, came along and, to my surprise bought six pots of jam. 'Gosh,' I thought, 'he must have a sweet tooth!' He stayed for the whole afternoon and I ended up asking him back to my place for a drink and, inevitably, supper. He needed to talk and did just that, telling me about his wives who had sadly died, one of them quite recently. I am a good listener so heard the full story, with all his embellishments. It was a sorry tale, the deaths being precipitated by trips abroad with him on holiday. Both were unexpected and quite sudden, difficult for anybody to cope with. So I was sympathetic and agreed to have dinner with him later in the week to continue the conversation.

In the meantime, I wanted to sing again and found a choir called The Singing Tree. A friend, a member of the choir, was giving a party which they would attend so I was invited along to check out the singing. What impressed me most was that they seemed to manage without any sheet music. This included African, Spanish, Croatian and French songs in other words 'World Music.' They made a wonderful sound and seemed a great bunch of people. As usual there were not many men amongst them, but I did catch the eye of one of the tenors. Later, I would join them and in fact I still sing with them, though the venue has changed and the leader is now a lovely lady called Lizzie.

One day when Douglas and I were working in the garden together he told me he had a terrible pain in his back and right leg. He had been loading a shredder with twigs and branches, a hard job, and had become exhausted. I suggested he see his doctor. He did, and returned with the devastating news that he had a tumour on his back which would have to be removed. It was a terrible time for Eileen, driving him to Cheltenham for the operation and for radiotherapy over a period of months. He struggled hard to recover but it was terminal. He ventured out into the garden on his sticks but never fully recovered from the huge operation; he also lost his appetite and, not surprisingly, his sense of humour.

Oliver by now had started to become part of my life with the occasional dinner at my place or at his. The change happened when he told me he was going to Portsmouth for the submariners' reunion dinner. This was something my father had done every year for as long as I could remember and I knew they would have a lot in common. They had both been in the Royal Navy so would immediately have something to talk about. That year my father was not going because he had not been well. Oliver went and on the way back came to meet my parents as I had conveniently gone to stay with them. Mummy had cooked her usual amazing Sunday lunch and was particularly put out because Oliver did not mention the meal: he was too busy chatting to my father about mutual friends.

We both had come in our separate cars and when Oliver left, I quizzed them about him. They said he was much too old for me: he was, indeed, ten years my senior. I did not mind. He had become a good friend and we both needed the company of each other to express our ambitions and expectations in later life. Early on in the relationship, he had indicated to me that there would be no sex because he had had a serious illness which had made him impotent. I thought it would be fine because, at this stage of my life, I did not want any physical relations. I had had enough sex and the complications that inevitably accompany it - for a lifetime.

Since I arrived in Herefordshire I had heard of an initiative to build a special home for severely disabled youngsters. The fund raising was spearheaded by a parent of such a child and it would be called the 'Martha Trust'. It sounded just the place where I should be working. I wrote with my credentials and thankfully they wrote back interested in some art therapy. I started with them as soon as the home was up and running. It was a very special place and I continued there, once a week, for the next eight years. It was enough for me for the clients to remember who I was and to know they looked forward to their painting. Many could not talk or hold the brush so I would paint for them, holding the brush in their hand under mine.

Everything was beginning to take shape and I was getting settled into my new life in Herefordshire. It was a gentle relaxed place and moving at a pace of its own, so unlike London. But it could not remain peaceful for long - the next dreadful thing that happened was that I received a call from my mother to tell me that my father had had a stroke. Leaving the cat in Eileen's care and taking the dog with me, I set off at once for Chichester Hospital to see him. I drove like a bat out of hell until the car started overheating and choking badly. I was nearly there - so I put on the fan, cut the engine, and free-wheeled as much as I could until I arrived. I rushed to the ward where I found the entire family at his bedside. He was in a coma. We stood around him in a kind of a trance, in absolute disbelief that this could be happening to a man who, right up to the end, had kept reasonably fit, doing push-ups on a regular basis.

On my visit a few weeks earlier, he had told me to take his car if anything happened to him. When I was alone with him, I explained the trouble I had had with my car on the way there. Although he could not actually talk, I felt he wanted me to take the car as we both knew mine had had it. I was convinced that he gave me a little squeeze, agreeing to it. It was a sad time for all the family, feeling most inadequate and not being able to do much except love him totally. On leaving I filled my radiator with water and managed to get it safely back to Aldwick, where I would stay to comfort my mother for the next few days. We continued to visit Daddy in the hospital. The house was very strange without his presence.

I transferred the insurance from my car to my father's car and drove it back to Hereford. It was a relief to be driving something that felt as if it had enough power; mine had become rather inadequate. I had left it at my mother's and would sell it later. When I got back to Breinton, Douglas was still not well but trying to make a slow recovery. It was a miserable time because I soon heard that my father had died, never having regained consciousness. I went back to Aldwick for the funeral. My sister Trisha had been there the day Daddy died, so she had done all the necessary things like registering the death and making the funeral arrangements. Oliver came with me to the funeral, and was a great support at this difficult time.

The funeral was a magnificent affair. It was in their local church which they had attended for some considerable time. They were well respected in the community and he was known as the 'Captain' because of the medals he wore on Armistice Day. All their friends and the larger family were there; it was quite a crowd and I felt we gave him a good send off. The four siblings had planned the funeral, choosing the hymns and the readings. Each one of us did our bit and read something. I had arranged for a friend to come and sing 'Panis Angelicus' which he sang beautifully. Oliver was supportive and a great help - giving out the Order of Service and showing people to their seats.

Everybody was invited back to the house where we had all contributed to making canapés and sandwiches. We drank to Daddy's long life in champagne and talked about the family which now had become pretty dispersed. It was an opportunity for me to introduce Oliver to everybody because no one really knew who he was until then. We stayed with Mummy for a few days and then set off for Hereford again. On our return Douglas was making slow progress but he was not himself. It was a subdued Christmas. I was coming to terms with my father's death and Oliver was good to have around at this time. I, on the other hand, was miserable company for him.

January is always a slow month and it seemed to take ages to pass. In February Douglas sadly died. The night before I had cooked him his favourite meal, which was kedgeree. Whenever I prepare it now it reminds me of a dear, kind man who had become a surrogate father to me, with my parents being so far away. Again, there was a funeral to arrange, at St Michaels. Our vicar Graham made a suitable service for him and the church was packed. At the reception I tried to cook some delicacies he would have liked; it was quite a spread. It was the end of an era for many there, including me. I remember sitting with the gardener and chatting about our respective plans.

I struggled to keep my spirits up. For the first time in my life I felt really sad and depressed. I continued to do my work with patients and at Martha House and also attended my various classes. I was now seeing Oliver on a regular basis; he had become the man in my life and certainly helped me through this difficult stage. One of the things we discussed was taking a holiday together. He came up with the idea of going on safari to Kenya. As this was something I had always wanted to do, I agreed wholeheartedly and we spent the next month making the necessary arrangements. Eileen was not adverse to my leaving her as she was suffering her own grief and needed time alone to make her own plans to move out of the house. Mummy, however, was not so pleased because on previous occasions both Oliver's wives had died as a result of a holiday with him!

It was exciting when we finally set off from Heathrow, and I was beginning to feel a bit more cheerful. I had packed some summer things as it would be warm: Oliver had his African shirts from the time he had lived in Angola. We had bought a safari package where we would have our own driver who collected us from the airport and took us to our Nairobi hotel. We spent a couple of days in the capital, after which he came back and collected us to take us to our first destination - the Maasai Mara Safari Park. We were pleased to have the driver to ourselves, instead of having to share a minibus with four other couples. There had been a murder on one of the parks recently and people had been too scared to come to Kenya.

It was thrilling to be there and be driven by a knowledgeable man who, during our time with him, told us a great deal about the politics of this developing country. After a long drive we arrived at the Mara Lodge and settled into our new surroundings where we would stay for a week. The next morning our first excursion was breathtaking. We had an early breakfast with the sun rising as we set off. We were soon out on the wild savannah. Almost the first thing we saw was a cheetah with her three cubs. What a stroke of luck ! They were magnificent. We drove on through herds of Thomson's gazelles beside the Mara River and saw hippos enjoying themselves in the water. I had bought a new camera, so we were both taking shots of the wild life. It was a photographer's paradise. A memorable moment came, when, on our way back, a lioness approached and stole the kill of a deer from our cheetah, only to have it taken away again by a big male lion. We held our breath as we saw the cheetah trying to hide her cubs in the long tufted grass. She did, and they remained safely among the reeds, away from the hungry lions.

I had brought my paints with me and made a few sketches of the huge luminous skies and vast landscape. I literally just had to step outside the room and the view was right there in front of me, with wart hogs dashing around with their young. Another fabulous moment was when, one evening, a group of incredibly tall Maasai came to perform for us. What they were actually doing was a war dance from years before which they had perfected for the tourist trade. They were beautiful people, thin and graceful, dressed in vibrant colourful clothes with loads of beads around the women's necks which jangled as they moved up and down. It was strangely hypnotic and most impressive as the men jumped, feet into the air, holding their spears.

We then moved north to another park, passing Mount Kenya and stopping in a place which I called Noah's Ark. It had been built especially to observe animals coming to the waterhole to drink. You walked across a bridge to board the building which was designed rather like a boat. We sat up half the night watching various wild life appearing to drink, the most impressive being the elephants. There was one baby with them who was finding his way and practising squirting water over the others. It was a truly memorable experience. The next morning we were on our way again, stopping at an enormous waterfall and a shimmering lake with hundreds of flamingos - great photo opportunities.

Knowing Kenyans like to barter, I had brought some wood-carving tools with me, which I had purchased reasonably from Chris Pye. I planned to exchange these tools for a carving. We stopped at a gallery bursting with examples to select from. We took our time choosing what to buy; the quality varied greatly, so one had to be careful. Eventually, I chose a family group of Maasai standing together carved in jet - a hard, almost black wood. It was beautifully worked and they wanted plenty for it. I showed them my tools and their eyes opened wide; they had never seen anything like them before as they carve with knives.

We negotiated a good price for this group carving along with others. As we left, the trader said, holding a tool with a smile, 'I will use this one for circumcision.'

Our final visit would be to Amboseli, a special park reserved for a large herd of elephants. With Mount Kilimanjaro looming in the background, we were driving towards the lodge when our driver noticed a leopard; unbeknown to us, this was a rare sight. The driver left the road to follow the beast, although he was not supposed to do so in this reserve. The beautiful leopard leapt up into a tree some distance away from us, but luckily we were able to have a good look at him through our binoculars. We arrived safely and elated by our adventure and checked in. We had a drink in the bar, having dressed for dinner later in the splendid dining room. At this Lodge we would spend many wonderful hours following the elephants. They were always in families, usually with a matriarch in front keeping an eye on the mothers with youngsters running at their feet. So glorious to see how tender they are to the young and to each other. There was one with a damaged foot which they all seemed concerned about and were keeping a watchful eye on.

On our last day, having had a good rummage in the shop and drinks on the terrace, we moved into the dining room for our final meal. The food was good with an excellent selection, both hot and cold dishes. Oliver ordered champagne, which was rather special, and I wondered why. Over dinner, he broached the delicate subject of our future together. I said that it was a little early to think too seriously about such things because his second wife had only recently died and I did not want to insult her two sons. I had met both of them and certainly did not want to hurt them in any way. But it did make me think though: with the success of this holiday behind us, maybe it could work if we were to get married. With these thoughts buzzing in my head, we packed our bags for the airport.

We flew to London, collected the car, and drove back to Herefordshire where Oliver dropped me off in Breinton. He was living in Ross-on-Wye at the time and my thought was that I certainly did not want to live in his house as everything there was in another's taste. I had a long discussion with Eileen about the future and realised that we both had to move out within the next few months. I told her how things had developed with Oliver and said there was a real chance we would marry. She was delighted but a little concerned that he was ten years older than me; my mother was also a little hesitant. I assured them both that we got along well, and said it was not exactly a passionate relationship, but an affectionate, powerful companionship, and most importantly, we loved each other.

Things started to move fast now and we agreed to look for a house together. We decided it should be situated between Ross and Hereford as we both had commitments in our respective towns. Oliver made the first gesture and selected a number of properties for us to look at in Ross. None was suitable. I did not want to be near a busy road because of my animals and I would also be sure to have more. So I suggested I had a look and decided to search near Fownhope as it was situated half-way between the two places. I looked for an estate agent in the Yellow Pages and found one in Woolhope which I thought would be fine. I called him. He immediately said he had a suitable house for an artist with animals in Kings Caple and I arranged to meet him there the same day. He gave me good directions, I jumped in the car and drove the few miles from Breinton to the house.

It was just perfect - a beautiful Herefordshire stone cottage, about three hundred years old with an acre of garden. It needed a lot of work doing to it, but it was selling at a reasonable price because of the condition. Despite everything it was a good buy. Situated near the River Wye, it would be a marvellous place to walk the dogs, with space and privacy to paint. The other surprise was that I had looked at this very building and complimented the lady in the garden on her flowers. On leaving I had turned to the dog and said that we would be back. It all seemed quite karmic and too good to be true. It was thrilling to find something that you feel with all your heart could be your next home. But I still had to show it to Oliver. Would he like it or would he feel that there was too much work to do? He had not been able to come with me so we made an appointment for the following Saturday for him to see it.

We arrived together and I invited him to walk through the garden first, swinging him around to show him the house from the front. It looked like a Queen Anne residence with the original sash windows in place though in fact it is a Herefordshire farmer's stone cottage. It had apparently originally been used as a pub called the 'Old Boar'. Admiring it from the front, we eventually went in through the oak door. The staircase was before us. I said that would be the first thing we would have to change into a straight up and down staircase, thus opening up the top floor and making it safer for the elderly, such as my mother. We proceeded, noting everything which needed to be done, such as insulation, damp coursing, new bathrooms, kitchen, and electrical rewiring, and central heating.

It was exciting to see the house in a sad state but at the same time, knew that a competent builder would be able to do wonders with it. It was wonderful to have good feelings about the property and feel that you could happily live there, perhaps for the rest of your life. We were both in high spirits about it, and decided to celebrate in the local pub with a beer and fish and chips. Over this insalubrious meal Oliver proposed to me properly; I said yes. He did not have a ring with him so we decided to go into Cheltenham to buy one the following week.

Although the house was not actually on the market, as probate had not yet been completed, we heard that somebody else was interested. So we thought it sensible to make an offer. The next day we called the estate agent and put in our bid, and to our great delight we heard later that if we increased it by £2,000 - the property would be ours. We readily did so and then waited patiently until probate was completed and we could start making arrangements to renovate. In the meantime Oliver had put his house on the market and thankfully it sold quickly. Finally, we were ready to go ahead just as soon as the builders could start work.

I had discovered some reliable men who happened to be engaged on a project next to my cottage in Breinton. I had agreed to feed the cat there while my neighbours were away. In doing so I had met these two lovely brothers who were renovating their house. They were East Enders, having moved to Hereford when they were youngsters, and were making a good living for themselves specialising in upgrading old buildings. They were still busy next door when we were negotiating for 'Shieldbrook' so I invited them to come and have a look at the property to get their opinion. They were thrilled with it and could see the enormous potential. Rob, the brother in charge, did a costing for us and provided a realistic price for what had to be done. Although the roof needed replacing we decided to wait until later to do that and the studio. They would have a separate estimate later.

As well as organising things for the renovation, such as having a staircase made and bookshelves, not to mention ordering a mantelpiece and kitchen equipment, we started to make plans for the wedding. I told Eileen of our intentions and said that we wanted to get married at Breinton church as I wanted Graham Sykes to officiate for us. I also wanted Sophie to be one of my bridesmaids.

He had to get special dispensation from the Bishop because I was a divorcee and had already been married in church. I mentioned to her that it would be lovely to have the reception in my garden and asked if that would be possible. It would mean putting up a marquee and our friends walking through the orchard to my place from the church. She agreed and of course she would be guest of honour, seated at the top table!

We were married in Saint Michaels and All Angels Church, Breinton on 26 September 1998, with The Singing Tree providing some African songs to greet people as they came in. Graham conducted a beautiful service, and Mummy was one of the witnesses. Graham welcomed the guests warmly and made a great effort to make my day special. I had made his daughter Sophie's dress, and she along with Trisha and Annukka were my bridesmaids They looked amazing and by the end of the service everybody's spirits were lifted. It poured with rain as the service finished but most people managed to arrive safely at the reception with food and drinks for all.

A friend did most of the catering and I helped with some dishes. My sister arranged magnificent flowers in the marquee. We did not have to put any flowers in the church as harvest festival was about to be celebrated, and was already full of flowers, fruit and vegetables and smelt strongly of apples - most appropriate. A mate of Oliver's played his synthesiser and various friends and family did a turn. There were many special people there, Mummy being the most important. Sadly, Daddy missed my second marriage but he was in my thoughts. My mother looked fabulous, being a young ninety at the time, in a shocking pink suit, orange hat and a fluffy orange silk scarf at her neck. I wore a pale grey skirt with a large checked, knee-length silk jacket, lined in orange. So we went well together, which of course we had planned. A friend of mine from college had arrived from Sweden for the wedding and we all three had slept in my bed the night before the great day. My Dutch friend

Marjan also came with my two godchildren. She wore a velvet dress of mine from my boutique days.

Many friends and the family stayed overnight so that they could come and see the new house 'Shieldbrook' before leaving for their respective homes. We would be having another party there before everyone set off for their final destinations. The reception had been a great success and had gone on for a while with some choir members being the last to leave. The happy bride and groom went to stay the night at the Pilgrim Inn in Hereford. We decided our real honeymoon had been our trip to Kenya, so one night was sufficient.

After a late breakfast, we drove to 'Shieldbrook' and did a final clear-up to prepare for our guests. We had painted the walls pale yellow, terracotta pink and a delicate blue, and I had stencilled the skirting boards with a colourful motif; new carpets had also been laid. Some furniture was in place so it looked clean, spacious and just beautiful. We were ready to toast our new home in champagne and pizza. It was wonderful to see friends and family there and let them discover the garden's hidden corners.

At the end of a memorable weekend we both went back to our respective homes and would not be moving in properly for a couple of weeks. It was Oliver's birthday in October and we wanted to be there for that. The kitchen needed to be completed and the electrical fittings had to be finished. The furniture was moved in and we managed to get the curtains up. I hired a white van to get mine over and Oliver arranged for a proper removal van to move his furniture. It was not until the beds were placed that we finally spent our first night at our new home. It was wonderful to wake up to the sound of birds and to be aware of the river as it passed the end of the garden.

CHAPTER NINETEEN
SUE SHARP AND 'SHIELDBROOK'

You're getting to be a habit with me

The builders had done a great job getting 'Shieldbrook' ready for us to move into. I realised early that it would be a work of art getting the place to be just as we wanted it. This was the first time I had been able to do anything like this, so I wanted it to have a good feel about it and loads of atmosphere - which I knew could be created with the clever use of colours. There were still things that needed doing but we decided to have a break from the builders until the following spring. Then we would do the studio and lay the floor in the kitchen and hall. That would involve moving out for a week as the screed had to be laid and levelled before the floor could be glued in place. The dog could come with us but the two cats, one belonging to Oliver, would be boarded out whilst all the flooring was being laid.

Almost as soon as we moved in there was a terrible flood; apparently, one of the worst for years. The water came up the lane as far as our kitchen - within about twenty yards of the door. Everybody assured us that the floods never came into the house, so we believed them. The River Wye floods most years but has never come inside the house, so we were pretty relaxed about it. The flooding in our area has been controlled somewhat as the Environment Agency has put in preventative measures upstream. Despite this changes, the flood plain and surrounding fields are often knee deep in water. When they built our home, they knew exactly where to build the houses just above the highest flood level, so for the moment - all is well.

Our first Christmas at 'Shieldbrook' was a special one. The family decided to come to me for a change, which was lovely. Mummy and my sister Trisha came and it was a great thrill for me to be able to do the full works for once for our festivities. A beautiful free-range turkey was delivered by our butcher. Everybody helped - Mummy brought her especially delicious pudding and made the brandy butter on the day. Trisha prepared the vegetables and made an amazing fruit salad. We watched the Queen's speech and went for a splendid walk across the bridge to Sellack over the Wye. The bridge and the river banks always feel rather like our extended back garden. The house is a good place to have a party, and before the family had arrived - I decorated it with holly and mistletoe from the garden.

We celebrated the new year with our nearest neighbour, Audrey. She had invited many from the village so it was a good opportunity for us to get to know more people. Also to hear some of the stories about the area which are always interesting. Some of those present could remember when our house was a shop and children would come to buy sweets at the window. Apparently we sold a few basic supplies such as flour and shoe polish. This was the last village shop and was really missed by the youngsters. Then there was the story of why they decided to build the bridge. There used to be a man who would ferry customers across the river for a small fee. One day the vicar wanted to cross to officiate at a funeral, but the ferryman was drunk so the vicar had to go right round to Sellack Church by road - and the funeral was late!

I was looking forward to tackling the mature garden in front of the house. It had been well looked after by the previous owner, so in the beginning it was a case of weeding and keeping everything cut back. I also introduced some new plants. However, the field at either end of our garden was overgrown with nettles and docks, and needed radical clearance and landscaping. In February we discovered wonderful bulbs which had been planted in the garden over the years. The hellebores were also quite spectacular. The first to come out were snowdrops, aconites and hellebores, followed swiftly by daffodils and tulips. Each year I planted more of each so now there are hundreds of bulbs in the garden which come up and flower regularly.

During our first spring we moved out for a week in order for the floor in the kitchen and hall to be laid. We went to stay at the 'Cottage of Content', because we were able to take Teal and it was our nearest family-orientated pub. The cats went happily into a cattery and we collected them at the end of the week, none the worse for wear. Our stay at the pub was memorable in as much as we would eat our way through their comprehensive menu and listen to some of the landlord's stories over endless bottles of red wine.

It was a relief to move back into the house which finally had a feeling of completion about it. The work had amalgamated the whole of the ground floor with wood throughout. The next thing to be transformed was my studio. This is attached to the house, having previously been two potting sheds and before that, stables. The areas were made into one space and one of the doors to the outside was blocked off. The floor was raised to make it even and the roof was insulated to keep in the warmth. I had a sink put in the corner for a much-needed fresh-water supply and daylight-saving bulbs for good light in the early evening. It was a perfect space for painting for me and for my students.

I continued my work at the Natural Therapy Centre in Hereford with Anna. I commissioned a weaving by one of my students, which hung on the landing at the Centre; this colourful tapestry greeted people when they arrived. I was also painting with clients at the Martha House Trust. It was satisfying bringing a little colour into the lives of these profoundly disabled young people. It was a specially built care home providing many different forms of therapy. This kind of treatment is not widely available in the rest of the country, hence the long waiting list for places. They are now in the process of building another home because of the demand.

I celebrated my sixtieth birthday in the July with a 'Green Party' where everybody was asked to wear green and, if they felt like it, to bring a plant. Many did and I was inundated with gifts of flowers and shrubs, including several floribunda for the rose garden which I planted in special beds in the bottom field. I hired a gazebo for a band to play in, with a small floor for dancing. It was a wonderful day and the place was packed with friends. My mother came with Trisha and her family. The Singing Tree singers arrived and to everyone's astonishment, we sat down and sang a few numbers. The weather was perfect with a clear blue sky and a slight wind.

By now I was performing regularly with The Singing Tree. They met every Thursday in Garway and I was usually collected by my tenor friend as he lived nearby. I got to know him well over the next few years as he was a person who needed to talk. At one point the choir made a recording of some of our songs in Garway Church, which has an excellent acoustic and the resulting CD was amazing. We used to sing in the music room of the leader's house, which was a bit of a squash but always fun - followed by a few drinks in the pub. I continued to listen to my friend and pointed him towards colour and painting, which would help him. I also suggested he take a course at Hereford Art School. I intended doing a life class there myself so we ended up doing the class together, and now he is painting happily.

I enrolled in the RHS horticultural course at Hartpury College and enjoyed finding out about every aspect of cultivation. Almost the first thing I did was to design what we now call the 'Healing

Garden' in the top field. I wanted it to be somewhere I could invite clients from Martha House to visit. It therefore had to be wheelchair friendly as many were not able to walk. I had been taught all gardens need a focal point, and as the only thing in the top field was a big old pear tree - this became the focal point. All gardens also need a pond or two, so in front of the pear tree we dug one with a substantial rockery at one end, made with all the earth we had excavated out of the pond. It was exciting standing inside it and digging, your eyes parallel with ground level. We laid a pond-liner and the best part was putting in the water followed by the aquatic plants. Without the course I would never had known how many tons of rock to order for the rockery (six to be precise). Also whilst at Hartpury they happened to be clearing a pond of overgrown water lilies and I was offered some for ours.

The next thing on my list was to ask a landscaper to come and lay the paths. He did a wonderful job because my design had very few straight lines and some of the curves were very difficult to lay. The slabs had to be well concreted in and quite substantial as they needed to carry the weight of wheelchairs. When the paths were finally laid, I started the planting. I wanted as many trees, shrubs and grasses as possible. All they needed then would be space to grow and not too much maintenance. Thankfully, they would only require the occasional cutting back and mulching to keep weeds at bay. Where possible, I also put down a liner to discourage the weeds.

I have to admit my planting was a little precarious, due to my lack of experience. I often did not appreciate how big a tree or a shrub might grow. There is such a thing as replanting shrubs and flowers, and I had to do that a few times. On one of my visits to the Chelsea Flower Show, I had great fun ordering a splendid greenhouse, which had to have special footings put in place before it could be satisfactorily erected by my builders. It was wonderful having it for tomatoes, cucumbers and courgettes not to mention potting up and starting seeds in. I foolishly put a fig tree in it and although it bears fruit, it is much too big and needs moving.

The garden was beginning to take shape and I was learning a great deal about the special nature of the shrubs and trees which I had established. I wanted to use the coloured foliage and phallic shaped leaves to their best advantage. The phormium family were a favourite group which impressed me. They are focal points in themselves, with their long pointed leaves. I used many different species of this group, the only problem being that I discovered they were not entirely frost friendly. I also developed my skills at propagation with plants such as chrysanthemums, hostas and geraniums. I was sorry that neither my father nor Douglas were alive to offer advice and appreciate everything I was trying to do. They both would have been thrilled and amazed to see the garden I have achieved in such a short time.

The lawns were prepared and the grass seed spread by hand. And we placed a number of trees and shrubs in position in the Healing Garden such as six silver birch and a tulip tree. I also put a quercus rubra in the middle of a lawn which one day will be the biggest tree in the garden but not in my lifetime. I then invited an expert to come and talk to us about grasses. I planned to buy quite a quantity for the garden as they are good focal points and survive the winter. It was interesting to have a professional perspective and my friends and myself ended up buying a number of them for our respective gardens. The grasses continue to flourish even after the harshest of winters.

It was now autumn and leaves were falling all over the place and I was beginning to think about Christmas. As nobody was really expecting us and as neither of us have any children, we decided to holiday in Jamaica. Both Oliver and I had spent time there before, so it would be fun to rediscover some of our favourite places. We had many good memories of it and it is always good to see how somewhere you know well has developed over the years.

A friend, with whom I do pottery, was also going to be there so we arranged to meet up. Coincidentally, we were staying in the same resort, Ocho Rios, if at opposite ends; ours being the cheap end - with all drinks and food included in the price. Our Herefordshire friends were staying at the Jamaica Inn, which is rather special. We spent a couple of days on their beach and had a few meals with them. One day we went rafting - floating down a river in boats and being serenaded by the boatman. I had a swim in the river, which was really cold but exciting. The whole day was hilarious and most exhilarating.

I was thrilled to be back in Jamaica remembering the marvellous times I had when I lived there. I could not resist returning to Montego Bay to see one of the shops I had worked in. Although it had new owners, to my great surprise and delight they were still selling designs I had made thirty years earlier! As they were summer fashions - cruise and beachwear - these clothes did not exactly go out of fashion. We drove around the island ending up in Negril, and had a meal in one of the hotels which had been built on the beach since my time. I swam out to sea and thought of my tenor friend at home who was still pretty depressed. There was not much I could do for him and ultimately we each have to take responsibility for our own lives as best we can.

We returned to discover that Mummy had been taken ill over Christmas. She had had a series of mini strokes and was not her normal self. So I suggested she came to stay with us for a while so that I could care for her and help her recovery. I went down to Sussex to collect her and brought her back with some of her things. We had anticipated that she would come and live with us at some point so we had prepared for this turn of events. I had fully anticipated putting a bed in the dining room but for the moment it was not necessary. Mummy was feeling rather miserable and was as frail as I had ever seen her. She seemed unable to stand up straight and had little appetite. She said things like 'This is it, my life is over.' I assured her that it was not. During the following month she recovered somewhat and started talking about wanting to go home to see her friends in Sussex.

After some serious discussions about this plan, I agreed to let her return to her own place as she seemed determined to do so. I made the necessary care arrangements for her through a local agency and went to stay with her while the process was put in place. After a few days it all seemed to be going well. Someone would come in the morning and help her to get up, and there would be the same arrangement at night to be sure she was in bed safely. I got some supplies in for her and on the day I was leaving arranged for Bundy, an aunt and great friend of my mother, to come and spend some time with her. I went back to Hereford, trusting all would be well.

On arrival I heard she had fallen over on the way to open the door to Bundy, who was able to get into the house to help my mother as luckily Bundy had a key with her. The consequence of the fall was that my mother soon needed twenty-four-hour care and within a week had taken a turn for the worse. I drove back to Sussex but everybody concerned, including her GP, thought she would be better off in a nursing home. By the time I arrived, it had all been arranged by my brother and the doctor. Now my mother was going somewhere we had all promised her she would never go.

It was dreadful dressing her in her best nightie and packing a bag for her to be taken, by ambulance, to the home. My sister and I went with her to help her settle in. Mummy was limp with exhaustion and could not speak. We tried to give her a drink but she could not take anything by mouth. It was the saddest ending to her marvellous, colourful life, but one blessing was that her four children were there for her and in our own way - said our goodbyes. It was awful to leave her in that dreary place where, sadly, she died the following day.

We assembled back at the house to discuss things. We hoped and expected her to recover and to come back to her home. I then set off for Kings Caple and was in Herefordshire when I heard the terrible news of her death from my brother. It was a shock, even though we knew she was very frail. Simon and his wife Jo, who lived nearby in Alverstoke, did all the necessary arrangements for the registration of the death and the funeral. The arrangements were similar to my father's in as much as it was the same church and the same undertakers. We selected special hymns and readings and I invited another friend to come and sing 'Ave Maria.'

We had a special family meeting to finalise the plan for a splendid send-off for her, and invited all her colleagues and our relatives to come. The more we got into the arrangements the more I realised why she wanted to return home so much. She wanted her funeral to be in the same place as my father's and to be close to where so many of her friends lived. Mummy had been so active with the Sussex Flower Arranging Club and other organisations like the WI. She had exhibited her flowers all over the county, and had even had one on display in Westminster Cathedral for some celebration, meeting the Princess of Wales. All her friends and colleagues were there - it was some turn-out.

Losing both parents so near together, seemed massive at the time. They had both been healthy without many serious illness for most of their lives. Being the eldest child made me realise I may well be the next, not a happy thought, but these things go through the mind when you are arranging a funeral. All the family members came and it was good to meet cousins we had not seen for ages. It was also a treat to meet many of my mother's friends who had been part of her life in Aldwick. Again Oliver was a great support; he knows so well how to behave on these occasions. None of us had had much experience of them. It was a fitting service for our beautiful, precious Mummy who was special to so many people.

The house smelled of lilies, her favourite flowers, and my sister had made impressive arrangements. We drank to her life in champagne and wished her Godspeed. After all our guests had gone we sadly and silently cleared up the mess and put their precious things away. It was decided to leave our brothers to plan what to do regarding the house and their papers. I helped sort out some of our parents' possessions, which we shared amongst us. It was incredibly sad going through her jewellery box and giving various items to each family member. I was given her aquamarine engagement ring and her gold watch which I treasure and use. Sorting out their clothes and books was also really upsetting. After we had taken what we could use, the rest was given to charity shops. It made me realise that it was a good idea to offload as much as you can along the way.

CHAPTER TWENTY
SCULPTURE EXHIBITIONS AND NEW AWAKENINGS

*For age is an opportunity no less
Than youth itself, though in another dress*

Life had to go on, so I started devoting more time to the garden and to creating my own art - increasingly concentrating on sculpture. Although I continued to attend classes, I also did more woodcarving at home. I bought a bench from Chris so was able to carve in the studio. I started to make bigger pieces to display outside; it was a good way to spend a day, alone with your thoughts, banging at a lump of wood. My brother John sorted out the probate and the will and a few months later, we were all pleased to receive a substantial amount from our parents' estate. This enabled me to complete the garden as I had planned it originally, and to have regular help with the heavy work.

In the spring, I decided to visit Marjan and Patrick, my friends in Holland. They were living in Heerhugowaard with their children; the twins - Anna Rose and Blathnet who are my godchildren. Marjan and Patrick also had a new baby, Secoya. I wanted to see how they were growing up and if they could remember their English. I was very glad to see them again.

As soon as I arrived in Holland, Oliver phoned to tell me that Teal had died. Great sadness again - my faithful girl had reached the grand old age of ten, and passed away peacefully in her sleep. Oliver made arrangements to have her buried in the garden and a friend dug her grave.

Despite such sad news, somehow I managed to enjoy my stay in Holland - going on cycle rides on the dunes and for long walks. During my visit, Patrick arranged for us both to go to a sculpture workshop. A Zimbabwean sculptor was giving a course, working in serpentine, a relatively soft stone, which originates from that country. It took place in a sculpture garden with a number of pieces on display which I really enjoyed looking at in the break. I had a wonderful day, carving a dog's head, which I polished up beautifully and brought home to put on Teal's grave. When we got back I played with the children, in particular with Secoya, enjoying getting to know her better. We also discussed the next plan which was for them to visit us at 'Shieldbrook' later on in the year.

On the flight home I started to think about the possibility of having a sculpture exhibition on my own land. The work on display in Holland had really inspired me. I was producing some reasonably large pieces myself especially for that purpose; why not ask a few local sculptors to exhibit with me? The next few months were taken in research, looking at work and seeking out artists from all over Herefordshire. For the first exhibition I aimed to have a dozen sculptors who would use a whole range of different materials such as wood, stone, alabaster and metal. The mix needed to be exciting and unusual as well as weather-hardy as they would be exhibited outside throughout the summer and possibly remain in the garden over the winter. Hopefully it would become a tourist attraction. The following spring I started making all the necessary arrangements to open to the public in June.

On my return from Holland I called the breeder from whom I had bought my two previous pointers and asked what the situation was with puppies. I cannot be long without a dog and miss their presence in my life so much. Thankfully she had a litter on the way and I soon would have another puppy to train and look after. When they were born I was invited to go to select a bitch and sometime later, in the summer, after teaching on the Curative Eurythmy

Course in East Grinstead, I went to collect her. We named her Flora; of my three pointers, she was the most difficult to train.

We had started going to our local church as soon as we got here but on the whole it was poorly attended and was usually a non-event for me. For important occasions like Christmas and Easter, we went to our beautiful cathedral in Hereford. It has a wonderful warm atmosphere and is always so welcoming. The service which I found so spiritually rewarding was held on Good Friday, so I have made a point of always attending that particular event. As we live in Kings Caple village, we are connected with what is going on in the church and one activity we got involved with is the annual village fete. Once we held it in the 'Shieldbrook' garden and managed to raise good money for the church with splendid teas being laid on by the ladies of the village. A book stall, tombola and an art exhibition were some of the events.

Since we met, Oliver has been going on a Monday morning to Probus which he enjoys enormously. I think of it as being a gentleman's WI. It is a group of professional men who meet, sometimes having a visiting speaker, or they will talk about their own career life and work. There has been many occasions when Oliver has spoken about his career in the navy and subsequent travels around the world. I trust he has not repeated himself too much as he tends to forget what he has already told them. There are three groups in Ross and two women's groups, one of which I have given a talk to on art therapy.

The wonderful thing about living in Herefordshire is the festivals and the various events that happen in the course of the year. The first one I discovered soon after my arrival in Breinton was the Hay-on-Wye Literary Festival which is now the most famous of its kind in the world. It happens every Whitsun, and has grown beyond all recognition since my first visit. Then it took place in the local school which would close for half-term for the book events to take over. Now they have leased a field especially for the duration and a village of marquees arises. The parking is often a nightmare if the weather is wet, which it invariably is. The Hay Festival is something everybody in the area looks forward to. Like everything else, it seems to get more expensive every year but hopefully they will not price themselves out of the market.

The garden continues to give hours of satisfaction, now with a slightly different purpose as I am making areas for exhibiting sculpture. I have decided that it will be a memorial to my parents as I know they would have approved and enjoyed the various events. With the help of my inheritance and gardeners, I have developed interesting corners or rooms in order to show the sculpture to its best advantage. We also needed more car-parking areas for when a great quantity of people visited the garden and exhibition. We used old railway sleepers to make out the space finishing it with pink Herefordshire gravel. Finally, we built a gazebo in which to run sculpture workshops and to exhibit some of the pieces in. On special occasions we also use the local farmer's field for parking.

That Christmas we decided to go to Malta as we both had spent time on the island - Oliver in his days as a naval officer and me when I was living with my parents. My father had been stationed there twice and I had gone on my honeymoon there (from my first marriage.) We booked a 'Christmas Special' at the Palace Hotel in Mdina, the ancient capital of Malta. It was a marvellous old building where, strangely, friends had lived before it was converted. The rooms were spacious and the food amazing. We hired a car to visit the places we both had known before or were interested to see new ones for the first time.

I could not resist calling my old boss at the pottery in Attard where I had worked. He invited us to lunch, before which we visited the building I had laboured in all those years ago. Unbelievably it was exactly the same, almost nothing had changed, even the pieces for sale on the shelves were virtually identical with only a few new products. Most amazing of all, there was a tiled panel I had painted in the sixties of Saint Paul landing on the island. The owner had decided not to sell it and had kept it on display for all those years. I always have to buy a plate or a bowl to remind me of a visit so we purchased something before having a memorable lunch.

We spent the rest of our holiday visiting our favourite places, especially the ancient sites on Gozo and on Malta itself - such as the Hal Saflieni Hypogeum which dates back to 4000 BC. It was rediscovered over a century ago and is thought to have been hacked out of the rock as a funeral site and temple. There are some extraordinary pre-Christian frescos on the ceiling which are still visible and well worth seeing. We spent some time in the Valletta art gallery and had a meal looking over the magnificent harbour. We went to see the Caravaggio paintings in St John's Cathedral, which are always a surprise to find there. The artist spent some time in Malta when he was trying to escape from his enemies in Rome.

Oliver did all the driving on this occasion as I had not brought my driver's license which was perhaps just as well; it meant that I did the navigation. He found it hard work and was pleased when it was over and we were heading for the airport. It had been special to be in Malta for Christmas. We went for Mass in the Cathedral in Mdina, but after three hours quietly left without taking communion. There were about two dozen bishops present with lots of pomp and circumstance. There was also rather a lot of incense, which is not my favourite, but we were grateful and happy to just be part of the congregation.

When we got back to Herefordshire, I soon began to put the summer sculpture exhibition in place I gathered together names of sculptors to whom I wrote asking if they would be interested in contributing. The majority were positive and replied with photographs of their work. All were accepted and I then prepared the catalogue. I needed an A4 sheet of information about each sculptor along with a few words about what inspired the work, plus a photograph. I had a smart white folder printed in green with 'Shieldbrook Sculpture' on the front. This would take the loose sheets of information about the exhibitors to present to each visitor. This was time consuming, but worth it. My mother's money enabled me to do it. The invitations for the private view followed.

The exciting moment came when the first sculptor brought his work and together we placed it in the garden. There were many places to choose from and it was done on a first-come-first-served basis. Eventually there would be sixty pieces on show with everybody happy with their space. The other important thing to organise was the running order of the exhibition. Each sculpture was numbered in the price list so that pieces could be easily identified and sold. This would always be the final thing to do as some contributors would arrive at the last minute with new work. Visitors would then be able to go round with the catalogue and enclosed price list, often taking an hour or so to find everything.

The big opening day of the sculpture garden arrived! Sculptors, friends and the press were invited; it was quite a celebration with wine and canapés to keep everybody happy and chatting. The first sale was an owl I had carved in oak. Sculptors and close friends stayed on for dinner afterwards. By the end of this exhilarating day, from the preparations, the entertaining to the clearing up - we were totally exhausted. Oliver, as always, did his bit meeting and greeting our visitors not to mention pouring the wine. The show continues to get bigger and better each year; now it has been going for eight years with up to a hundred exhibits.

There have always been beautiful gardens to visit in this area and 'Shieldbrook' is now one of them. I thought it would be good to offer some of the proceeds to the National Gardens Scheme. I contacted Antony Evans, the chairman of the organisation in the county and invited him to come to see if the garden was good enough to participate. He came and was delighted with what he saw, especially as the garden is unusual with so many sculptures on display. He said I would have to get rid of the remaining docks or nettles which appear from time to time. When we bought the house there were many and are an ongoing problem, but under control now. We joined the NGS and are open every year for a weekend in June.

Living in the country is so special after spending such a long while in London. There was a time when I never thought I would leave the city, but now I would find it very hard to go back. The people are friendly and will always have a chat; and, when you are driving, you notice the difference in road manners. The best thing for me is the animals. We are surrounded by sheep, with their lambs in the spring. Often they get out of their field and end up on the road or sometimes in the garden. When we first moved here I heard a sound outside in the middle of the night, looking out of the window, I saw the garden was full of sheep - some eating my best delphiniums! I rushed out like a mad women in my nightie to shoo them away. We now have substantial gates to keep them out. We also have a racing stable in the village and when the ground is too wet for the gallops, they walk on the roads to keep fit. It is wonderful to see such beautiful animals passing by my kitchen window.

The next glorious event which happens each year is the Three Choirs Festival, a celebration of music and singing taking place in Hereford, Gloucester, or Worcester Cathedral. They are superb weeks and go in strict rotation - with each choir secretly trying to outdo the other performances; the standard, therefore, remains incredibly high. We attend as many of these concerts as we can. Elgar and other British composers are well represented alongside Mozart and Beethoven. Special pieces are often commissioned each year so there is a premier to attend, mixed in with a real cross section of music ranging from ancient to modern. This allows new composers the opportunity to shine in a beautiful environment. After a few years of attending concerts it became my ambition to sing in the cathedral and to participate in the Three Choirs Festival. Eventually I did both.

I joined the Hereford Choral Society when they were preparing to sing Handel's 'Israel in Egypt' to be performed in the cathedral. I had not sung this before and I particularly wanted the challenge of learning the difficult score. I attended the rehearsals and when it came to the moment for auditioning I was unable to do so as I had a terrible cold. Luckily for me, they forgot I had not passed the audition. I therefore was able to perform without one, fulfilling my ambition to sing in the cathedral. It was an exquisite experience to be singing where the acoustic is so good. Later in the season the conductor Geraint Bowen remembered some people had not auditioned. I did so in order to sing the Messiah with them. I am hopeless singing by myself, I need the rest of the sopranos to support me. But when I came to the audition, I was completely hoarse from the rehearsal I could not sing a note! Geraint looked at me in disbelief and said, 'Sorry, you have failed your audition. Try again next year'! I did not audition again, but moved on to another choir in Leominster where I sang medieval music in the town's Priory.

In the autumn there is usually a conference for art therapists held in Stroud. We meet up to discuss our work and generally share what we are doing with our patients: the successes and the downfalls. Often we will be working with a specific disease. On the first occasion I was unable to attend, but I continue to be on the mailing list of practicing art therapists in the area. Consequently a colleague who also trained at the Tobias School, called me saying he was at the conference and would like to visit. He wanted to have a look at Herefordshire as a possible place to live and practice. He was living and working in Northern Ireland and had recently married, but the marriage had broken down and his wife had taken their young son to Germany: he was absolutely heartbroken. I invited him to 'Shieldbrook' so that he could get a feel for life here - living next to the River Wye near to the Welsh border.

He was Hungarian and his name was Zoltan. He came to visit us after the conference, and both Oliver and I showed him the lay of the land and took him to various churches and schools - in particular, to see the Waldorf School in Much Dewchurch. He liked what he saw and wanted to try his luck here, always with the hope that his wife would one day come back and join him with their son Cartel. We decided to help, and funded him to hire a van to bring his belongings over from Ireland, and to store them for the time being in our shed, and he could stay with us for the next few months. There was plenty to do in the garden and he paid us back by gardening. During his time with us, he became rather like a surrogate son, as neither Oliver nor I have any children. It was enormously satisfying for us both.

Zoltan stayed with us for the winter months and has continued to help me with the garden ever since. He remained until my special Dutch family came over for their annual visit, when I needed the spare room. Marjan arrived in May with the children, along with her partner Patrick, who drove the family car here from their home in Holland - a challenging drive with a vehicle full of children but they arrived safely and in good spirits. We had a marvellous time going to local attractions such as Kilpeck Church, Sellack Church, and the Church of Saint Dubricius in Hentland. We had picnics and went for a walk on Hay Bluff, after spending the morning in the famous bookshops of Hay-on-Wye nearby. It was on this visit that we made a plan to hold a series of clay-modelling workshops with Patrick and his friend Nicolaas de Jong.

These events became another interesting and challenging aspiration for me to organise at 'Shieldbrook'. I was also having regular sessions in the studio with my painters, and now I would begin to hold some more serious anthroposophical events such as biography workshops. I met Gil McHattie, the facilitator who lived in Forest Row. I invited her to come and give a number of biography workshops to a small group of friends who agreed to participate. We made a commitment to do a series of six over as many years and almost without exception we managed to carry them through. There were us five women plus Oliver, being the only man in the group; he thoroughly enjoyed hearing the various stories from all of our biographies. We looked at the seven stages of our lives in depth, starting with childhood, teenage traumas, achievements, disappointments, struggles and relationships - all of which could be speculatively connected to the planets. It was an extraordinary and enlightening experience, looking back at our journey and noting the life-changing events. We have all travelled quite extensively and some came from a service background. In various ways we had similar stories, often with like-minded karmic events. We bonded well and I like to think we would do anything for each other as we grow older, especially supporting each other in any adversity.

When I discovered the Ledbury Poetry Festival, which takes place in July around my birthday, poetry visits have become my special treats. I go to as many sessions as possible. On one occasion when I was taking part in a creative-writing workshop a young man, called Harry Matthews, came and sat beside me. In these classes you may be given a series of words and be invited to write a poem using as many of them as you like. This was all rather new to me so I tentatively set about creating a poem. Then of course you had to read it out aloud, which was embarrassing for me but at least I had tried my best. Harry, to my surprise, offered to read his out first and it was quite amazing. I was so impressed: it was a beautiful, sensitive poem, written in fifteen minutes. My thought was that this young man was a talented poet!

After the workshop we went for lunch and chatted about our respective lives, especially his. He was a journalist and had just returned from a dramatic assignment in Amsterdam. He had been interviewing some hippy types from the sixties who had been and were still involved in drugs. He was also a poet and trying to get his work published. Harry has become a firm friend over the years, though I am old enough to be his mother. He visits regularly and we hear about his adventures and setbacks. He was still suffering the effects of drugs which had been inadvertently given to him in Amsterdam. I encouraged him to paint, as it can help the healing process.

Another interesting poetry event during the year is the Thomas Traherne Festival at Credenhill Church, which was Traherne's parish church when he was living in the area at the time of the English Civil War. Each year the members of the Traherne Society meet to celebrate the poet and mystic's life. Traherne is buried in Teddington, Surrey, where he died. Recently, some important manuscripts of his work have been found and there is an enormous interest in his work. I have taken Harry to these Traherne events and he much appreciates them. There are various lectures and activities during the day, usually followed by a concert. The Singing Tree have performed twice at the Traherne Festival.

It is always a pleasure to sing in a church with beautiful acoustics, and it is lovely to have an audience. Recently some lovely stained glass windows have been installed in the cathedral to celebrate Thomas Traherne's life. On October 10th the Birthday Lecture is given at College Hall by an academic - an excellent opportunity to learn more about Traherne and his work. On one occasion, I introduced Harry to the Dean, Michael Tavinor. I especially asked the Dean to look after my young friend, because I felt he needed more spiritual help than I was able to give him. He agreed. Harry was desperately trying to get his strength and energy back after his disastrous time in Holland, and the Dean has been a great support to him over the years.

The Herefordshire Council is particularly helpful and encouraging to its artists, so one of the exciting events I am involved with was h.Art. Many Herefordshire artists open their studios to the public, and visitors come and meet participants to look - and sometimes buy - their work in a relaxed and informal way. In my case this happens to be in the garden, with smaller, more fragile pieces of sculpture on display in the studio. When h.Art began in 2002, it was funded by the European Arts Fund and the Arts Council. Originally, the artists participated free of charge but now without EU funding, the artists have to pay for the privilege of appearing in the superb brochure. At 'Shieldbrook' we make a special effort to promote the programme of h.Art events, along with anything else one might arrange during that time. I usually put on a concert in the garden for Peace Direct, which is something we have done successfully for the last two years. It is a wonderful occasion and people come from near and far in September to visit artists' studios all over the county. It is something we look forward to enormously, even though it is incredibly hard work.

As with the life of a garden, there is a magical rhythm to the year and there are always dramas along the way. There was a dreadful moment when some of my conifers died. Two of my junipers just shrivelled up and went brown at the end of one summer along with a few other trees. We cut them back and dug them up; being a member of The Royal Horticultural Society, I sent a piece of the dead root off to Wisley, their headquarters, to have it tested. I had the dreaded letter back which said, 'I am very sorry to tell you that you have honey fungus in your garden'. As a gardener, this is a devastating thing to hear as there is little you can do apart from provide good maintenance. Everything has to be burned to stop the spread of the infection and you have to remove all the soil from around the root. We did this and shipped in some fresh soil for new planting and hoped for the best.

I had an alternative idea, however, which I carried out the following spring. As planned, I had invited my Dutch friends Patrick

Steensma and Nicolaas de Jong to come and do a workshop, in particular, working with the Elemental Beings in the garden. Most people have heard of gnomes, but there are other small spiritual elements at work on our land, unbeknown to us. Mostly, they do their work uninvited and, sadly, unappreciated. It is possible to assist them, to get in touch with them and try to understand them better. This was the purpose of the workshop, with my specific problem in mind. There are various activities and things you can do to facilitate this: singing, clay modelling, and even talking to them. Nicolaas is sensitive to where they are and encouraged me, through the exercises we did, to get in touch with my little friends. I was therefore able to work with them in fighting the honey fungus. The important thing was to thank them for their contribution in helping me to get rid of it, which they did.

At some point Zoltan, who had become our regular gardener, decided he wanted to do a Waldorf teachers training and therefore would not be able to do much gardening for us in the next few months. The same week he told me this, a young couple arrived asking for work. They were charming and I agreed wholeheartedly to their request. They had come from Romania to pick strawberries for the season in Kings Caple. The picking work was now finished, and they had decided to stay in the UK. After they made sure that they had the necessary registration papers, they returned to tell me all was well and that they were ready and willing to work in the garden or the house.

They worked well and hard in the garden. Then they told me that Mychaela was pregnant and that they would have to leave the accommodation they had on the farm. I pointed them in various directions to find something, but I said that if they could not find anything they could stay with us in return for some gardening. They could not find anything suitable so I soon found myself clearing the spare room for them, suggesting that they stayed until the baby was born, and they did exactly that. When the baby had arrived they found somewhere else to live.

It was lovely having a young couple in the house and to be part of the excitement of the imminent birth of their first child. Traian is a strong young man able to do heavy work such as sawing up logs for the fire and bringing in the coal. Mychaela helped with the cleaning and we all settled in for the winter and the birth. They were here for their first English Christmas and I tried to do the full works for them. As she neared her time, Mychaela was able to do less and I think became quite uncomfortable because the baby was very big. January moved into February and the snow fell. On the night of the worst snowfall, Mychaela went into labour so we let the hospital know we were coming and nervously set off for Hereford. Traian drove slowly and carefully as it was still quite early and the snow was fresh. The car was slipping and sliding about, and Mychaela was looking anxious. I was thinking 'Please God, don't let it happen in the car because I am not sure if I really know what to do apart from say Push!' They were ready for us at the hospital, and Mychaela was taken to the special delivery room. The first thing they suggested was that she have a warm bath; this apparently helps the baby along. Mychaela did that while I popped out to an arranged dental appointment. The surgery was nearby and surprise, surprise - I had a tooth out!

By the time I returned Mychaela was on the bed and labour had seriously started. With Traian on one side and me on the other, we held her hands and helped her as much as we could. Eventually after many hours, Mychaela was exhausted and an epidural was offered, which she gratefully accepted. Then it became apparent that the baby was getting distressed (as he was being monitored all the time). The midwife decided that the baby should be delivered by Caesarean section and, without too much hesitation, Mychaela was whipped off to the operating theatre. Both Traian and I were left pretty exhausted ourselves. I went to find a sandwich and a cup of tea for each of us as we were starving.

When I got back Traian was standing there - holding this beautiful baby and looking absolutely the proud father. He gave me the child to hold and I could not believe what a miracle the baby boy was. This was the first time I had been at a birth so it was a very special moment for me. As I was standing there with the infant, Mychaela was wheeled back into the delivery room. Traian rushed to be at her side and I was able to hand her the precious gift. It was such a beautiful moment for all of us. I stayed with them for a while and then left them to be alone and took a taxi home to tell Oliver the good news. Mychaela stayed in the hospital with the baby for a few days before they came home. He was named Gabriel and I was delighted to be asked to be his godmother.

After all that excitement, I had to get back to my routine of arranging the next exhibition. Earlier I had written to the sculptors who had exhibited in the previous year's show, at the same time inviting some new ones along. This gives them plenty of time to prepare their work as it does not start until June. It also gives me time to do the catalogue and some of my own work for the show. These days it has been made easier by the use of my friendly computer for e-mailing sculptors and being able to send photos over the Internet. Also our website has to be updated regularly in order to compete with all the other events in the area. It is interesting how only a few years ago we managed to arrange things without the Internet: now it seems imperative that the whole world should know what you are doing.

My sculpture has become important to me. All these years later, having wanted to do it so much in my early days at Chelsea, I am finally doing what I had hoped to do then; the difference being that I now share the space with a number of other artists. As a sculptor it can often be difficult to find places to exhibit your work and also to store it, so the garden resolves both problems for me and for friends. I work in wood and alabaster, a relatively soft stone that I carve with a different set of tools. It polishes up beautifully in the final process. The finishing of a piece is so important and how it is displayed can make all the difference when it comes to selling. At the end of the day this is what you are hoping to achieve.

In the months leading up to the exhibition I have plenty of time to produce a few numbers for the show. Sometimes I do a week's carving in Hoathley Hill where a friend has a studio. Here I can work uninterrupted for a week. We have known each other since my days at the Tobias School. She is a dedicated anthroposophical sculptor and often works with the planets and the zodiac, using concave and convex shapes. I tend to have a theme for my work which might be birds or organic shapes. She is also a great help when it comes to displaying a piece and offers useful criticism. I have bought a number of her pieces which are in the garden; they are three large sculptures in green oak originally from the exhibition.

The Hay Festival happens during the Whitsun bank holiday just before we hold the private view for the sculpture exhibition. Thousands of visitors converge on Hay-on-Wye at this time. Its residents, I am sure, have a love-hate relationship with the festival. On the one hand it brings many people to the area, all of whom spend their money; on the other hand, it causes absolute chaos for two weeks and it takes another two, at least, for the town to recover. It is an opportunity to hear writers talking about and promoting their latest books, poets reading their poetry, and often interesting general discussion on the important issues of the day, whether it be climate change or forest clearance.

The highlight of my year though remains the opening of our exhibition. It has been hard work and fun cajoling the sculptors to deliver on time and getting the work in position. The numbering and pricing is always last-minute and I breathe a sigh of relief when the list is finally accomplished. Then the catalogue has to be made up with the relevant information about each sculptor and the price list put into each folder. There is always at least one who is late delivering their work and as it is often too interesting to turn away - I usually say yes. I try to have everything ready the day before the opening, leaving Zoltan and me time to do a final clear-up with paths swept and overhanging branches cut back. We aim to have the garden looking at its best at this time largely because it is our most important week with our annual opening for the National Gardens Scheme following at the weekend.

The moment comes when people arrive, having parked in the field kindly lent for the evening by Keith, our friendly farmer. Oliver is the main greeter who gives a drink and the catalogue. I rush around doing a host of things like putting out cards and the visitors' book. There are delicious nibbles which have to be heated up and passed around and always the important person, who may be buying, to chat up. Towards the end of the evening it is friends and sculptors who remain. Time for another drink and food which may be a lasagne or salmon or whatever I have dreamed up for supper. This is my favourite evening of the year and we are hopefully celebrating the sale of a few pieces of sculpture. Recently, the private view is something I have done in aid of the 'Haven' in Hereford, a charity for breast cancer, or St Michael's Hospice in Bartestree. With guests paying to come to the evening and the proceeds going to the charity plus a percentage of sales, it is a means of getting a few hundred pounds for them which seems to be appreciated. The garden now will be ready for the NGS opening. The few days before are spent removing any last weeds. The roses need dead-heading but are always looking their best as I have timed it so, and my climbing rose is also in its prime at this time.

Being a NGS garden keeps you on your toes looking after the grounds and planting new areas. It also raises funds for local and national charities, which is the added bonus. Although times are hard, people are good about supporting us. June is a very busy month to open, but it is the best time for the garden with the roses, lupins and some late tulips in full bloom. I put on a splendid English tea with a choice of tea and cakes, some of which I make myself. I tend to open just before Wimbledon, because one year I opened the garden at the same time as the tennis tournament – with disastrous results.

One of my great loves is poetry and I have started to write a little myself. Over the years I have been inviting a group of friends round for soirees; we read the work of other poets often with a theme such as rivers, mountains, or animals. Occasionally when we are feeling brave, we read one of our own poems. Paul Groves, an established writer, is part of our group and encourages us and will criticise when necessary. I am very grateful to Paul for giving me guidance with this book. I have arranged some readings at Monmouth Priory with the help of the Welsh Academi (now named 'Literature Wales'): these have always been well received. We have had some wonderful events there with poets such as Ruth Bidgood, Anne Cluysenaar, and Sam Harcombe reading.

As a result of these poetry evenings, Margot Miller and I were invited to edit an anthology relating to the River Wye and the English and Welsh borders. We had a brilliant few months collecting material and inviting poets to contribute to the book. Finally, *Landscapes on the Edge – Poems of the Wye Valley and Welsh Borders* was published by a local publisher Fineleaf Editions with some beautiful engravings by Robert Gibbings. I was pleased with the final result. We launched it in the summer of 2010 and it is now selling reasonably well in local bookshops.

One of my lifetime ambitions has been to have a litter of puppies, but for various reasons it has never happened. I chose a bitch especially for the purpose - a springer spaniel rather than another pointer. I naively thought a smaller springer would be easier to control. I found a puppy locally and named her Sophie. She was the sweetest dog and I thought she would make a good mother. When she was old enough - about two and a half - I arranged to put her with a local dog called Bill. He was lovely with a gentle nature and I thought they would make beautiful puppies. The deed was done and we waited patiently, sixty days to be precise, through the gestation period. I decided to do this in the winter because there was so much going on in the summer. Traian had built a special whelping box for her out of an old homemade bed and we waited for the moment with bated breath. One cold day in February 2010, Sophie started to give birth. The first puppy arrived on the kitchen floor and I had to get Sophie and the little boy into the whelping box for the births to continue. The first one had arrived at about two o'clock and Sophie proceeded to give birth until ten in the evening. There were finally nine puppies altogether: six boys and three girls. Both Sophie and I were exhausted afterwards as I had sat with her and helped her by putting each puppy on to her for suckling and had cut and tied the umbilical cords. By the end of the birthing, Sophie seemed very confused, and wondering what on earth was happening. I left her for the night to sleep it off with them and could not wait to get down in the morning to see if all was well. Mother and babies were fine except the last-born - a little girl and the weakest. I realised that I would have to hand-rear her as she was always getting knocked off the tit, and I had to keep putting her back on to her mother as the others fought for their position. In the end, I got some special milk from the vet and fed her three times a day, as well as putting her on to Sophie. The puppies grew very fast and were soon strong and big enough to get out of the box. Traian built a run for them out of my painting boards, and we covered the floor in newspapers. By now at least half the kitchen was taken over by them. It was wonderful but tiring work, a beautiful sight to behold over the weeks as they grew and grew. I knew why I had wanted to do it for such a long time - and finally I had achieved it. Each little dog was different and had its own personality. I had decided that I would like to keep one, and felt very attached to the smallest girl, which I had called Lucy Locket, but she was one of only three bitches so it was unlikely I would be able to keep her. They were all so perfect - I would not have minded keeping any of them. At one point when sales were slow, I thought I might be left with four puppies to bring up.

One day I noticed that one of the boys had a bit of a manky tail which might need to be docked. It is now illegal to dock a dog's tail unless if was medically necessary. I took him to the vet who said it was necessary to operate. I had to leave the little dog with the vet to have an anaesthetic and the operation. It was awful leaving this tiny puppy to have his tail chopped off, and I cried as I walked along the street as I waited for him. He came through well and was the only one of the litter with a docked tail so now he could be a working dog. As luck would have it, the man who bought him, wanted him for just that - so it was fine in the end. The vet cost the amazing sum of one hundred pounds!

After their first injections, I advertised them in the local press and people started coming to choose their puppies. The first person was my niece Tonia who arrived with her husband Mikey and their four children. It was lovely having the house full of children and puppies. They wanted a girl so they had first choice of the bitches and spent time playing with them before they made their choice. They chose one which I had called Dawn French because she was a greedy puppy - but she was also the best bitch. When they took the puppy back to London, they renamed her Truffles. I was very anxious about Truffles' safety, and warned them all to be sure to keep doors and gates closed. A few months later, I had the dreaded call that Truffles had been run over by a Royal Mail van. The whole family were devastated by the accident, especially Tonia and me - and we cried buckets over it.

After the second injection the puppies were able to go to their new owners. They all found good homes except for the one which I had decided to keep - the eldest boy, Jack. At some stage in the proceedings, Oliver had fallen into the puppy pen on top of Jack and I was worried that the dog had been damaged. Jack was traumatised at the time and I had to hold him close for ages before he stopped shaking. Thankfully, the beautiful dog came through and I am very proud of him. Jack had some problems initially but I took him to a doggy chiropractor, who straightened out his shoulders and spine and all seems to be well now. It was a worthwhile experience to have had a litter but all the work entailed was exhausting. Sophie seemed to grow up quickly, hardly more than a puppy herself. Now I had three dogs and two cats - quite a family to have under one roof, but they all get on well. Jack the lad was rather bumptious with the cats, but they can look after themselves.

We soon settled back into a routine and started preparing for our annual opening. Zoltan was back on garden duty and helped me prepare everything for the two most important events of the year. This year he made something himself which we placed in the orchard - it was a table with a bench attached, made from a lovely piece of oak.

Soon after the exhibition open day, I had to have an operation. I had noticed some slight bleeding probably brought on by the puppies. Knowing this was not a good omen, I went to see my doctor, and she sent me to see a specialist at the hospital and I quickly found myself with a date to have a hysterectomy. Cancer was found in my womb and it was suggested that I have radiotherapy in the hope that it would not spread further. Reluctantly I agreed to do it and I had to go to Cheltenham Hospital. It is at moments like these that you find out just how wonderful your friends are. They rallied round and drove me to the hospital for treatment, often waiting around for ages for the process to be completed. It was all most unpleasant and left me feeling depleted and sorry for myself, but you cannot stay miserable for long.

Like many people I get loads of junk mail telling me I have won a million or something else like a cruise or a holiday. On one occasion I took up one of these offers to discover it was to invite me to buy a timeshare with a company called RCI. The holiday was in Tenerife at a resort called Pearly Grey. I took my sister and her daughter the first time and we had an excellent time. The second visit was after my operation. I went to Grand Canary this time and had a relaxing week by myself - just what I needed. So I ended up buying a share in the resort although it does not mean I have to go to the same place every time. There are plenty of other venues to choose from all over the world. So now at the end of a hard season, I go away on a well-deserved holiday.

The next thing to celebrate was Oliver's birthday. He is in his eighties now and getting rather frail. I usually organise an evening for him where we have a few friends round for dinner and we read poetry between the courses. They have become a popular event and there is a core group of people who come. I noticed that he was not quite on the ball the last time and could not remember all their names. I know it happens to everyone as we age but his memory loss was becoming quite serious. After the celebrations I made an appointment for him to visit the Mental Health Clinic in Ross-on-Wye, for the second time as he had been the previous year for a check-up.

He had been diagnosed with dementia then but now it was becoming more serious and was beginning to affect his quality of life. The consultant thought that the DVLA should be informed about this. He was still driving but only to Ross; venturing further was not a good idea. I had read about some medication for the problem called Aricept and I asked if it could be made available for Oliver. I knew it was expensive so I was delighted when they agreed to give it to him. It was a success and he has continued to use it and I am delighted to say it helped him with his memory loss problem. Sadly, his driving licence was taken away - which upset him very much. We are both somewhat apprehensive about the future but you must keep your head up high and soldier on. For the moment all is well and we just have to wait and see what the prognosis will be.

It is at times like these that I find myself drawn back to the cathedral for spiritual support. The services are beautifully conducted with our wonderful choir in full voice. It seems extraordinary to me that I seem to have gone full circle, starting with our regular church visits as a family when we were young, then moving away from the church as a student and trying to find my own spiritual path as a young woman. In times of trouble I always go back to my Christian roots but then I branched off into anthroposophy whilst I did my training, only to come back to the cathedral under the watchful eye of the Dean, Michael Tavinor. He is a good friend and shares my love of music, history and art.

The cathedral has become a great sustenance for me and I am pleased to be more involved. It is truly satisfying to have joined the many volunteers and to be part of cathedral life. In particular, taking after my mother, I have joined one of the flower-arranging teams and was delighted to do the flowers for the tomb over Easter. I am also on the committee for the Art Fest which is an annual exhibition held in the Bishop's Palace where more than forty artists exhibit their work in beautiful surroundings. It has now been going for six years and each year is more successful than the last, raising necessary funds for the cathedral and its various activities. I also became a member of the Tuesday prayer group which I enjoy enormously.

When I set out to write about my life I really had no idea where it would lead. It has taken me a couple of years to complete, working mainly in the winter months because I am so busy with my sculpture and the garden in the summer. It has been a cathartic experience, thinking about my childhood, the family and above all my friendships which have been the framework and backbone of my existence. I feel so blessed and grateful that during my life there have been many marvellous friends to share it with.

It was exquisite to remember the beautiful moments where often the least expected was such a thrill. I would rate singing 'Israel in Egypt' in the cathedral as one of those moments and Sophie having her nine puppies. Not to mention getting married - twice - to two wonderful men. I have been very lucky in my life and appreciated every moment. I have also been blessed with pretty good health, so far. Let's hope it continues and that life at 'Shieldbrook' will inspire all those who come across its threshold. It is always special to open the garden to the public with another exhibition of sculpture, hoping that it will be well received.

We continue to have our annual family get-togethers, usually to celebrate a birthday. Oliver, myself and Trisha, along with Simon and Jo converge on John and Maria's comfortable home in Beckenham and catch-up. We discuss all of their children's careers and their children's children. I am now a great-aunt! The best thing is that Trisha is now a Granny with the birth of Lola - Billy and Fabiana's little girl.

Over several years whilst I was writing this book, I have had plenty of time to contemplate the good times and my achievements, along with my failings - thinking about where I have gone wrong and how I could have done better. The saddest thing for me was the loss of Sam in the car crash in Jamaica. He was my groom and looked after my horse, and he lost his life sitting beside me in my car as we collected bedding for the horse. I too should have been killed that dreadful day, but I felt God's hand on my shoulder. When I look back on it all, I realise there were things I had to do with my life. Indeed, there is still much more for me to do and I look forward to it.

It is a special moment when you complete what for me has been quite a journey in itself. My great thanks to the many friends who have helped me on my way, without whose help this book would not be as presentable as I hope it is.